Absolute Authority in Mark's Gospel

© 2021 Julius Kithinji

Published by Borderless Press
Phoenixville, Pennsylvania
www.borderlesspress.com
info@borderlesspress.com

All rights reserved. No part of this book may be reproduced or transmitted in any form or by any means, electronic or mechanical, including photocopy, recording, or any information storage and retrieval system, without prior permission from the publisher, except by a retriever who may quote brief passages in articles or reviews.

Although every precaution has been taken to verify the accuracy of the information contained herein, the author and publisher assume no responsibility for any errors or omissions. No liability is assumed for damages that may result from the use of information contained within.

ISBN: 978-1-7331221-1-5

First edition

Printed in the United States of America

ABSOLUTE AUTHORITY IN MARK'S GOSPEL

A POSTCOLONIAL ANALYSIS OF POWER ABUSE IN KENYA

JULIUS KITHINJI

To my wife, Meg, and to our children,
Kimaita and Jemima, for all their support

CONTENTS

Foreword v
Acknowledgments vii
Abbreviations. ix

INTRODUCTION xi
Background Issues xii
Impunity: A Kenyan Problem xv

CHAPTER ONE Decolonizing Ἐξουσία in Mark 1:21–28
Introduction 1
Mark's ἐξουσία. 2
Mark's Construction of Jesus's ἐξουσία 5
A Postcolonial Appraisal of the Gospel of Mark 11
    Imperial Representations in Mark's Gospel 14
Reading Ἐξουσία in Mark's Gospel 17
    The ἐξουσία in Mark 1:21–28 18
Impunity and Empire Tactics of Ἐξουσία in Mark 1:21–28 19
    Binarism. 20
Ἐξουσία in the Rest of Mark 23
Conclusion 27

CHAPTER TWO Social Memory and Kenyan Impunity

Introduction...29
The Culture of Impunity in Kenya................................30
Faces of Impunity in Kenya......................................31
    The Cultural Face of Impunity 34
    Gendered Perspectives.....................................37
    Hybridized Impunity.......................................38
    Mimicked Impunity..39
    Ambivalent Impunity......................................40
Impunity and Building Empires of Corruption....................41
The State of Corruption in Kenya...............................42
Corruption and the Empire 44
Impunity and Connectedness 46
Impunity and Postcolonial Identities in Kenya..................47
    Tribe and Ethnicity.......................................48
        Tribe and Ethnicity in Kenya..........................51
    Colonial Period (1895–1963)...............................52
    Jomo Kenyatta Period (1963–1978) 54
    Daniel arap Moi Period (1978–2002)........................55
    Mwai Kibaki Period (2002–2013)............................57
    Ethnic Identities and Impunity in Kenya 59
    Poverty, Subalternity, and Impunity 61
    Poverty Realities and Markers of Impunity 65
    Impunity and the Law......................................68
Impunity as Empire Resistance 71
Resistance through Violence 73
Conclusion...75

CHAPTER THREE Reading Otherwise: Mark's Ἐξουσία and Kenyan Impunity

Introduction...77
Bible Reading in "Ordinary" Readers' Terms 81
    Foregrounding Contextual Issues 82
    Selective Readings..83
    Retrieving Submerged Ordinary Resources 84
Ordinary Readers' Analysis within Contextual Bible Studies.........85

Reading Mark 1:21-28 for Impunity: Reading with
the Key Respondents 91
Restating Ordinary Voices 102
    Authority in Kenya as Derived from Mark's ἐξουσία.............. 103
    Kenyan Authority as Mimicked and Hybridized Power 103
    Empire and Impunity in Mark 1:21-28 105
    Postcolonial Feminist Concerns in Mark 1:21-28............... 107
Conclusion 108

CHAPTER FOUR Dethroning Empires of Impunity

Introduction... 111
Contrapuntalism and Mark 1:21-28 112
Divination and Mark 1:21-28 115
    Divining Mark 1:21-28 for Impunity 118
    Divining Applause of Ἐξουσία in Mark 1:21-28.................. 121
    Finding a Postcolonial Hermeneutical Key for Mark 1:21-28...... 124
Reading "Possession" in the Kenyan Context 125
    "Possessed" by Impunity 126
    "Possessed" by the Powerful 127
Kenyans as Reformists... 128
Kenyans as Conformists 130
A Hermeneutics of Impunity 132
    Postcolonialism and Impunitism 133
    Analysis of Impunitism as a Hermeneutical Tool 134
    Impunitism and Service to God 135
Conclusion 136

CHAPTER FIVE Beyond Empires of Impunity

Introduction... 137
Impunity and Mark's Legacy..................................... 138
The Debate Goes On 140

References 145
Index 161

FOREWORD

Borderless Press is a knowledge Activist charitable publishing organization. We operate with an understanding that knowledge production, distribution, and consumption have, for the longest time, privileged the Minority World (Europe and USA) scholars and writers at the expense of the Majority World (Africa, Asia, and Latin America). Consequently, our publications are works primarily written by Majority World scholars and knowledge activists. Like all academic publishers, we are committed to rigorous peer-review processes, celebrating scholarship that makes important contributions to academic discourse. Beyond this tradition, we seek to decolonize knowledge production and distribution through equality, creativity, and justice. This focus guides us not only in manuscript selection, but also in the ways we approach our work and organizational structures.

Most of our books are published through generous financial donations. Postcolonial Networks would like to thank our donors for making it possible for us to publish this book.

All inquiries should be addressed to the publisher Dr. R.S. Wafula at drwafula@borderless.press.com.

ACKNOWLEDGMENTS

Without the generous cooperation of many people, the writing of this book would have been severely hampered. Among those to whom I am deeply indebted for their valuable contributions are Prof. Philomena Mwaura, Dr. Humphrey Waweru, Prof. Deborah Krause, Prof. Niles Damayanthi, and Dr. Jeff Moore. I also acknowledge Rev. Dr. Stephen Kanyaru, a former presiding bishop of the Methodist Church in Kenya, for his mentorship and friendship.

I would also like to acknowledge Kenyatta University; St. Paul's University in Limuru, Kenya; Hekima College in Kenya; and Eden Theological Seminary in the USA for offering me research spaces at various stages of my writing. I would also like to thank Prof. Esther Mombo for supporting me to write this book. To the various churches and Christians who participated in interviews and contextual Bible studies, I express my sincere gratitude.

My sincere thanks to Postcolonial Networks and the Borderless Press team for accepting my manuscript and for shepherding me through the publication process. Special thanks to Dr. Joe Duggan, founder of the above organizations, who also substantially financed costs for revision on the manuscript. My gratitude to Dr. John Ndavula and Dr. Andrew Mbuvi, who at various stages provided invaluable advice. I would like to thank Dr. RS Wafula, who took a personal interest in my work and provided expert advice and guidance through the mesh of publishing intricacies. This book would not have been published had it not been for the dedicated work of the Borderless Press team and Dr. Wafula. Finally, let me thank my production editor, Melody Stanford Martin, for her diligence in producing this book.

Special thanks go to my wife, Meg, and our children, Kimaita and Jemima, who provided me with all the support I needed during the entire process. To all the "others"—peripheral subalterns who are still in the margins, and under the shadow of the empire—I have retrieved your submerged voices and foregrounded them in this work. *Mungu awabariki nyote* (God bless you all).

ABBREVIATIONS

ACK — Anglican Church of Kenya
AFRiCOG — Africa Centre for Open Governance
AG — Attorney General
AICs — African Instituted Churches
AIPCA — African Independent Pentecostal Church of Africa
AMICC — American NGO Coalition for the International Criminal Court
AMISOM — African Mission in Somalia
ASR — African Studies Review
CBD — Central Business District
CBS — Contextual Bible Study
CE — Common Era
CPI — Corruption Perception Index
DFRD — District Focus for Rural Development
DN — *Daily Nation*
DP — Democratic Party
EACC — Ethics and Anti-Corruption Commission
FIDA — International Federation of Women Lawyers
FGDs — Focus Group Discussions
FORD — Forum for Restoration of Democracy
GEMA — Gikuyu, Embu, Meru Association
GTM — Grounded Theory Method
HPI — Human Poverty Index
ICC — International Christian Centre
ICC — International Criminal Court
ICPC — International Centre for Policy and Conflict
ISB — Institute for the Study of the Bible
JBL — Journal of Biblical Literature
JETS — Journal of Evangelical Theological Society
KACC — Kenya Anti-Corruption Commission

KAG — Kenya Assemblies of God
KAMATUSA — Kalenjin, Maasai, Turkana, and Samburu
KANU — Kenya African National Union
KKV — Kazi kwa Vijana
KNCHR — Kenya National Commission on Human Rights
KTN — Kenya Television Network
LDP — Liberal Democratic Party
LXX — The Septuagint
MCK — Methodist Church in Kenya
MRC — Mombasa Republican Council
NACC — National Aids Control Council
NARC — National Alliance Rainbow Coalition
NAK — National Alliance Party of Kenya
NACOSTI — National Commission for Science, Technology, and Innovation
NDP — National Development Party
NHIF — National Hospital Insurance Fund
NPC — Nairobi Pentecostal Church
NRSV — New Revised Standard Version
NT — New Testament
OT — Old Testament
SDP — Social Democratic Party
TNDT — Theological Dictionary of the New Testament
TRC — Text, Reader, Context
UNDP — United Nations Development Program

INTRODUCTION

The Markan Jesus is an authoritative personality, towering over and above everyone else due to his close relationship with God the Father. Mark uses the word ἐξουσία (*exousia*—"absolute authority") to distinguish Jesus's authority from that of the other world authorities. To what extent does the word ἐξουσία, particularly in Mark 1:21–28, construct and perpetuate imperial ideology? In what ways can this ideology be constructive in understanding contemporary imperial ideology? In what ways can the study of Markan ἐξουσία help us understand the abuse of power through the concept described as impunity?

To address these and related questions, I employ a postcolonial reading framework to argue that the Markan gospel is influenced by the imperial setting of his day to construct a Jesus who is all powerful and all knowing, and who exercises power without fear of any personal punishment, harm, or loss. He has ultimate and final power, and beyond him there is no other authority that can hold him responsible for his actions or words.

If my portrayal of Jesus as stated above is true, what consequences and repercussions does this understanding and redeployment have on contemporary generations of Christians and world leaders who appeal to stories such as this one for their imaginations and construction of authority? How has Markan ideology influenced political processes in a country such as Kenya (my case study)? How can we read Mark differently to create an environment where absolute power is not abused or misused? Or how can we reconstruct the Markan message such that absolute power is not vested in a single person but in a bureaucratic system of checks and balances?

Background Issues

In writing this book, I am inspired by widespread voices that deem impunity an emerging social problem in the Kenyan community, and one that needs to be eradicated.[1] I am also inspired by the fact that biblical studies have increasingly turned to a postcolonial reading strategy to address questions of authoritarian power, both in biblical texts and contemporary times, and the resultant issues of impunity.[2] Simply stated, impunity refers to situations where individuals or groups assume so much power and authority that they deliberately fail to be accountable to anyone else. Consequently, they commit all sorts of crimes without fear of being punished. For Leah Kimathi, impunity refers to

> ...behavior that culminates from a null expectation of punishment and develops into a culture especially in countries that suffer from corruption or that have entrenched systems of patronage, or where the judiciary is weak or members of the security forces are protected by special jurisdictions or immunities.[3]

Although, as Kimathi states, impunity is rampant in weak democratic systems, I would add that impunity is a global problem to the extent that it has drawn the attention of the world community, which desires to find ways to eradicate the problem. For example, the United Nations special rapporteur Louis Joinet calls on the world community to be united to combat impunity.[4] The worst-hit continent with the problem of impunity is Africa, where the efforts to hold senior government officials and rebel leaders accountable for torture, murder, rape, and other serious crimes against humanity have been hampered by the same leaders' ability to evade the rule of law. Recognizing this problem, the United Nations

---

1. See for example Mwangi wa Gĩthĩnji and Frank Holmquist, "Reform and Political Impunity in Kenya: Transparency without Accountability," ASR 55, no. 1 (2012): 53–74.

2. See Henry Schwarz and Sangeeta Ray, eds., *A Companion to Postcolonial Studies* (Oxford, UK: Blackwell Publishing, 2005); Pramod K. Nayar, ed., *Postcolonial Studies: An Anthology* (Hoboken, NJ: Wiley Blackwell, 2016), and R. S. Wafula, *Biblical Representations of Moab: A Kenyan Postcolonial Reading* (New York: Peter Lang, 2014).

3. Leah Kimathi, "Whose Truth, Justice and Reconciliation? Enhancing the Legitimacy of the Truth, Justice and Reconciliation Commission among Affected Communities in Kenya," *International Peace Support Training Centre* 6, no. 1 (2010): 1–40, 17.

4. Louis Joinet. Impunity Watch (July), accessed June 3, 2017, http://www.impunitywatch.org/en/publication/2.

INTRODUCTION

Council formed the International Criminal Court (ICC) in July 2002 to help countries address cases of impunity.[5]

The situation of impunity in my home country of Kenya, which I will use as a case study in this book, can be traced back to colonial history. Philip Alston, who was the UN special rapporteur to Kenya immediately after the 2007 postelection violence, describes Kenya as a place where impunity is a culture that has gained increasing momentum since independence.[6] The postcolonial Kenyan leadership state has continued to refine and sharpen the art of oppression and control bequeathed by the colonial state. It is no wonder, therefore, that between independence in 1963 and 2017, the Kenyan constitution been amended over thirty times, most with the singular purpose of consolidating the powers of the presidency.[7]

Pondering on these changes, Mbai argues that throughout the 1970s, 1980s and 1990s, personal rule by the incumbent presidents promoted repression, abuses of human rights, ethnicity, nepotism, patronage, and widespread corruption. Within this context, the institutionalization of the use of violence, manipulation of ethnicity for political and economic gains with concomitant marginalization and inequality in access to resources, as well as the breakdown of state institutions became the defining characteristics of the state. The repeated failure to stem the ethnically-based political violence, to evade purging official impunity and to hold perpetrators of human rights abuses to account created a climate of impunity that often led to cycles of violence.[8]

The violence that erupted in Kenya immediately after the 2007 general elections, and the continuous rampant disregard for the rule of the law that exists, can be interpreted against this backdrop. The fact that Kenya has had its current president and deputy president tried at the

---

5. AMICC, accessed June 3, 2017, http://www.amicc.org/docs/Conservative%20.pdf.

6. Philip Alston, *Promotion and Protection of All Human Rights, Civil, Political, Economic, Social and Cultural Rights, Including the Right to Development: Report of the Special Rapporteur on Extrajudicial, Summary or Arbitrary Executions, Philip Alston—Mission to Kenya* (Geneva: United Nations—Human Rights Council, 2009), 5.

7. Odhiambo Mbai, "The Rise and Fall of the Autocratic State in Kenya," in *The Politics of Transition in Kenya*, ed. Odhiambo Mbai, P. Wanyande, and W. Oyugi (Nairobi: Heinrich, Boll Foundation, 2003), 51–95.

8. Mbai, "Rise and Fall," 55.

ICC as suspects for crimes against humanity can be interpreted as a lack of capacity by the country to offer justice to her citizens.[9]

But how is the Kenyan impunity situation related to the Bible, and more specifically to the Markan depiction of Jesus? In general terms, several scholars have pointed out how the Bible has influenced the Kenyan political scene. For example, by revealing how initial European missionaries were counterparts of colonial masters, Humphrey Waweru has argued that the Bible was used by the missionaries to legitimize colonial control in Kenya.[10] Julius Kiambi argues that the Bible has influenced the ever-widening gap between the rich and the poor in Kenya.[11] Kiambi is probably relying on the idea that Christians comprise 82 percent of Kenya's population.[12] Owing to this fact, and with the observation that in Kenya the Bible is highly esteemed, it follows that the Bible forms a central aspect of the population's thought pattern. If this is true, there could be a relationship between the hearing and reading of the Bible in Kenya, as far as Mark's exposition of Jesus's authority in Mark 1:21–28 is concerned. Consequently, it is imperative to read Mark in the context of the use of the Greek term ἐξουσία and how that relates to the reception of the biblical message in Kenyan communities.

Mark 1:21–28 is extensively used in this book because its usage of the term ἐξουσία dictates the construction of authority in the rest of the gospel. Thus, I use ἐξουσία to explore empire traits in the text that influence the picture of authority by paying special attention to the characters in the gospel who are employed to exercise it.

---

9. The ICC website contains details of the prosecution of Uhuru Kenyatta and William Ruto for various crimes against humanity. These cases were on account of the pair being alleged sponsors of the 2007 postelection violence in Kenya. See https://www.icc-cpi.int/kenya/kenyatta and https://www.icc-cpi.int/kenya/rutosang.

10. Humphrey Waweru, "Postcolonial and Contrapuntal Reading of Revelation 22:1–5 Part 2." *Churchman* 121, no. 2 (2007): 139–62.

11. Kiambi Julius, *Postcolonial "Redaction" of Social-Economic Parables in Luke's Gospel; Bible and Making of the Poor in Kenya* (Berlin: LAP Lambert Academic Publishing, 2011), 61–62. Kiambi uses a postcolonial framework to do an "otherwise" reading of socioeconomic parables in Luke's gospel. Kiambi concludes that such a reading exposes binary relationships embedded in these parables that give a divine mandate for the poor to be poorer and the rich to grow richer.

12. According to the recent demographic survey published after the 2019 census, Christians in Kenya are 85.5 percent of the population (47,564,296), "Kenyan Population and Housing Census," accessed April 15, 2020, http://www.scribd.com/doc/36670466/Kenyan-Population-and-Housing-Census-PDF.

Introduction

Impunity: A Kenyan Problem

Although impunity is not a singularly Kenyan problem, Kenya needs to address the issue quickly because there are serious and increasing cases of disregard for the rule of law. Impunity is a major cause of the disregard for the rule of the law, leading to social disintegration, ethnic intolerance, corruption, and ultimately violence and bloodshed in Kenya. There are many examples of impunity shared in this book, but the fact that many Kenyan leaders are not tolerant of or patient with judicial systems, regulatory bodies, and common sense in maintaining a community of workable systems is a clear indication that impunity is the norm. Because of this, many Kenyans can willingly break the law because they are assured of triumphing over the consequences through other means, which are discussed in this book.

The good news is that the search for a fair and just society in Kenya is being advanced from many quarters: by many civil groups and nongovernmental organizations (NGOs), like the United Nations Development Program (UNDP), International Federation of Women Lawyers (FIDA), and Bunge la Mwananchi,[13] among others. Moreover, the implementation of Kenya's current constitution that was promulgated on August 27, 2010, continues to make major inroads in promising an impunity free society. This book provides a religious tributary of thought that equips the church to address the issue of impunity in Kenya.

---

13. Bunge la Mwananchi is a platform that was started in 2008 to discuss the social, political, and economic status of citizens of Kenya. It is involvement in governance by ordinary members of the community. It is a people's parliament and, in every aspect, unofficial.

CHAPTER ONE

Decolonizing Ἐξουσία in Mark 1:21–28

²¹And they entered Caper′na-um; and immediately on the sabbath he entered the synagogue and taught.²² And they were astonished at his teaching, for he taught them as one who had authority (ἐξουσία), and not as the scribes.²³ And immediately there was in their synagogue a man with an unclean spirit and cried out; ²⁴ saying, "What is it you with us, Jesus of Nazareth? Have you come to destroy us? I know who you are, the Holy One of God."²⁵ And Jesus rebuked him, saying, "Be silent, and come out of him!"²⁶ And convulsing him the unclean spirit, cried with a loud voice and came out of him.²⁷ And they were all amazed, so that they were discussing among themselves, saying, "What is this? A new teaching! With authority (ἐξουσία) he commands even the unclean spirits, and they obey him."²⁸ And immediately his fame spread throughout the whole region neighboring Galilee.

Introduction

The task of this chapter is to examine how Mark uses the term ἐξουσία in Mark 1:21–28. The aim of such a reading is to concretely identify how Mark weaves the ideology of power and authority in his ἐξουσία and the various ways in which he intends his readers to understand it. This helps to center the priority of the concept of ἐξουσία in Mark's gospel in addressing impunity in Kenya.

Mark's ἐξουσία

Discussing Mark's concept of authority begins where most Markan scholars begin their engagement with Mark. That is, by acknowledging, as most scholars do, that Mark is the earliest of the gospels to be written and that it provides a framework by which the other synoptic gospels (Matthew and Luke) are worked and reworked.[1] In spite of its historicity, Mark is also rich in theological interpretation. Indeed, most critical scholars conclude that Mark is deeply theological in his orientation and that he shapes his story in ways that fit his view of things. In other words, we do not just get in Mark history as it really happened, but we get a theological interpretation and faith proclamation.[2]

Consequently, there is a structural tension between spiritual and political authority. Although a number of scholars, such as Dennis Nineham, have rejected the idea of structure in Mark, citing that this is "attributing to the Evangelist a higher degree of self-conscious purpose than he in fact possessed," the gospel is not entirely devoid of a structure.[3] It is within Mark's redactional genius that his structure is conscripted; otherwise there would be no need of studying how and why Mark arranged his traditions.

Within his structure, Mark plays out a spiritual and political ἐξουσία that is not easily smoothed out. On the one hand, in the gospel, Jesus is the Messiah and Son of God, who as the suffering servant gives his life as a ransom for many. Jesus is presented in purely spiritual terms. He is a spiritual leader whose key qualities that lead to his exaltation and glory revolve around service, suffering, and humility. In Simon Samuel's words, "Mark fundamentally interprets the Kingdom of God as a present reality realized within the faith of the community as it exhibits spiritual insights and understanding (Mark 12:28–34)."[4]

On the other hand, in Mark we encounter a Jesus who has absolute authority to disrupt political authority and instate his own views. Jesus

---

1. See for example Robert Stein, *Mark* (Grand Rapids, MI: Baker Academic, 2008); Carl Holladay, *Introduction to the New Testament: Reference Edition* (Texas: Baylor University Press, 2017); Herman C. Waetjen, *A Reordering of Power: A Socio-Political Reading of Mark's Gospel* (Minneapolis: Fortress, 1989); and Simon Samuel, *A Postcolonial Reading of Mark's Story of Jesus* (London: T&T Clark, 2007), among others.

2. Herman C. Waetjen, *A Reordering of Power: A Social-Political Reading of Mark's Gospel* (Minneapolis, MN: Fortress Press, 1989), 56.

3. Dennis E. Nineham, *The Gospel of St. Mark* (New York: Penguin Books, 1963), 29.

4. Simon Samuel, *A Postcolonial Reading of Mark's Story of Jesus* (New York: T&T Clark, 2007), 125.

not only has authority on earth to forgive sins, calm storms, and raise the dead, but also to superintend over all human affairs.[5] In Mark, therefore, is a structure that tries to fix this tension of a Jesus who is authoritative in his spirituality and authoritative in his politics. It is this last point—the note of authority as exemplified in this structural tension and built up in his concept of ἐξουσία—that remains my focus.

Mark's first mention of ἐξουσία is in a summary passage (1:21–28), and it refers to Jesus's authority in the teaching and performance of miracles. In John Hargreaves's opinion, there are three parts to this story: Jesus's teaching (vv. 21–22), his healing (vv. 23–26), and the effect of his work on others (vv. 27–28).[6] These verses are part of a longer section (vv. 21–45), which tells of the sort of work Jesus was doing while at Capernaum. According to Jack Dean Kingsbury, it is in these verses that Mark introduces a conflict built around ἐξουσία, which dominates other conflicts in the gospel.[7] Whether or not this is true depends on the interpretation of ἐξουσία in this passage and other occurrences in the gospel.

Herman C. Waetjen understands Mark's usage of authority in two ways: first, as a condemnation of an old order, which is represented by the temple, and by the power of Jewish and Roman establishments.[8] Second, he sees Mark's authority as characterized by binary exclusion (for example, in the formation of the in-group against the out-group), hierarchical oppression, and economic dispossession (systemic impunity).[9] Accordingly, in Waetjen's reading, Jesus's order and use of authority typify and signify the possibility of a new community that is characterized by love and inclusiveness.

According to Michael Cline, ἐξουσία is used ten times (1:22, 27; 2:10; 3:15; 6:7, 13; 11:28, 29, 33; 13:34) in the gospel of Mark to denote authority and power.[10] There are other times when the authority of Jesus is much more implicit, arising more from his actions than his words. It hides in the background of his evaluations of present-day Judaism and the

---

5. See Samuel, *A Postcolonial Reading*, 125, who also tends to (though not in such a direct way) decipher and ascribe this kind of tension in Mark's presentation of his Jesus.

6. John Hargreaves, *A Guide to St Mark's Gospel* (London: SPCK, 1994), 45–52.

7. Jack Dean Kingsbury, *Conflict in Mark: Jesus, Authorities, Disciples* (Minneapolis, MN: Fortress Press, 1989), 78.

8. Waetjen, *A Reordering of Power*, 47–48.

9. Waetjen, *A Reordering of Power*, 49.

10. Michael Cline, "The Gospel of Mark and Authority," accessed June 16, 2018, http://reclinerramblings.com/2009/03/gospel-of-mark-and-authority.html.

religious establishment (e.g., 8:33, 9:7). Jesus's ἐξουσία is demonstrated in the power of his words, which produce the healing and expulsion of unclean spirits. The term reveals the element of freedom in his authority and shows that Jesus's power is unmatched. James Edwards argues that Mark deliberately packs too much into his usage of the term ἐξουσία.[11] The specific assertion is that ἐξουσία as used by Mark derives not from human origins but from the authority of God that Jesus receives at his baptism (Mark 1:9-10), and that it constitutes the essence of his divine sonship and unique confidence to act on God's behalf.

Much focus is put by scholars on this word, ἐξουσία, and in all instances it connotes the dawn of a new order. Read through a historical-critical lens, the usage of ἐξουσία in Mark's gospel does not reveal as much. However, read through a postcolonial lens, several observations begin to emerge about Mark's construction of the authority. For example, the authority of Jesus is taken for granted and obeyed without question, just as the authority of the Roman colonialists would have been obeyed without question.[12] For Tat-Siong Benny Liew, Mark mimics the Roman colonial discourse of power in order to enforce its own brand of imperial tyranny, boundary, and might.[13] Liew emphatically argues that ἐξουσία as taken up in "Mark's politics of *Parousia* remains a politics of power, because Mark still understands ἐξουσία as the ability to have one's commands obeyed and followed, or the power to wipe out those who do not."[14]

Insofar as postcolonialism is concerned, Stephen D. Moore exposes the construction of imperial authority in Mark by showing that the gospel refuses to relinquish its dreams of the empire.[15] Richard Horsley works with various facets of Mark's gospel in a similar manner, and commands great authority in dealing with the gospel and the entire New Testament.[16]

---

11. James R. Edwards, "The Authority of Jesus in the Gospel of Mark," *JETS* 37, no. 2 (1994): 217–33.

12. See for example Mark 11:1–11 where Jesus enters Jerusalem. The smoothness of that narration depends on the obedience of his followers

13. Tat-Siong Benny Liew, "Tyranny, Boundary and Might: Colonial Mimicry in Mark's Gospel," *JSNT* 73 (1999): 7–31.

14. Liew, "Tyranny," 25.

15. Stephen D. Moore, *Empire and Apocalypse: Postcolonialism and the New Testament* (Sheffield, UK: Phoenix Press, 2006), 1–23.

16. Richard A. Horsley, "Submerged Biblical Histories and Imperial Biblical Studies," in *The Bible and Postcolonialism*, ed. R. S. Sugirtharajah (Sheffield, UK: Sheffield Academic Press, 1998), 152–73.

Joerg Rieger also deals with Mark from a postcolonial biblical perspective.[17] In his seminal work *Christ and Empire*, Rieger reads authority in Mark by elucidating how a theological depiction of Christ was laden with colonial biases.[18] This author goes back and forth, leaning on this "earliest" gospel to propose a decolonized image for Jesus's authority. His strength lies in his unique incorporation of church history in postcolonial biblical studies and the usage of Mark's gospel as a source for that history.

The studies on Mark's usage of authority are creative, pointed, and contextual. I have incorporated as many as I could in this book. However, it is important to note that it is unlikely that the authors mentioned above have shown in detail how the authority that Mark has ascribed to Jesus as "the holy one of God" (ὁ ἅγιος τοῦ θεοῦ) (Mark 1:24) can be construed as impunity. This is the unique contribution that I hope to make in this book. I work with both the socio-historical and socio-literary dimensions of the text to argue that Mark's construction of ἐξουσία can be used to construct impunity, and later in this work, I show how this perception and persuasion can be addressed.

Mark's Construction of Jesus's ἐξουσία

Mark 1:21–28 raises questions on what precedes and what succeeds these verses. The section forms a perfect harmony with the rest of the gospel, which Robert Stein views as belonging to an anonymous gospel that church tradition and contemporary scholarship overwhelmingly ascribe to John Mark of Jerusalem, who was the abbreviator of Peter.[19] This Mark is likely mentioned in Acts 12:12, 25; 13:5, 13; and 15:37, and in four New Testament epistles, Colossians 4:10, Philemon 24, 2 Timothy 4:11, and 1 Peter 5:13. Mark writes from Rome, and for an audience that was predominantly Gentile. He writes in the simplest of styles, not only to document the life and works of Jesus, but also to present his understanding of Jesus. Although Mark has other themes that he presents in his multilayered discourse, it should be noted that, regarding his main purpose (the life of Jesus), Mark is straight to the point, starting with the public ministry and ending with the death of Jesus. This has caused sev-

---

17. Joerg Rieger, *Christ and Empire: From Paul to Postcolonial Times* (Philadelphia, PA: Fortress, 2007), 269–301.

18. Rieger, *Christ and Empire*, 287.

19. See Robert H. Stein, *Mark: Baker Exegetical Commentary on the New Testament* (Grand Rapids, MI: Baker Academic, 2008). See also Eusebius (*Eccl. Hist.* 3.39, 1–17).

eral scholars to note that Mark is a gospel of an abrupt beginning and an abrupt ending.[20] Although this trajectory can be followed in other works, the most important dimension here is to note that Mark was originally written to help imperial subjects learn the hard truth about their world and themselves, through the lens of Jesus's life.[21]

Most studies of this gospel agree that the narrative of 1:21–28 falls into a section that is part of the continuing discourse that starts from Jesus's announcement of the εὐαγγελίον ("good news") in 1:14–8:22. Eugene LaVerdiere terms this section an action story.[22] This is probably because, in Mark's and Luke's gospels, this exorcism constitutes the first miracle that Jesus performed, with the synagogue being the perfect background scene. It has less discourse than the previous section and is the home of the so-called Markan καὶ εὐθὺς ("and immediately") narrative trope that elucidates the fast-paced nature of the gospel. Moreover, it is important as a section because, according to Stein, it introduces the story of exorcism as part of the longer "teaching-by-action" ministry.[23] Moreover, in Stein's view, there is a need to take note of the importance that authority plays in all these appearances and "acts" where Jesus is starring. Mark 1:27 can be singled out as "the summary of Jesus' authoritative teaching in Mark 1:21–27."[24] The section is followed by an account of exorcism containing an additional statement about his authoritative teaching.[25] For Mark, therefore, this is a "new teaching with authority"—a new form of ἐξουσία.

In this way, Mark can be construed as having "taken a traditional story of an exorcism by Jesus, placed it at the beginning of his ministry, and edited it to emphasize the authoritative teaching ministry of Jesus."[26] Given this, it is persuasive that Jesus is the subject of the story: "His teaching and accent of authority, the supernatural aura of His person,

---

20. See for example Robert H. Gundry, *Mark: A Commentary on His Apology for the Cross* (Grand Rapids, MI: William B. Eerdmans, 1993).

21. Ched Myers, *Binding the Strong Man: A Political Reading of Mark's Story of Jesus*, 2nd ed. (Maryknoll, NY: Orbis Books, 2008), 11.

22. Eugene LaVerdiere, *The Beginning of the Gospel: Introducing the Gospel According to Mark* (Collegeville, MN: The Liturgical Press, 1999), 37.

23. Robert H. Stein, *Mark* (Grand Rapids, MI: Baker Academic, 2008), 83–91.

24. Stein, *Mark*, 84.

25. Stein, *Mark*, 85.

26. J. R. Donahue and D. J. Harrington, *The Gospel of Mark* (Collegeville, MN: The Liturgical Press, 2002), 83.

His reaction to evil, His ringing command and sentence of expulsion; these are the points that arrest the attention of the reader."²⁷ Therefore, who Jesus is in terms of his authority forms part of the "Good News" (τὸ εὐαγγελίον) that Mark introduces (Mark 1:1).

Scholarly agreement cites this pericope as a genuine account of Mark because it does not deviate from the more familiar Markan method of narration. Moreover, at this point, the narrative richly "abounds in primitive features," which is a key characteristic of the Markan style.²⁸ Thus, the hand of Mark is seen in all the verses, including his simple Greek grammar betrayed by the frequent use of καὶ ("and"), followed by εὐθύς ("immediately"), which are Markan literary characteristics.²⁹ Mark attempts to explain all other instances in this section except the fact that Jesus was seen "as having authority" (ὡς ἐξουσίαν ἔχων). He offers a slim explanation of this in Mark 1:23-28. Stein points out that in Mark 1:23-28, Jesus's authority is contrasted with that of the scribes (οἱ γραμματεῖς), probably because he spoke as one with authority to make own pronouncements on the Torah rather than appealing, like the scribes, to authoritative texts or teachers.³⁰

However, it can be noted that a scribe is a professional person who possesses the ability to write and interpret texts. This was once a secular position, but in the NT times it was associated with religious duties such as interpreting religious texts and serving as guardians of the tradition. It is important to note, however, that the contrast between the authority of Jesus and that of the scribes is possibly because all along in the gospels, the scribes act as the (un)necessary "other" and are mostly "othered," isolated, and portrayed in Mark as bitterly opposed to Jesus (see e.g., Mark 2:6, 16; 11:27-33; 15:33). Jesus's teaching is contrasted with that of the Pharisees because his teaching possesses ἐξουσία ("authority"). Some scholars have suggested that the difference between them lay in the fact that Jesus's authority was spiritual while that of the scribes was intellectual, hence worldly.³¹

Although this is not my main argument here, there is a need to question this simple explanation of ἐξουσία that is given and go beyond the

---

27. Vincent Taylor, *The Gospel According to St. Mark: The Greek Text with Introduction, Notes and Indexes*, 2nd ed. (Grand Rapids, MI: Baker Book House, 1988), 171.

28. Taylor, *Gospel According to St. Mark*, 171.

29. See Tolbert, 1989, 59–78; Beavis, 1989, 35–37.

30. Mary Ann Beavis, *Mark* (Grand Rapids, MI: Baker Academic, 2011), 54.

31. See Stein, *Mark*, 86, among others.

meaning that Mark intends in his insertion of Jesus's authority at this stage. There is a need to invoke David Penchansky's model for reading the Bible ideologically "by examining the cracks or fault lines in the text and the points of dissonance."[32] Therefore, in this section just as it is done in popular movies, Mark prepares his readers for the ensuing action by propping up the main character, Jesus. This section, apart from being an exorcism account, points out the unique authority of Jesus that elicits amazement and wonder. Authority must be Jesus's companion for Mark to sustain the central thesis of his argument. This authority manifests itself in political or spiritual forms. It is authority with something new; Jesus needs only speak and the demons must obey.

Authority in Mark is far more than just Jesus's spiritual prowess. It is also a form of "imperial power," in the sense that Jesus has power over all humans in the echelons of power. He controls what they cannot. For Mark, Jesus must be able to control the empire of demons, whom the reader must understand as being human rivals from time immemorial. According to Edwards, beginning with this story (see also Mark 3:7-12, 5:1-20), the exorcisms in Mark present the gripping conflict between the empire of God and the dominion of Satan; between the one anointed with God's Spirit and those held captive by unclean spirits.[33] The in-breaking of God's kingdom in Jesus begins, according to Mark, not in the human arena but in the cosmic arena, to bind the "strong man" (Mark 3:27) who exercises power over the natural order. Indeed, as supernatural powers themselves, the demons recognize the mission and authority of Jesus before humanity does (Mark 1:24, 3:11, 5:7). Nevertheless, the encounter is a no-contest event. All that can be mustered by the evil spirits is mere complaint: "'What have you to do with us, Jesus of Nazareth? Have you come to destroy us?' cried the demoniac. 'I know who you are, the Holy One of God'" (Mark 1:24).

As seen above, Mark puts human beings and evil forces at loggerheads. The world of demons is portrayed as superior to and more powerful than that of human beings.[34] In this power differentiation, Jesus becomes the powerbroker on the side of human beings against demons. By assigning Jesus this power, Mark subtly introduces imperialism. He creates ideological spaces for the center (Jesus) and the margins (human beings),

---

32. David Penchansky, "Up for Grabs: A Tentative Proposal for Doing Ideological Criticism," *Semeia* 9, no. 34 (1999): 35–56.

33. Edwards, "Authority of Jesus in Mark," 217–233.

34. Taylor, *St. Mark*, 171.

the "Other" and the "othered." In Mark 1:22, Mark uses the Greek verb ἐξεπλήσσοντο ("astonished") to express great amazement or being awestruck. Several times, this verb is used in Mark to express the crowds' amazement at Jesus's authoritative power (cf. Mark 6:2, 7:37, 11:18). It is the authority of Jesus, which the crowds are not accustomed to, that causes their amazement.[35]

The differentiation of power is not just with the common crowds; it is also between Jesus and religious leaders. The word ἐξουσία appears in Mark 1:22, where those listening to Jesus in the synagogue "were amazed at his teaching, because he taught them as one who had *authority*." This perceived authority is then contrasted with that of the teachers of the law, the Jewish religious leaders of the day.[36]

Jesus's power is not only reported in his activities; it is also placed on the lips of the crowds in the synagogue. In Mark 1:27, Jesus has just performed an exorcism and the crowd is amazed, saying, "What is this? A new teaching—and with authority! He even gives orders to evil spirits and they obey Him." Here, Jesus's authority links with his ability to cast out evil spirits.

In Mark 1:23, as in 1:21, καὶ εὐθὺς ("and immediately") appears, which is characteristically Markan, and is used not only to show the rapid sequence of events after he entered Capernaum, but also the rapid ascendancy of his authority. The word ἀνέκραξεν ("to cry aloud") indicates strong emotion that presents some ambiguity. As Taylor observes, it is difficult, if not impossible, to determine whether it is the demons crying or the man himself.[37] Important to note, however, is that many times in Mark πνεῦμα ἀκάθαρτον ("unclean spirit") is interchangeably used with demons. Apparently, the man identifies himself with the demon and speaks in the name of the class to which he belongs, which Mark indicates is a class below that of Jesus.

In verse 24, the question of the demons possessing the man, ἦλθες ἀπολέσαι ἡμᾶς; οἶδά σε τίς εἶ, ὁ ἅγιος τοῦ θεοῦ ("Have you come to destroy us? I know who you are, the holy one of God"), is another place to locate Mark's construction of Jesus's ἐξουσία. For example, there is the sudden change from plural (ἡμᾶς—"us") to singular (οἶδά—"I know"), which not only reveals a plurality of voices but also an expression of the person

---

35. Mary Hooker, *A Commentary on the Gospel According to St Mark* (London: A&C Black, 1985), 63.

36. Hooker, *St Mark*, 62.

37. Taylor, *St. Mark*, 174.

in the demons or the demons in the person. According to Hooker, the phrase ὁ ἅγιος τοῦ θεοῦ ("the Holy one of God") expresses a deeper truth about Jesus's authority unknown to the bystanders but recognized by the demon, who is assumed to have supernatural knowledge.[38] In the comprehension of this saying and in determining what this phrase means, a decision must be made with the understanding of how "the messianic secret" is interpreted.[39]

Jesus's power is further enhanced in 1:25-27. Here Jesus rebukes the unclean spirit, and commands it to be silent and come out of the affected man. According to Hooker, Jesus uses the word Φιμώθητι ("come out!"), which was used in the ancient world in magic spells for binding people and demons.[40] This could mean that Mark is constructing a magician Jesus or, in LaVerdiere's view, it could imply that Markan Jesus shared the belief in demon possession.[41] The Greek word ἐπετίμησεν ("rebuked" or "chided") is meant to heighten the ἐξουσία of Jesus. In 1:27 Mark employs two more words: ἐθαμβήθησαν and κατ' ἐξουσίαν. The word ἐθαμβήθησαν ("to be amazed") is used to express great astonishment. It is employed metaphorically to denote that they were totally silenced. It is also remarkable that Mark ascribes this word and its impression to Jesus since the Jews were quite familiar with exorcisms.[42] For the ignorant crowd, the astonishment is because Jesus casts out the spirit with a word and not with a magical formula.[43] Unlike verse 21, the new teaching is now the point of authority. Most importantly, what now arouses astonishment for Mark is possibly not the action but the ἐξουσία in the "new teaching" (διδαχὴ καινή) and the note of authority.

In 1:28, Mark closes his narration of this miracle story by heightening the effect of Jesus's authority. He does this by a reference to the spread of this "new teaching with authority" (κατ' ἐξουσίαν) and by the use of the word ἀκοὴ ("was heard"), which marks the urgency with which the news about Jesus's ἐξουσία spread. Notice also the third εὐθὺς ("immediately") in this short passage. Luke's account, despite its verbal agreement with

---

38. Hooker, *St Mark*, 64.
39. Taylor, *St. Mark*, 64.
40. Hooker, *St Mark*, 65.
41. LaVerdiere, *The Beginning*, 71.
42. See also Hooker, *St Mark*, 65.
43. Taylor, *St. Mark*, 176.

Mark, omits all εὐθὺς, probably because ἐξουσία is not part of Luke's theological purposes.

A Postcolonial Appraisal of the Gospel of Mark

Mark's gospel, like many other New Testament texts, has largely been read from a historical-critical point of view, with a focus on themes such as the messianic secret, or as a passion narrative with an extended introduction.[44] The gospel has also been read for its advocacy on discipleship, priority among the synoptics, Christology, and eschatology.[45] However, in the last decade or so, and with the entry of postcolonial biblical criticism, other ways of reading Mark have emerged. These new ways have brought to the surface issues of colonizer-colonized relationships that are present in the gospel. In this regard, a reading of ἐξουσία in 1:21-28 interrogates for colonial nuances the spiritual authority inherent in the text.

Postcolonial readings of Mark may be classified into at least four main models.[46] These are (1) the model that reads Mark as an essentialist postcolonial resistant literature;[47] (2) the model that reads it as a resistant as well as colonizing discourse;[48] (3) the model that sees it as a colonial mimetic discourse representing tyranny, boundary, and might;[49] and (4) the model that views Mark as a colonial archive with traces of postcolo-

---

44. It was William Wrede (see Hooker, *St Mark*, 66) who, in 1901, first attempted to explain the theme of secrecy (which he termed "messianic secret") in the gospel by suggesting that it reflects a tension between the belief of the early church in Jesus as messiah and the un-messianic character of Jesus's ministry. Jesus's command to secrecy, he argued, cannot be taken as historical but was a dogmatic device to explain why he was not acknowledged as messiah during his ministry. The interpretation of Jesus's words and deeds as messianic belongs to the post-Easter faith of the community and has been imposed upon the tradition. This claim by Wrede has not had easy explanations, but it is agreeable to most scholars that Jesus was widely recognized as the messiah (in Christian sense) in the light of the post-Easter traditions.

45. Taylor, *St. Mark*, 653-60.

46. Samuel, *Mark's Story of Jesus*, 76.

47. Horsley, "Submerged Biblical Histories," 153.

48. Mary Ann Tolbert, *Sowing the Gospel; Mark's World in Literary-Historical Perspective* (Minneapolis, MN: Fortress Press, 1989).

49. Liew, "Tyranny," 28.

nial heteroglossia.[50] A brief appraisal of these models becomes important for the ongoing argument.

Richard Horsley's reading of Mark suggests that Mark's narrative efficiently obscures and submerges the histories and aspirations of imperially subjected peoples and therefore needs a radical overhaul. He states that

> a postcolonial biblical study includes in its agenda the emancipation of previously submerged or distorted histories of the movements that produced the literature that was later included in the Bible—partly by avoiding, opposing, and replacing the essentialist and depoliticizing categories and approaches of imperial western biblical studies.[51]

For Horsley, if Mark is an "on-the-way" gospel, then it becomes the story of the "othered" people, and these are the people who, when viewed through postcolonial lenses, are "out-of-the-way" people. These are the people who not only resist Roman imperialism but also resist the new and subtle empire the Jesus model seems to condone.

Thus, Horsley notes that "Mark provides a metanarrative that enables a movement to maintain its own identity and solidarity over against the pretensions of the imperial metanarrative."[52] Consequently, a postcolonial reading of Mark's story offers a chance to recover the stories of those who are othered—the peasantries, the opponents of the empire, and those who oppose the kingdom of Jesus. In other words, Mark uncovers the immorality of authority in othering and hegemonization, and exposes ἐξουσία as exercised by Jesus, disciples, and demons as a scapegoat for impunity. Horsley does this by revealing that Markan construction of authority for each of these categories is not "innocent" but is an intentional power play.

Second, reading Mark as "resistant as well as a potential colonialist literature" reveals the Markan text as a story that is a "perfect medium for religious propaganda or edification of a people who are rootless and lost restlessly searching for security."[53] Mark is hence a resistant as well as ambivalent literature that originates from the margins. It represents

---

50. Jim Perkinson, "A Canaanitic Word in the Logos of Christ; or the Difference the Syro-Phoenician Woman Makes to Jesus," *Semeia* 75 (1998): 61–85.

51. Horsley, "Submerged Biblical Histories," 167.

52. Horsley, "Submerged Biblical Histories," 161.

53. Samuel, *Mark's Story of Jesus*, 78.

those from the marginal groups in antiquity who were excluded from access to social, economic, political, and religious power and were in constant danger of concrete persecution and repression by those presently holding that power.[54]

Mark further reveals that the audience of Mark per se lived as a colonized people under an imperial power. In this case, Mark might be understood in retrospect as an example of a colonial or even anti-colonial literature. Mark may be construed as denouncing colonial collaborators, though in the end it is uncritical of the neocolonialism that the "beginning" (ἀρχή) heralds. What emerges here is that Mark, in advocating a resistant postcolonial rhetoric against the colonialists, mimics a rival imperial ideology. Mark, like the Roman Empire, enjoins the tactic of invoking violence against the "enemies." This conjures up images of how impunity works in Kenya. The one who has the authority (ἐξουσία) to coerce and run over the subaltern "other" is foregrounded and endowed with economic, spiritual, and political power that he can use for his own selfish ends.

Third, reading Mark as "colonial mimicry of tyranny, boundary and might" reduplicates and internalizes the colonial ideology of the Roman colonialists. In this manner, Mark propagates an imperial regime of impunity.[55] Mark attributes absolute authority to Jesus, preserves the insider-outsider binary opposition, and understands the nature of legitimate authority. Mark also presents Jesus in categories of authority in relational and hierarchical terms. Jesus is the fulfillment of the scripture and the "master scribe." He enjoys "tyrannical" authority to interpret, change, or break scripture. This claim becomes an effective ideological weapon that leads to absolutism. It leaves no room for comparison or competition.[56]

Mark also creates total subservience between the colonizer and the colonized. Following the strict requirements set by Jesus as a precondition for becoming an insider, all others remain outsiders. This leaves no room for criticism or alternative thinking. The fate of outsiders is marked as annihilation at the end in the *Parousia*. As Liew notes, "this in

---

54. Samuel, *Mark's Story of Jesus*, 78.
55. Liew, "Tyranny," 31.
56. Samuel, *Mark's Story of Jesus*, 80.

effect duplicates the colonial (non)choice of 'serve-or-be-destroyed.'"[57] In this case, Mark represents insidious colonial tyranny as a service where wrongs are made right by the master (Jesus). In a similar manner, impunity in Kenya is often marketed as "righting" of wrongs by the ruling elite.

Last, when Mark is viewed as "colonial archive with traces of postcolonial *heteroglossy*," it forms a colonialism that played a crucial role in shaping the Christian scriptures.[58] The gospel made its way into the NT canon because of its "inkling towards domination."[59] For example, in rereading the story of the Syrophoenician woman (Mark 7:25–30), one sees that "the colonial voice of Jesus, though abounding, fails to silence the Canaanite subaltern voice from emanating and speaking for itself."[60] In fact, she can be read as valorizing Jesus's own politics by introducing and representing the "little ones" in her discourse.[61]

The models outlined above are important for the progressing argument in this study, and more so for decolonizing Markan ἐξουσία. They help uncover the colonial bias that Mark's gospel is laden with. They buttress the central thesis of this book, which is that Mark's conception of power and authority evokes a rival imperial ideology and provides a template for seeing the gospel as both a colonial resistant and a potential colonialist literature without any contradiction. More importantly, the models help in the ultimate reading of Mark from a postcolonial perspective that may enable the retrieval of Mark as a narrative of imperially subjected peasantries. Again, this can be done "without subalternizing a narrative that aspired (achieved) hegemony."[62]

IMPERIAL REPRESENTATIONS IN MARK'S GOSPEL

Fernando Segovia argues that postcolonial studies must take the empire seriously because the empire is "an omnipresent, inescapable and

---

57. Liew, "Tyranny," 23.

58. Samuel, *Mark's Story of Jesus*, 81.

59. Perkinson, "A Canaanitic Word," 61–85.

60. In Matthew's gospel (Matt. 15:21–28), she is termed a Canaanite woman. Although Perkinson buys into Matthean language, the label remains that she is a gentile woman. It is probable that Matthew took Mark's original version and modified it for his audience.

61. Perkinson, "A Canaanitic Word," 61–85.

62. Samuel, *Mark's Story of Jesus*, 121.

overwhelming reality in the world," as it was in biblical times.⁶³ Since colonization is not just about soldiers and weapons, but also about forms, images, and imaginings, postcolonial inquiry is helpful in investigating the issues of empire, nation, ethnicity, migration, human subjectivity, race, and language.⁶⁴ Imperialism, according to Musa Dube, is an ideology of expansion that takes diverse forms of methods at different times, as it seeks to impose its languages, trade, religions, democracy, images, economic systems, and political rule on foreign nations and lands.⁶⁵ In empire building, the colonized are rearranged according to the interests and values of the imperializing powers. Though Dube sees this domination as involving suppression by use of conquest through military might and cultural texts, many other critics suggest that the use of ideology and religion cannot be underestimated. Imperialism therefore becomes the "process of building an empire through the imposition of political, economic and social institutions of one nation over a foreign one."⁶⁶

Postcolonial biblical scholars have been exploring issues of imperialism in the gospel of Mark for a while now. Many have noted the role the gospel plays in the process of empire building.⁶⁷ The process seems to involve maintenance and hegemonization of a class that requires a constituent subaltern class. In Mark there is an ambivalent view of the empire. Although Mark in his βασιλεία τοῦ θεοῦ (Kingdom of God) concept lacks a sustained hostility toward the Roman Empire, there is no reason to assume that it is pro-empire. One thing that should be noted in Mark is that βασιλεία should not casually be translated as kingdom; properly understood, βασιλεία in Mark stands for empire, and therefore every occurrence should be read as "empire." In Mark, the empire of God is shrewdly set against the Roman Empire. On this subject, Mark is ambivalent. It is hostile and not hostile; it is attracted and repelled, forming a complex simultaneous liking, and disliking of the Roman imperial

---

63. Fernando F. Segovia, *Decolonizing Biblical Studies: A View from the Margins* (Maryknoll, NY: Orbis Books, 2005), 56.

64. Edward W. Said, *Culture and Imperialism* (New York, NY: Vintage Books), 16.

65. Musa Dube, "Reading for Decolonization (John 4:1–42)," in *The Postcolonial Bible*, ed. R. S. Sugirtharajah (Sheffield, UK: Sheffield Academic Press, 1998), 297.

66. Musa Dube and Jeffrey L. Staley, eds. *John and Postcolonialism: Travel, Space and Power* (Sheffield, UK: Sheffield Academic Press, 2002), 47.

67. See Hans Leander, *Discourses of Empire: The Gospel of Mark from a Postcolonial Perspective* (Atlanta, GA: Society of Biblical Literature, 2013). See also Fernando Segovia and R. S. Sugirtharajah, eds., *A Postcolonial Commentary on the New Testament* (London: T&T Clark, 2009).

power. There is pro-empire and anti-empire rhetoric appearing in his Jesus, the disciples, and his audience (see for example 12:17; 15:29; 20:10). In Mark, empire structures are maintained by pitting the center versus the margins, a process that involves *othering* from both fronts. Mark falls prey to the Roman divide-and-rule strategy of societal organization. The gospel incorporates imperial dimensions of subaltern repression, representation, and representability, thus succumbing to key characteristics of imperial literature.

Consequently, Mark can be interrogated for imperial motives and contamination at the point where it overtly or insidiously dips into historical events of imperialism.[68] If imperialism is "a system of economic, political and cultural force that disavows border in order to extract desirable resources and exploit an alien people," then Mark's gospel seems to support this state in the way it predicts the replacement of Rome with a $\beta\alpha\sigma\iota\lambda\varepsilon\iota\alpha$ (kingdom) that is similarly scripted.[69] Thus Mark, like other "canonical scripture plays a highly significant role in the ideology of imperialism."[70]

In view of the foregoing, Mark's gospel can no longer be viewed as innocent, and must be read with suspicion. This calls for a reading of Mark that involves a reading for decolonization whereby, according to Dube, decolonization stands for

> awareness of imperialism's exploitive forces and its various strategies of resisting domination, the conscious adoption of strategies of resisting imperial domination as well as the search for alternative ways of liberating interdependence between nations races, gender, economies and cultures.[71]

What this means is that, in postcolonial biblical studies, Mark's gospel must be interrogated for the role it plays in empire building, including the cultural values it condones to achieve this course. Thus, situating the empire as Mark does forms a good springboard for interrogating the theme of impunity. This is important because impunity thrives in a climate of othering, particularly an othering buttressed and secured in imperial settings such as that found in Mark's gospel.

---

68. Musa Dube, "Toward a Postcolonial Feminist Interpretation of the Bible," *Semeia* (1997): 17.

69. Jon L. Berquist, "Postcolonialism and Imperial Motives for Canonization," in *The Postcolonial Biblical Reader*, ed. R. S. Sugirtharajah (Oxford, UK: Blackwell, 2006), 30–36.

70. Berquist, "Postcolonialism," 34.

71. Dube, "Decolonization (John 4:1–42)," 298.

Reading Ἐξουσία in Mark's Gospel

The concept of ἐξουσία is a central driver of Mark's gospel and a key ingredient in his construction of Jesus and power relations. In recent times, authority in Mark has attracted several voices. Narry F. Santos, for example, writing from a perspective of the "Paradox of Authority and Servanthood in the Gospel of Mark," has argued that the "gospel of Mark is a paradoxical gospel, a riddle that teases its readers' response, and a narrative that possesses an enigmatic and puzzling character."[72] Using this paradox motif, Santos reveals that paradox of authority serves as a key Markan rhetorical device that urges readers to show servanthood in the exercise of authority within the community of believers and beyond.

Samuel depicts Mark as "the discourse of a subordinate minoritarian community that attempts to map a space in-between the Roman colonial and the relatively dominant native Jewish discourses."[73] In summing up the gospel in such a manner, Samuel views the gospel as a discourse of power, and one in which the author crafts his characters to serve this motif. Liew also situates Mark's story of Jesus in its multilayered imperial framework.[74] In his analysis, Liew concludes that "while Mark may contain critiques of the existing colonial (dis)order, it also contains traces of colonial 'mimicry' that reinscribe colonial domination."[75] Similarly, Brenda Schildgen, who studies Mark from the viewpoint of a reception motif, argues that there are glaring gaps and silences in Mark's gospel that are the source of interest for many commentators. Her central thesis is that Mark's authority is present in our lives and absent at the same time in the silences it enjoins.[76]

According to Stein, Mark's gospel has a Christological authority, which forms the dominating theme.[77] For him, Mark's portrayal of Jesus Christ as the Son of God, although multifaceted, has discernible ἐξουσία, and hence Mark's view of Christ is not innocent. In fact, as he argues, Mark may have "created a majority of his traditions to explain to his readers

---

72. Narry F. Santos, "The Paradox of Authority and Servanthood in the Gospel of Mark," *Bibliotheca Sacra* 154 (1997): 452–60.

73. Samuel, *Mark's Story of Jesus*, 108.

74. Liew, "Tyranny," 7–31.

75. Liew, "Tyranny," 26.

76. Brenda Deen Schildgen, *Power and Prejudice: The Reception of the Gospel of Mark* (Detroit, MI: Wayne State University Press, 1999), 21.

77. Stein, *Mark*, 25.

why the life of Jesus was so '*un-messianic*' and that Jesus became the messiah only after his resurrection."⁷⁸

A further sampling of other relevant scholars of Mark's gospel reveals that Mark rejects the imperialistic Roman oppression, repudiating the temple's exploitative economy, and advocates for building a just and egalitarian community.⁷⁹ Waetjen understands Mark's ἐξουσία as "a condemnation of an old order, which is represented by the temple and the power of the Jewish and Roman establishment, and also characterized by binary exclusion, hierarchical oppression and economic dispossession."⁸⁰ Instead, Jesus's "new order" (ἐξουσία) according to Waetjen's reading of Mark, is typified by egalitarian and familial relationships.⁸¹

Given such a broad spectrum of approaches, one can argue that though there are diverse ways of reading Mark, imperialism nuanced with the idea of ἐξουσία forms a central place in most of the Markan readings. However, none of these readings seem to relate ἐξουσία to impunity or to show the dangers of its extremities. My reading of Mark's gospel hopes to fill this gap.

THE ἘΞΟΥΣΙΑ IN MARK 1:21-28

Most historical-critical readers of Mark view the gospel as an innocently "sacred" text. It is a spiritual story—a gospel that only "repudiates the temples exploitative economy, and advocates building a just and egalitarian community of sharing and mutual service by way of the cross."⁸² However, in light of current developments within postcolonialism, there is a need to invoke a "hermeneutics of suspicion" and to question the one-sidedness of these Markan readings.

Recent trends in Markan scholarship have started turning attention to this issue. Let us look at two scholars, Tat-Siong Benny Liew and James Edwards. Liew reads Mark as a gospel that duplicates colonial ideology in Bhabhan colonial mimicry terms. Mark uses Roman structures to model the authority of his Jesus.⁸³ Mark is also involved in "colonial worlding,"

---

78. Stein, *Mark*, 25.
79. See Ched Myers, *Binding the Strong Man: A Political Reading of Mark's Story of Jesus* (Maryknoll, NY: Orbis, 1988), 34.
80. Waetjen, "Reordering of Power," 116.
81. Waetjen, "Reordering of Power," 117.
82. Liew, "Tyranny," 18.
83. Liew, "Tyranny," 8.

which involves both the construction of the colonizers and the internalization of that constructed world on the part of the colonized.[84] Another characteristic of ἐξουσία in 1:21–28 is that it is full of anti-authority rhetoric. Nevertheless, when it comes to the allocation of an absolute authority to Jesus, "one may question if Mark is concerned with breaking up the very makeup of authority, or merely wishes to replace one authority by another."[85] In Mark 1:21–28, (the first healing miracle) and Mark 2:1–12 (the first controversy story), Mark contrasts the teaching and authority of Jesus with those of the Jewish leaders. This seems to suggest that the issue for Mark must do more with categories of authority (whether new and substantial, or traditional and hollow) than with constitution.

The second scholar, Edwards, shows how Mark opens Jesus' public ministry in 1:21–28 by establishing his supremacy over the highest authorities in both the temporal and supernatural realms.[86] The temporal realm is represented by the scribes, whose erudition and prestige among the people are legendary. The scribes stand in the tradition of the fathers (and mothers) (Mark 7:8–13); however, whereas they receive their authority from the Torah, Jesus receives his authority directly from the "Father" (Mark 1:11). Thus, Jesus appeals to a superior authority than the scribes.[87]

Impunity and Empire Tactics of Ἐξουσία in Mark 1:21–28

Considering Mark's duplication of colonial ideology, and his rhetorical and emotional power, we are reminded of Susan Stewart's argument that when an anti-hegemonic movement turns hegemonic, it often involves gigantic emotions of obedience, loyalty, and faithfulness.[88] One of the tactics that Mark 1:21–28 employs to reduplicate colonial ideology is to present an all-authoritative Jesus who eventually annihilates all opponents and all other authorities. For example, in the question in verse 24, "Have you come to destroy us?," the demons that Mark introduces in his narration seem to be conversant with this arrangement.

Again, as I have argued, Mark maintains the colonial tension and (non) choice colonial mentality of "serve or be destroyed," which is reproduced

---

84. Liew, "Tyranny," 13.
85. Liew, "Tyranny," 13.
86. Edwards, "Authority of Jesus in Mark," 217–233.
87. Edwards, "Authority of Jesus in Mark," 223.
88. Susan Stewart, *On Longing: Narratives of the Miniature, the Gigantic, the Souvenir, the Collection* (Baltimore, MD: Johns Hopkins University Press, 1984), 70–103.

in his Jesus. Unfortunately, this form of arrangement is the very seedbed of impunity. Impunity recreates and socializes its own law and hierarchy, and demands to be submitted to. It has no fixed or written law. It makes its own laws as the situation demands. These laws are engineered to reduce victims to subservient objects even when it defies logic to do so. It remains at the top and asserts itself as the dominant consciousness. With such a tactic, Mark creates a Jesus who functions to justify and sustain impunity. The gospel presents a "hierarchical, punitive and tyrannical concept of ruler and ruled, while claiming that it was all for the best."[89]

If, as Lewis Mudge proclaims, it is the case that "impunity is the wife of power,"[90] what are the relationships and outcomes of impunity in a situation of (over)powering, as found in Mark? Two things stand out when this question is pursued: binarism and othering.

BINARISM

According to Bill Ashcroft, Gareth Griffiths, and Helen Tiffin, signs have meaning not by a simple reference to real objects, but by their opposition to other signs. Thus, signs by their difference form the framework in which binarism thrives.[91] A binarism framework considers extreme forms of difference. Such oppositions, as Ashcroft, Griffiths, and Tiffin show, are quite common in the cultural constructions of reality.[92] The problem with such binary systems is that they suppress the spaces between the opposed categories such that many overlapping regions end up appearing between the expected categories. Postcolonial studies have demonstrated the extent to which such binaries entail a violent hierarchy, in which one term of the opposition is always dominant—for example, man over woman, birth over death, white over black—and that, in fact, the binary opposition itself exists to confirm that dominance.

Adoption of binary conceptualization acts as an imperial tactic when any activity or state that does not fit the binary opposition becomes subject to repression. For instance, the indeterminate stage between child

---

89. Samuel, *A Postcolonial Reading of Mark's Story of Jesus*, 47.

90. K. G. Kannabiran, *The Wages of Impunity: Power, Justice and Human Rights* (New Delhi: Orient Longman, 2004), 12.

91. Bill Ashcroft, Gareth Griffiths, and Helen Tiffin, eds., *Post-Colonial Studies: The Key Concepts* (London: Routledge, 2007), 19–20.

92. Ashcroft, Griffiths, and Tiffin, *Post-Colonial Studies*, 19–20.

and adult (youth) is treated as a suspicious category, a rite of passage subject to considerable suspicion and anxiety. Subsequently, the state between the binarism, such as the binary colonizer or colonized, will evidence signs of extreme ambivalence manifested in mimicry, "cultural schizophrenia," or various kinds of obsession with identity.[93]

Moreover, as Ashcroft, Griffiths, and Tiffin show, the binary logic of imperialism is a development of that tendency of Western thought in general to see the world in terms of binary oppositions that establish a relation of dominance.[94] A simple distinction between center and margin, colonizer and colonized, metropolis and empire, and civilized and primitive represents very efficiently the violent hierarchy on which imperialism is based and that it actively perpetuates. Binary oppositions are structurally related to one another, and in colonial discourse a variation of the underlying binary of colonizer/colonized may be rearticulated in any context. Clearly, the binary concept becomes important in constructing ideological meanings in general, and extremely useful in imperial ideology.

Although binary distinctions are not always motivated by a desire to dominate, the tactic in Mark 1:21-28 is to set up conditions fit for binarism with an intention to control.[95] In other words, in Mark 1:21-28 and other places in the gospel, Mark constructs binarism in such a way that the "other" cannot be avoided in his discourse of power. Binarism must reorder social relations to pave the best way for the colonizer, and this is what we see in the introduction of Jesus's authority right from verse 21. Jesus's presence necessitates the opposite presence of possession and demons. The witnesses become an intervening binary presence in this power matrix. Therefore, the ἐξουσία of Jesus comes to expression in social relations that create binarism. In Mark 1:21-28, and by use of the word ἐξουσία, Mark pits the scribes against Jesus. Fundamentally, Mark employs the tactic of binarism to present a conflict of Jesus and the religious authorities. Mark heightens the intensity of this conflict with the authorities by *absolutizing* the authority of Jesus.

---

93. Ashcroft, Griffiths, and Tiffin, *Post-Colonial Studies*, 20.

94. Ashcroft, Griffiths, and Tiffin, *Post-Colonial Studies*, 21.

95. David Spurr, *The Rhetoric of Empire: Colonial Discourse in Journalism, Travel, Writing and Imperial Administration* (Durham, NC: Duke University Press, 1993), 103.

OTHERING

"Othering" is another empire tactic that Mark employs in 1:21–28 to make absolute Jesus's ἐξουσία. "Othering" has to do with representation and the making of differences to affirm one's identity. In postcolonial studies, the term refers to the process by which imperial discourse creates its "others."[96] Simply stated, this is the conception of existence as them versus us. This "other" becomes the focus of inquiry, especially when it is construed in the arena of power. Therefore, whereas the "other" corresponds to the focus of desire or power in relation to which the subject is produced, the "other" is the excluded or mastered subject, created by the discourse of power.[97] "Othering" describes the various ways in which colonial discourse produces its subjects. In Spivak's explanation, "othering" is a dialectical process because the colonizing *Other* is established at the same time as its colonized *others*[98] are produced as subjects.[99] In any case, in postcolonial discourse, the construction of the "other" is fundamental to the construction of the "Self."

In Mark 1:21–28, "others" are created using the term ἐξουσία in verse 21 and verse 27, and the fact that it requires a subject and an object. Mark does not leave the authority of Jesus in a vacuum. On the contrary, Markan Jesus is the "Other" who creates his corresponding subordinates ("others") using the term ἐξουσία. Since impunity relies on "othering" by creating others in order to take root, it can be argued that Mark's conception of Jesus's ἐξουσία in verse 21 and verse 27 paves the way for the treatment of Jesus and his subjects in the rest of the gospel, unless for Mark it cannot be excused why Jesus transgresses the laws of the "others" to reinstate his "Other" law. This prepares the ground for the sprouting of conflict and the contours that impunity takes in Mark's gospel.

---

96. Ashcroft, Griffiths, and Tiffin, *Post-Colonial Studies*, 123.

97. Anna Virkama, "From Othering to Understanding: Perceiving 'Culture' in Intercultural Communication, Education and Learning," in *Cross-Cultural Lifelong Learning*, ed. V. Korhonen, (Tampere, Finland: Tampere University Press), 47.

98. The capitalization of "Others" here is to differentiate the center and the margins: "Others" for center and "others" for the margins.

99. Gayatri C. Spivak, *Selected Subaltern Studies* (New Delhi, India: Oxford University Press, 1988), 67.

Ἐξουσία in the Rest of Mark

Apart from 1:22 and 27, ἐξουσία is used eight other times in the gospel of Mark.[100] In Mark 2:10, the ministry of Jesus in Capernaum is crowned with his claim to possess the authority to forgive sins. In 3:15 and 6:7, Mark narrates the calling of the first disciples. In each case, Mark concludes his narration by stating that Jesus gives them authority to cast out demons. Again, in an interaction between Jesus and the religious leaders in Mark 11:27–33, the term ἐξουσία is used four times as Mark introduces a whole section (which runs from 11:27 to 12:44) on the question of Jesus's authority after the cleansing of the temple. Jesus shows his authority in the confrontations and controversy narratives without directly answering their questions. In this section, Mark makes it clear that Jesus possesses unique ἐξουσία to do everything.[101] A final occurrence of the word is symbolically placed in the conclusion of Mark's little apocalypse in his parable of the man on a journey—Mark 13:34. The man leaves for the journey, giving each servant ἐξουσία over some part of the household responsibilities until he returns. It is this last ἐξουσία that symbolically sums up the extent of Jesus's final ἐξουσία in Mark's narration.

There are other times when the authority of Jesus is much more implicit, arising more from his actions than his words and hiding in the background of his evaluations of present-day Judaism and the established Roman systems.[102] The implicit ways that Mark does so are all over the gospel. The examples of Jesus's actions that perform this function include his healings, utterances, exorcisms, restoration of the dead, and various clashes with Jewish law, coupled with his subsequent reinterpretation, ability to forgive, power over creation (wind, waves, material goods, and many more), and connection with the Father (Mark 9:7).[103]

In Mark 8:33, in contrast to Peter, Jesus unreservedly claims to know the things of God, which is also a definite claim to authority. There are two instances that appear to stick out in Mark: Jesus's capacity to forgive sins and his right to judge the religious system of the day (including the popular reinterpretation of the Mosaic Law). Though these two are not the most common examples—like the healings and exorcisms—they are the two instances where the authority of the religious leaders directly

---

100. These occurrences are in 2:10, 3:15, 6:7, 11:27–33 (four times), and 13:34.
101. Stein, *Mark*, 528.
102. Edwards, "Authority of Jesus in Mark," 218.
103. Tolbert, *Sowing the Gospel*, 12.

clashes with the authority of Jesus, and where the authority of Jesus is most questioned.

Whether implicit or explicit, in each use it can be observed that the term ἐξουσία refers to that abstract notion of the right and power to act, to command, and in some sense to rule over people and overrule circumstances. Jesus has this right to control and command, and to have power and authority because of his divinity. That is, Jesus reorders social and political priorities, redefines Torah commandments, and claims prerogatives that are otherwise God's alone. In all these verses, it can be deduced that Jesus has the capacity to dispense this power to his disciples, hence the idea that he is the ultimate source of all authority. On a broader scale, he is the one who has divine ἐξουσία.

This uniquely Markan ἐξουσία is also seen within the wider space of Mark's intentions in building up the portrait of Jesus. The construction of this Jesus's ἐξουσία in Mark cannot be construed as innocent. Accordingly, and due to his authority, Jesus's ἐξουσία is well clarified by this passage from Liew:

> Jesus can quote and modify scripture to justify his own actions and teaching whether it is about the Sabbath (2:23–28), the practice of speaking in parables (4:10–12), ritual cleanliness (7:1–8), responsibility to parents (7:9–13), the acceptability of divorce (10:2–12), the assurance of eternal life (10:17–22), the operation of the temple (11:15–17), the credibility of resurrection (12:18–27), the first commandment (12:28–31), the relationship between David and the messiah (12:35–37), or the apocalypse (13:24–27).[104]

Mark does not stop at this. He goes on to offer authorial comments that further silence any contrary thinking on Jesus's authority from his critics. Mark 11:18 states: "And the chief priests and the scribes heard it and sought a way to destroy him; for they feared him, because the multitude was astonished at his teaching." Similarly, Mark 12:37, with the words "and the great throng heard him gladly," demonstrates that Jesus's freedom in the use of scripture was recognized as authoritative and valid by the crowd as well as the scribes.

Mark heightens this authoritarian figure of Jesus by taking his words and actions beyond any temporal imagination. In all of this, Mark appeals to one absolute authority, God! For this reason, Liew shows that

---

104. Liew, "Tyranny," 14.

this ideological construct is buttressed by effectively positioning three scripts, one at the beginning of the gospel (Jesus's baptism—Mark 1:9-11), one in the middle (Jesus's transfiguration—Mark 9:2-8), and one at the end (Jesus's crucifixion—Mark 15:33-40), to declare Jesus as God's son and thus "superimpose a script of divine approval and involvement of all Jesus' activities."[105] Tolbert also points out that presenting Jesus in such a manner gives Jesus an air of omniscience.[106] Thus, the Markan Jesus becomes an authority in himself. His directives become decisions without discussions. When put in terms of "Foucault's theory of power which suggests that power is omnipresent,"[107] the Markan Jesus becomes the very embodiment of that omnipresence.

The fluidity of this kind of absolute authority is evident in the fact that the Markan Jesus cannot even sustain its demands for himself. Since the minimum definition of impunity is refusal and inability to adhere to the rule of law or to denigrate authority, Jesus is seen falling into a trap of his own absolute authority. Several times, Jesus cannot adhere to the demands of this absolute authority and he is sometimes forced to override the instructions that he himself gives others to follow. For example, while he rebukes the scribes for exploiting the livelihood of poor widows (Mark 12:40-44), he allows an undistinguished woman to anoint him with a jar of expensive nard oil that could have been sold and the money given to the poor (Mark 14:3-9). He also faults the Pharisees and the scribes for neglecting their parents (Mark 7:9-13), yet he himself justifies the reason for his decision to ignore and shame his mother and his siblings (Mark 3:31-35).

At another point, Mark constructs the authority of his Jesus by deconstructing that of his disciples. As Patrick Brantlinger notes, the disciples are reduced to playing "sidekick" roles as the royal satellites or virtually "personified colonies" of the messiah.[108] Although Liew reads this treatment of disciples as training or apprenticeship, he concludes that "apprenticeship or Mark's discipleship is often just another name for

---

105. Liew, "Tyranny," 16.

106. Tolbert, *Sowing the Gospel*, 259.

107. Richard A. Lynch, "Foucault's Theory of Power," in *Michael Foucault: Key Concepts*, ed. Dianna Taylor (London: Routledge, 2011), 15.

108. Patrick Brantlinger, *Rule of Darkness: British Literature and Imperialism, 1830–1914* (New York: Cornell University Press, 1988), 57.

slavery or Mark's servitude in human history."[109] This is how Mark builds his ἐξουσία, by reducing disciples to extremely subordinate status.

Another way in which Mark fosters the ἐξουσία of his Jesus is by enjoining familial discourse. Colonial discourse has alerted us to the realization that even language of the family may encode oppressive and dominating relations. In Mark, this may be represented by deliberate obstruction of the "fatherly" authority. In Mark 3:33–35, the vocabulary of "father" is conspicuously absent in Jesus's definition of the new family. As Liew rightly observes, this should not be equated with the dismantling of authority or hierarchy, for Mark goes on to reintroduce an authoritative "father" in the person of God. As such, "Jesus' definition of family does not automatically eliminate the interplay of power and subordination; quite the contrary, power always resides with the one who has the authority to define."[110]

One last thing about familial discourse that needs to be noted is the inclusion of the "child statuses" in Markan discourse (Mark 9:36–37). This is the posture necessary for inclusion and continuing participation. On several occasions, Jesus explicitly refers to his disciples as "children." Even if one understands children as a symbol for something else, "infantilization is still an insulting form of patronization at its best, and an extreme form of victimization at worst."[111] More often than not, such demeaning relations are meant to shield the empire when it acts with impunity and to silence those who would speak truth to power by questioning its ἐξουσία to act.

What is noticeable in Mark 1:21–28 and cannot be redeemed in Mark's gospel is his obsession with the status quo of his irredeemable socialization in imperial and hierarchical power constructions. These powers act with impunity since they are assumed to act on behalf of their cognate empires. Mark retains an extremely hegemonic worldview, which is also seen as stemming from his vantage point from what Walter Brueggemann terms the "dominant consciousness."[112] Mark refuses to diffuse the thinking of the dominant and hegemonic community, and moves alongside and uncritically of that thinking. His critical thinking is numbed by his obsession with the royal culture of the day, which relies on the

---

109. Liew, "Tyranny," 19.

110. Liew, "Tyranny," 20.

111. Liew, "Tyranny," 21.

112. Walter Brueggemann, *Hopeful Imagination: Prophetic Voices in Exile* (Minneapolis, MN: Fortress Press, 1986), 80.

mainstream meta-narratives for their construction of the image of Jesus and his "others." Unfortunately, a Jesus who heralds "Good News" (τὸ εὐαγγελίον) and is meant to be a liberator employs the same tactic as the oppressor with impunity and ends up mimicking the Roman Empire in inaugurating his kingdom. In all this, a tentative conclusion can be made, which is that Mark constructs a supreme Christology from below, on which he relies to represent a portrait of Jesus who is vulnerable to an impunity interpretation.

Conclusion

In this chapter, I have discussed current trends in Markan biblical postcolonial studies as far as they relate to Jesus's ἐξουσία. We see that Mark oscillates between resistance (anticolonial) and collaborative (colonial) ideologies. When Mark reinscribes imperial power, he mimics the Roman colonial discourse that produces tyranny, boundary, and the "Other."[113] He uses the colonizers' cultural categories by making use of the imitation with a difference as a model of self-assertion. Initially pretending to "represent" the subaltern "other," the Markan Jesus ends up colonizing the "other."

This in-betweenness in Mark's gospel can be exploited to sustain the current studies on impunity in contexts where Mark is heard and read. In fact, Mark's mapping of Jesus evolves an in-between cultural space, which necessitates that power must be applied to the subject by the one on top to those below. This power must be submitted to, obeyed, and respected at all costs by those below. The imagination of an alternative community that emerges from the dominant one almost becomes elusive. The alternative becomes a counter-disregard of the power of this Jesus. This is the true seedbed for impunity.

---

113. Samuel, *Mark's Story of Jesus*, 109.

CHAPTER TWO

Social Memory and Kenyan Impunity

Introduction

To link Kenyan impunity with Mark's gospel, it is important to present its manifestations. The major task of this chapter, therefore, is to align more closely the notion of impunity to the elements of the life and history of Kenya through a postcolonial lens. I use a postcolonial framework to trace and analyze several examples of impunity in Kenya.[1] More importantly, I situate the genesis of impunity in contact with the colonizer's ideologies in literature and worldview. On one front, and within a postcolonial framework, impunity in Kenya can be examined as a by-product of "othering." According to Newton Fairclough, "othering" enjoins a discourse that normalizes formations between "we" and "they," producing divisive relationships that threaten safety and survival in the long term.[2] In pitting "them" versus "us," "othering" creates difference from sameness, and this permeates all sectors, including economics, culture, penal institutions, and at a larger scale, the organization of society.

On another front, and still within a postcolonial framework, impunity in Kenya can be viewed as a product of colonial "mimicry." Mimicry that describes the ambivalent relationship between the colonizers and the colonized also depicts the situation where the colonized Kenyans mimic their colonial masters' cultural habits, assumptions, language, institutions, values, and voices to conjure the culture of impunity.

---

1. Presentation of such Kenyan examples assumes that they take their bearings, whether directly or indirectly, from contacts with Mark's gospel or biblical Christianity at large.

2. N. Fairclough, *Discourse in Organization Studies: The Case of Critical Realism* (London: Sage, 2005), 119.

I will also engage ethnicity, political institutions, penal institutions, and poverty, as fertile ground where impunity has been sown and grown in Kenya. I begin by briefly mapping the road taken by Kenya prior to independence. Later, and to get a broader picture of how impunity has stalked Kenya, I survey the extent to which the country has been affected by colonialism and show the ways impunity could be a result of previous contacts with the culture of empire.

The Culture of Impunity in Kenya

There are sufficient grounds to argue that impunity has not only become ingrained in Kenyan social practices, but has become a culture in itself. A substantial body of writing on social, economic, and political issues in Kenya reveals the link between impunity and culture.[3] N. W. Sobania, for example, underscores the fact that Kenya is not governed well, and concludes that this misrule has evolved odd cultures, including corruption and impunity.[4] Michela Wrong particularly exposes issues of governance and impunity in Kenya.[5] Though speaking for the empire, and full of a hegemonic imperial tone, Wrong not only aids in revealing the postcolonial psychology of Kenyan leaders, but also exposes the power struggles and the ἐξουσία that inform impunity. More importantly, she shows how contacts with colonization are replayed in the style of Kenyan authority and leadership.

Along similar lines, Leah Kimathi has sketched the history of impunity in Kenya.[6] Kimathi particularly argues that throughout the 1970s, 1980s, and 1990s, rule by the incumbent presidents promoted repression, abuses of human rights, ethnicity, nepotism, patronage, and widespread corruption. Kimathi further elaborates that, within that context,

> the institutionalization of the use of violence, manipulation of ethnicity for political and economic gain with concomi-

---

3. See for example N. W. Sobania, *Culture and Customs in Kenya* (Westport, CN: Greenwood Press, 2003); Bethwell Ogot, *Decolonization and Independence in Kenya, 1940–93* (London: Curry, 1995); Norman Miller, *Kenya: The Quest for Prosperity* (London: Gower House, 1984); and Mary Anne Watson, *Modern Kenya: Social Issues and Perspectives* (Lanham, MD: University Press of America, 2000).

4. Sobania, *Culture and Customs*, 27–34.

5. Michela Wrong, *It's Our Turn to Eat: The Story of a Kenyan Whistle-Blower* (London: Fourth Estate, 2009), 163–83.

6. Kimathi, "Whose Truth?," 12–18.

tant marginalization and inequality in access to resources, as well as the breakdown of state institutions became the defining characteristics of the state.⁷

For this reason, the repeated failure to stem the ethnic-based political violence, to evade purging official impunity, and to hold perpetrators of human rights abuses to account creates a climate of impunity that often leads to cycles of violence. As such, there is a terrain that impunity uses to arrive at where it stands in Kenya today.

Faces of Impunity in Kenya

It is hard to place a permanent face on Kenyan impunity. The type of impunity experienced in Kenya continues to mutate with every passing day. However, understanding impunity in Kenya using the category of faces can mainly be located within the spaces of the center in contrast to the margins, and their cognate liminal spaces. Postcolonial studies reveal sustained tensions between the center and the margins. Because of this, they have opened a window in which the empire is seen for what it is: a form of control and domination. Under postcolonial studies, therefore, the presence of the empire is unmasked till reality opens "a second world and a second life outside of the officialdom," or what Homi Bhabha terms the third space.⁸ In postcolonial politics, the official world must be unmasked and resisted. This is because the official world comes with imposing and hegemonizing tendencies that undermine the marginal world and threaten the very existence of the subaltern.⁹ As such, "more recent research has increasingly uncovered the fluidity of social structures and identities in Kenya in the late nineteenth century, and the haphazard and often casual violence with which the institution of colonial control and production emerged," and which are the products of the exchanges between the center and margins.¹⁰

---

7. Kimathi, "Whose Truth?," 15.

8. Richard Werbner and Terence Ranger, eds. *Postcolonial Identities in Africa* (London: Zed Books, 1996), 2.

9. See Feston Kalua, "Homi Bhabha's Third Space and African Identity," *Journal of Cultural Studies* 21, no. 1 (June 2009): 23–32.

10. Bruce Berman and John Lonsdale, *Unhappy Valley: Conflict in Kenya and Africa*, vol. 1, *State and Class* (Nairobi: Heinemann, 1992), 4.

In reconstructing the legacy of the empire and how it contributes to the architecture of placing faces on impunity in Kenya, one must be wary of whose history (*her*story) to follow. A large chunk of Kenya's history is, often, the memory of the dominant groups, which also exercise ethnic "othering." It means that stories of the subalterns have not been adequately captured as they lack representation, and so their stories are not told from a subaltern standpoint. As John Wekesa argues, the duality of understanding of memory raises the issue of whose history is to be recognized and whose memory forms a central component in the construction of the past.[11] Faced with such a revelation, postcolonial critics must contend with the issue of who controls and owns social memory.

Properly said, "the control of a society's memory—the regulation of what is remembered, how it is remembered as well as what is ignored or erased—is a valuable tool for maintaining and legitimating political power."[12] Therefore, a comparative analysis of memories constructed by the marginalized groups vis-à-vis those constructed by the larger groups or officially recognized enterprises becomes of paramount importance. The approach to Kenya's past therefore needs to pay attention to these views about dealing with the past, and particularly noting that Kenya's story of the past is partially a construction of the dominant class. Having inherited the political mantle from the colonialist, and in the interest of retaining such power for themselves, such groups made sure that the past was properly preserved within the mold of its colonial epistemologies.

Generally then, with the historical narrative in place, impunity becomes the "exemption or freedom from punishment."[13] It is "the impossibility, *de jure* or *de facto*, of bringing the perpetrators of violations to account—whether in criminal, civil, administrative or disciplinary proceedings—since they are not subject to any inquiry that might lead to their being accused, arrested, tried and, if found guilty, sentenced to appropriate penalties, and to making reparations to their victims."[14] The general understanding of impunity in Kenya can be condensed into one

---

11. John Wekesa, "Historicizing Negative Ethnicity in Kenya," in *(Re)Membering Kenya: Identity, Culture and Freedom*, eds. Mbugua wa-Mungai and George Gona (Nairobi: Twaweza Communications, 2010), 57.

12. Wekesa, "Historicizing," 58.

13. Kimathi, "Whose Truth?," 12.

14. Sheila Masinde, "Citizen Action: Key in Ending Longstanding Impunity in Kenya," *Transparency International–Kenya: Adili* (March 2011), 1–12, 2.

word that is common with the youth in the urban dialect Sheng: *uta-do?*[15] Literally meaning "what will you do?" *uta-do?* is a question commonly put to victims of impunity by perpetrators of impunity, asking them what they will do or where will they turn for help. By implication, the victims have nowhere or no one to turn to.

Several writers, for example Masinde and Kimathi, reveal that Kenya has had a long-standing history of impunity, so that one can speak of a culture of impunity.[16] These writers argue that indigenous Kenyans who took over power from the colonialists upon independence perpetuated the abuse of basic human rights and a vile culture among leaders that put self-service above service for all. Therefore, these leaders elected and appointed to serve the interests of the common people continued to reap where they had not sown, as many Kenyans wallowed in poverty and disease. Resources meant to end these problems were greedily and illegally siphoned into individual pockets.[17]

Over the years, impunity in Kenya has evolved into a culture that manifests itself in various forms—the ethnic clashes and violence that have long characterized general elections, the mysterious assassinations of charismatic leaders such as Pio Gama Pinto,[18] Tom Mboya, J. M. Kariuki, and Robert Ouko, among others, extrajudicial killings such as those

---

15. Sheng in Kenya is a language formed from a creative combination of many vernacular, Swahili, and English terminologies. It is very common with the youth and street gangs. It is not the language of hegemony or the dominant *mwenyenchi* ; on the contrary, it is the language of the subaltern, the common *mwananchi*. Per se, it is the language of mimicry in Kenya.

16. Kimathi, "Whose Truth?," 15; Masinde, "Citizen Action," 5.

17. Masinde, "Citizen Action," 5.

18. Pinto was the first Kenyan politician to be assassinated after independence. The gravestone at City Park Cemetery, Nairobi, where he is buried describes him as a socialist and freedom fighter, a political detainee from 1954 to 1959, and a Member of Parliament from 1963 till an assassin's bullet ended his life on the morning of February 24, 1965. By the time he died, he had become the main ideological strategist for Vice President Oginga Odinga's radical and left-leaning wing of Kenya's ruling party, the Kenya African National Union (KANU). Kenya History, accessed September 4, 2018, http://www.kenyahistory.co.ke/personalities.php?pg=personalities&id=53#sthash.oh10xazu.dpuf.

meted out by state security against followers of *mungiki*,[19] barefaced grabbing of public lands, including forests, in the face of global warming that threatens economic development, and unresolved corruption scams such as the Anglo-Leasing scandal and the Goldenberg scam, among an endless list of new and old corruption scams.[20] The list of incidences that indicates a face of impunity in Kenya is endless. Emanating from this, it can be argued that rampant corruption, impunity, and disregard for the rule of law in Kenya contribute to long-standing issues such as poverty, inequality, regional imbalances, lack of national cohesion, inequitable allocation of resources, and opportunities, among other injustices, and form the major face of impunity in Kenya. The face of impunity in Kenya hinges on the powerful, and the daring question that has been posed again and again to the citizenry is: *mta-do?* ("What will you do?"). What follows is more nuanced explication of the faces of impunity in Kenya.

THE CULTURAL FACE OF IMPUNITY

Together with other faces, impunity in Kenya has a cultural face. Cultural dimensions of impunity in Kenya today are supported by the presence of various precolonial cultural councils that were set up to deal with lawlessness. For example, writing about the customs of the Ameru of Kenya, Nyaga reveals that the Ameru historically had several governing structures that were set up to punish criminals and curb impunity.[21] The structures included the famous *njuri nceke*, which was the main

---

19. According to Margaret Gecaga, "Religious Movements and Democratization in Kenya: Between the Sacred and the Profane," in *Kenya: The Struggle for Democracy*, eds. Godwin Murunga and Simiyu Nasongo (London: Zed Books, 2007), 154, "*mungiki*" is a word in the Gikuyu language that has its etymological root in the word *muingi*, meaning masses of people: "Mungiki denotes a mass movement." However, the fact that a majority of its followers are from the Gikuyu community shows that it is an exclusively ethnic group. The ideology of the group is characterized by revolutionary rhetoric, Kikuyu traditions, and a disdain for Kenyan modernization, which is seen as immoral corruption. The group is banned in Kenya because of its association with criminal and violent activities.

20. According to Wrong, *It's Our Turn to Eat*, the scandal is alleged to have started when the Kenyan government wanted to replace its passport printing system in 1997, but it came to light after revelation by a government officer in 2002. It was among the many corrupt deals that were inherited from the KANU government that had ruled Kenya for twenty-four years under presidents Jomo Kenyatta and Daniel arap Moi. Even though the new NARC government that came to power following multiparty elections in 1992 promised to fight corruption, superficial efforts were made before being completely watered down by the magnitude of the Anglo-Leasing scandal.

21. David Nyaga, *Customs and Traditions of the Ameru* (Nairobi: East African Educational Publishers, 1997), 39.

council of elders.²² Under the watchful eye of the *njuri nceke*, impunity was minimized among the Ameru, and the people enjoyed a just society. This council retains its influence to date.

The cultural face of impunity becomes more glaring when a consideration of marriage and the dowry system is evaluated across most communities in the country. Marriage and the "dowry" or "bride-price" system in precolonial times had their usefulness and made for a lot of meaning in society.²³ However, they also had their disadvantages and created potential for misuse. Therefore, although dowry payments differed from community to community, the dowry system generally gave undue advantage to the man and his family over the woman's, and it became a cradle for impunity in marriage.²⁴ Although Mbiti ignores all the negative aspects of the dowry, blaming the problems on "outsiders," the dowry system remains the source of many inequalities in marriage.²⁵ During the contextual Bible studies I attended, several participants noted that impunity is prevalent even in today's marriages because the dowry system still exists and gives the male partner an upper hand in the union, contributing to marital impunity.

Apart from marriage and the dowry system, several other cultural institutions function as seedbeds for impunity, including traditions like tribal circumcision and systems of tribal leadership. In the place of initiation and circumcision, for example, Mbiti agrees that circumcision ceremonies present to the initiates specific ethnic privileges and give them advantages over the uninitiated. The ceremonies elevate the participants to another level of existence altogether. This elevation, if unchecked, creates several avenues by which impunity thrives in societies.²⁶

Given the presence and prevalence of impunity in culture, several Kenyan communities devised systems of governance that helped curtail but at the same time propel impunity. For example, Ahmed Saberwal, writing about the Embu people of eastern Kenya, observes that a council

---

22. Meru Council of Elders.

23. John, Mbiti, *African Religion and Philosophy* (Nairobi: Heinemann, 1992), 140.

24. See Mbiti, who uses several names for it: bride-price, gift, and so on. Although Mbiti refutes the notion that dowry is a payment, emerging trends in Kenyan marriages actually bear witness that the bride-price has been commercialized. This commercialization has bred its own source of social evils and impunity in marriage.

25. Such inequalities involve abuse of wives by husbands who regard dowry as a system of purchasing the wife (lit. woman).

26. Mbiti, *African Religion and Philosophy*, 146.

of elders maintained order in the community and hence fought impunity.[27] By presenting several cases in which elders' directives were disregarded, Saberwal reveals that impunity was rife among the Embu even before colonial contacts. At some point, he reveals that the body of elders did not always adequately deal with impunity. As such, it can be deduced from his argument that if the elders failed at whatever point, then the community would devise its own mechanisms of fighting impunity by recourse to fighting, bewitching, and sometimes cursing. For example, he writes:

> If a man [person] was determined to evade an obligation or a liability, his adversary could find little redress in the elders' council. The relationship between them would probably be strained and some informal sanctions applied. Individuals who had managed to antagonize many neighbors no doubt felt the force of informal ostracism; this could be made a formal act through the laying of a public curse.[28]

Several other Kenyan communities had ways of containing and managing their members, and hence mitigating impunity. The precolonial Akamba, for example, also had governments that ensured cohesiveness of the society. In the face of impunity and in cases of disregard of the law, Kimeu Ndeti writes that against individuals acting in ways that threatened the existence of the community, a most serious and collective retaliation was evoked.[29] The Akamba community took responsibility to protect itself against outlaws to the extent of killing some and banishing others.

The Agikuyu people, as Muriuki writes, had close-knit "family (*nyumba*) systems. Each family was regarded as a social and administrative unit under the headship of the father."[30] The father was supreme in all family matters. Beyond the family was the clan, or *mbari*, whose affairs were coordinated by an *mbari* council, and the Agikuyu controlled impunity through such means.

---

27. Ahmed Saberwal, *The Traditional, Political System of the Embu of Central Kenya* (Kampala: East African Publishing House, 1970), 73.

28. Saberwal, *The Traditional, Political System of the Embu of Central Kenya*, 81.

29. Kimeu Ndeti, *Elements of Akamba Life* (Nairobi: East African Publishing House, 1972), 104.

30. Gerald Muriuki, *A History of the Kikuyu: 1500–1900* (Nairobi: Oxford University Press, 1972), 28.

Unfortunately, in many African societies, many of these structures were male dominated and were controlled by a certain class of people. Therefore, impunity in precolonial Kenya can be seen to have had a gendered face, which was mainly patriarchal. *Different forms of patriarchy presented women with distinct "rules of the game" and defined for them how they were to live. Under patriarchy, life options were minimized, with varying potentials for active or passive resistance in the face of oppression. Under such options, conditions for the proliferation of impunity were multiplied. However, it needs to be noted that* impunity in precolonial Kenya, though given impetus by cultural elements and patriarchy, had a subtle face: it was not bold-faced.[31]

It is not in my interest to venture deeply into all cultural aspects of impunity. What can be noted is that there has been a cultural side to the face of impunity that is experienced in Kenya today, but whose history lies in the precolonial past. In other words, not all impunity being experienced in Kenya today emanated from the colonial system that governed Kenya for almost a century.

Impunity mostly postures in male-dominated structures, which not only compel, but also dominate structures of power and authority. This means that impunity and authority go hand in hand. It can also be said that although there was impunity in Kenya before contacts with the colonialists, it was not at the level that is experienced in the postcolonial Kenya of today. There is no doubt that colonialism gave impetus to Kenyan leadership's impunity and the face it wears today.

GENDERED PERSPECTIVES

As we noted, cultural transactions necessarily yielded impunity that has a gendered face. Although gendered impunity is detrimental to both genders, the worst affected are women. As was noted during the contextual Bible studies, women's experiences vary depending on their social location and proximity to the hegemonic centers, which in postcolonial studies form the basis for the empire concept. Their experience under any form of patriarchy is one of second-class or lower citizen status, and therefore gender perspectives become necessary in reading empire and impunity, because of the importance of gender positions during struggles for power.

---

31. Studies may need to be done on the prevalence of impunity in African matriarchal societies. A good place to begin would be Martha R. Robinson, *Matriarchy, Patriarchy and Imperial Security in Africa: Explaining Riots in Europe and Violence in Africa* (New York: Lexicon Books, 2012).

It will be acknowledged that Kenyan women have been victims of impunity in almost all sectors of life. In homes, from spousal abuse; on the roads, where women drivers are "bullied"; in employment spaces, where they are sexually exploited, harassed, violated, and silenced. In all these sectors, women bear the brunt of male impunity. This experience is worsened when seen to be given impetus by reading texts of the empire that presume a male governed world. Unfortunately, many narratives and sayings contained in the Bible often fall into this space because they subtly tend to propel a trajectory of male dominance and female subjugation.

Readings by a myriad of postcolonial feminist writers expose how the Bible conforms to its sociohistorical setting to condone patriarchy and impunity. This is to say that postcolonial readings expose discourses that condone relationships of profound inequality. Most of these relationships are driven by power plays that exhibit fear of difference while promoting the superiority of one gender over the other.

HYBRIDIZED IMPUNITY[32]

This section argues that impunity creates a third space, a liminality, as a response to some ills in the social setup. "Hybridized impunity" is therefore an imagination of how impunity operates in the in-between spaces, to resist in a subtle way. Simply stated, hybridized impunity connotes subversive opposition. Impunity in Kenya has a hybrid face. This can be taken to mean the "official face," or the face exhibited by those who are the dominant group and represent others in Kenya. When speaking of impunity in the official spaces, it is assumed that impunity has rank and its seriousness in practice, and effects seem to follow the top-to-bottom trend and the cause-and-effect matrix.

While the impunity of this type is serious, it is even more serious if the cause is at the top and the effect is at the bottom. Impunity committed by people in high places of power tends to reveal a connectedness that betrays an in-betweenness, a collaboration, and a contestation in identity between the rulers and the masses (the "other") in Kenya. It is easy for many in top positions to practice impunity because their behavior is condoned by the masses. For example, according to the Kenya National Human Rights Commission (KNHRC) report, leaders and administrators

---

32. Or third space impunity. Impunity that develops by default to disrupt the "official" impunity or impunity condoned by the empire.

allied to the political parties to which the executive belongs seem to be more prone to practicing impunity.[33] This is because they feel that the incumbent they placed in power can protect them from consequences. However, well-connected private or non-state actors also play a critical role either in initiating or abetting impunity in collaboration with their state partners. For instance, during the postelection violence and financial scandals such as Goldenberg, Anglo-Leasing, the Nairobi City Council Cemetery land, and National Hospital Insurance Fund (NHIF), individuals and companies have in the past been found to be the key purveyors of impunity in the public sector.

In the hybridized form of impunity, players or actors exhibit an overlap and displacement of identities. In hybridity, whether the players are aware of it or not, there is antagonism or affiliation, and new identities are produced performatively, producing multiple layers of existence. Hybridization, whether intentional or by default, yields cultural identities that were not originally intended in the transaction between the actor and the acted-upon. Just as in hybridity studies, hybridized impunity becomes a threat to the centers of power or colonizers because it becomes an inevitable by-product of the encounter.

MIMICKED IMPUNITY

Impunity in Kenya can also be construed as having a mimicry face. In postcolonial studies, mimicry stands for a situation where colonial subjects mimic by repeating the colonial masters; this is done to contest and disrupt colonial power, whether successfully or not. Applied to Kenya, this is the face worn by the masses or the Kenyan subaltern when they relay the impunity that is wielded in the power spaces. Unlike the hybridized impunity, which tends to confine itself to the high offices, mimicry's form of impunity mainly has its domain in the lower echelons of society. For example, the *matatu* (public transport) sector, on the roads by motorists, on streets in burglary and muggings, by junior ranking police officers taking bribes, corruption of city council askaris, and so on.[34] It is a by-product of impunity that is perpetrated in the high social spaces, which in turn trickles down to the masses. What is important to note in this form of impunity is that, in the repetition, the product is

---

33. Justice, accessed June 8, 2012, http://www.justice.go.ke/index2.php?option=com_content&do_pdf=1&id=25.

34. Interviewee #4.

never the same, and the repetition is not for repetition's sake. It is for the sake of fostering or layering other forms of impunity.

AMBIVALENT IMPUNITY

As already stated, ambivalence refers to a simultaneous attraction toward and repulsion from an object, person, or action. According to Bhabha, when adapted to colonial discourse theory, ambivalence is used to describe the complex attraction and repulsion that mark the relationship between the colonizers and the colonized.[35] Applied to the Kenyan situation, I would also assign this to the impunity practiced by religious people, and especially to Christian leaders and followers who are supposed to be the moral barometer of society. For Christians to abide by Christian principles while at the same time skirting the country's legal principles, this religious face of impunity can be described as the confluence of the struggle, which in turn poses a simultaneous attraction and repulsion to the narrow and wide way. It is a form of impunity that results from Christians, or Christian leaders, circumventing religious laws and the laws of the land to achieve their ends.

For example, the Ndungú commission that was formulated in 2003 to inquire into the extralegal allocation of public lands and lands reserved for public purpose to private individuals and corporate entities named churches and Christian leaders who were involved in land grabbing.[36] Put differently, this is the inability of some Kenyan Christians strictly to stick to the "narrow way" (Matt. 7:13–14), which in turn poses a simultaneous attraction and repulsion to the narrow and the wide way. It may not be so, but one cannot help but wonder whether the strict ethic that Jesus requires of his followers presents the Christians with constricted and constricting options such that the Christian is limited to an ambivalent reception of the same as a way out.

In summary, it can be noted that what goes on in Kenya today is more of a power and authority, which, conceived in colonial discourse terms, reveals the hegemony and the subaltern in continuous desire for domination of the other. In thinking about impunity, Kenya today may be suffering from power experimentations and improvisations in which

---

35. Bhabha, *The Location of Culture* (London: Routledge, 1994), 17.

36. *The Standard*, accessed June 8, 2012, http://www.standardmedia.co.ke/?id=1144019353&cid=4&articleID=1144019353.

everyone desires to indulge. In a climate of impunity, such as that in Kenya, the post-colony is centered within the philosophy of who represents and represses whom; the very traits that colonialism foisted on the citizenry. In this quagmire and in a bid to overpower, impunity inevitably becomes an ally.

Impunity and Building Empires of Corruption

The usefulness of postcolonialism as a discipline is seen in the fact that it acknowledges the severe impact of colonialism and recognizes the force of continuing neocolonization in the form of globalization.[37] Applied to the issue of impunity, corruption, and empire building in Kenya, postcolonialism becomes a useful theory in uncovering how neocolonial forces working with dominant forces collude to marginalize others through corruption and impunity. Put differently, postcolonial theory helps uncover authorities built and assembled through impunity and corrupt deals.

While we acknowledge that encounters and exchanges with the colonizers in Kenya produced a hybrid crop of Kenyans who were bent on sustaining imperialism, the masses have capitulated in their mimicry to the authorities and have been rendered ineffectual in resisting them. As Moore puts it, "colonial discourses regularly enjoin the colonizers to internalize and replicate the colonizer's culture."[38] If colonial mimicry involves the use of the master's tools, then the elite and privileged involved in corrupt deals in Kenya have perfected the use of the master's tools to build their own corrupt mini-empires.

Imperialism, "when characterized by the exercise of power through direct conquest or through political and economic influence," imbibes an expansionist ideology.[39] Under a capitalist system inherited from the British colonizers, Kenya became a suitable ground upon which empire-building ideology took root. The building of a corrupt political empire in Kenya takes the form of economic power, whereby "economic influence," which involves abdication of the consequences of the law through impunity, becomes the means to manipulate control.[40]

---

37. R. S. Sugirtharajah, *Voices from the Margin* (Maryknoll, NY: Orbis, 2006), 64.
38. Moore, *Empire and Apocalypse*, 13.
39. Young, *Postcolonialism*, 84.
40. Young, *Postcolonialism*, 85.

The State of Corruption in Kenya

Studies reveal that corruption is endemic in Kenya.[41] According to the 2020 report of Transparency International (Corruption Perception Index CPI), Kenya was one of the most corrupt countries in the world, at position 137 out of 180.[42] This means that the state continues to sink in the waters of corruption, and that efforts to tackle corruption have borne few results.[43] According to Martin Mutua,

> the political history and governance of the Kenyan state is a catalogue of gross human rights violations, the arrogance of power, and the commission of mind-boggling economic crimes.[44]

There have been attempts by various Kenyan regimes to uproot corruption cartels in Kenya. However, corruption is so entrenched that the poor ranking may not change for the better in many generations. Corruption, while used to entrench hegemonic empires, produces negative long-term consequences of an economic, political, and administrative nature that disproportionately impact the average Kenyan.

One could almost speak of corruption as a "normalized" way of life in Kenya. Corruption is practiced in both the high and low offices of government and private sectors; it is practiced by the state officers as well as the common *mwanachi* (citizen). The prevalence of corruption in Kenya can be illustrated by the fact that it is found in the public sector, private sector, and even in the religious sector.

Thus, the impact of corruption on governance in Kenya is impeding the upholding of the principles of good governance. To illustrate this, it has been documented that corruption is said to cost Kenya as much as

---

41. To date (2020), Kenya struggles with corruption perception. See for example Transparency International, accessed June 17, 2020, https://www.transparency.org/en/countries/kenya.

42. Transparency International Kenya, accessed June 6, 2020, https://tikenya.org/wp-content/uploads/2020/01/CPI-press-release-2019.pdf. Transparency International reports need to be taken with a pinch of salt. Sometimes the agency just exists to serve the interests of Western powers.

43. Transparency International Kenya, https://tikenya.org/wp-content/uploads/2019/01/Corruption-Perceptions-Index-2018-Press-Release-1.pdf. Kenya continues to score poorly in corruption perception measures that are monitored by Transparency International.

44. Martin Mutua, "Republic of Kenya Report of the Task Force on the Establishment of a Truth, Justice and Reconciliation Commission," *Human Rights Review* 10, no. 25 (2004): 17.

$10 million annually.⁴⁵ As Mitullah Waweru notes, theft, embezzlement of public resources, and fraud by public officials decrease the availability of government funds for development-related activities. The resultant financial impact gravely impedes the provision of essential public services to most Kenyans.⁴⁶ For example, in 2007 the Kenya National AIDS Control Council (NACC), which was set up to coordinate the prevention and control of HIV and AIDS, was discredited when it was discovered that senior staff had paid themselves inflated salaries and allowances, among other serious irregularities.⁴⁷ This not only led to the withdrawal of a US$15 million grant by the Global Fund to Fight HIV and AIDS, Tuberculosis and Malaria; it also led to apathy on the part of patients who were impacted the most by the lost resources to keep them alive.⁴⁸ This withdrawal continues to haunt many of the patients who are still alive.

The impact of corruption is also seen as impeding the upholding of the rule of law and promoting impunity.⁴⁹ For example, according to media reports, a former Kenyan attorney-general (AG), Amos Wako, was severally accused of misusing state powers by unilaterally using nolle prosequi (abandonment of a plaintiff's case) in cases of public interest and outright criminal activities.⁵⁰ Such was the case when Tom Cholmondeley, the Kenyan grandson of a former colonialist, was cleared of criminal liability after murdering a game warden on his ranch.⁵¹

These and similar cases have been investigated by the former Kenya Anti-Corruption Commission (KACC), now renamed the Ethics and Anti-Corruption Commission (EACC)), without much to show for it. This is not surprising, given that the KACC had no prosecutorial mandate (it only investigated, and the AG prosecuted on its behalf), which left its position

---

45. Transparency International Kenya, "2005 Bribery Index," accessed June 8, 2020, http://www.tikenya.org/documents/Kenya%20Bribery%20Index%202011.pdf.

46. Mitullah Waweru, "Local Political Systems of Nairobi," in *Nairobi Today: The Paradox of a Fragmented City*, ed. David Rodriguez-Torres (Nairobi: Mikuki na Nyota Publishers, 2010), 344.

47. *The Standard*, accessed June 8, 2018, http://www.standardmedia.co.ke/?incl=blogComment&id=1143998369&cid=&articleID=1143998369.

48. Michael Katumanga, "A City under Siege: Formalized Banditry and Deconstruction of Modes of Accumulation in Nairobi," in *Nairobi Today: The Paradox of a Fragmented City*, ed. David Rodriguez-Torres (Nairobi: Mikuki na Nyota Publishers, 2010), 343–65.

49. http://repository.up.ac.za/handle/2263/1222, accessed June, 8, 2018.

50. *Daily Nation*, "Amos Wako Rebuts Graft Claims after US Ban," accessed June 8, 2020, https://www.nation.co.ke/kenya/news/amos-wako-rebuts-graft-claims-after-us-ban-224806.

51. Gerald Muthui "A-G Defends Release of Delamere's Grandson," *East African Standard*, May 25, 2005.

undermined by allegations of impropriety and of shielding prominent people in the government.[52] In the past, this led to public confrontations between the AG's office and KACC over the prosecution of top government officials allegedly involved in corrupt practices. Under the current constitution, the KACC has been transformed to encompass an ethical dimension in the EACC. It remains to be seen if its renaming and rebranding will grant it the wheels of justice to eradicate corruption. It also remains to be seen if renewed efforts to fight corruption by the current "Jubilee" Party administration will make any headway in this regard.

Corruption and the Empire

Corruption is seen as aiding in empire building when its proceeds are used by the *wenyenchi* (literally "those who own the nation") to further marginalize (*wanjikunize* or subalternize) the *wananchi* (citizenry). Corruption in Kenya comes in two forms. Petty corruption in Kenya occurs when citizens are asked for a bribe (*kitu kidogo*—"something small") for trivial reasons such as getting a document stamped, a service provided, or an infringement overlooked. The amounts are small, but hardly petty to the many people who can hardly afford the required petty amounts (also called *chai*—"tea").[53] Kenya also has corruption in high offices, or grand corruption, particularly in public funding, with purchases made at inflated prices, public benefits handed out to people who are not entitled, fictitious companies being paid for contracts that they never executed, and so on.[54]

Corruption in high offices conjures up the picture of imperialism. The mention of high corruption in Kenya quickly recalls several cases ingrained in the social memory of Kenyans, such as the Goldenberg and Anglo-Leasing scandals.[55] In recent years, there have been several other reported scams, including the flawed tendering process for the exten-

---

52. Mbugua wa-Mungai and George Gona, eds., *(Re)Membering Kenya: Identity, Culture and Freedom* (Nairobi: Twaweza Communications, 2010).

53. Interviewee #7.

54. Musambayi Katumanga, "A City under Siege: Banditry and Modes of Accumulation in Nairobi, 1991–2004," *Review of African Political Economy* 32, no. 106 (2005): 352.

55. In the Goldenberg export compensation scandal, Kenya lost billions of shillings in the early 1990s. According to witnesses, as much as 60 billion Kenyan shillings (US$850 million)—a fifth of Kenya's gross domestic product—was looted from the country's Central Bank through billionaire Kamlesh Pattni's Exchange Bank in 1991. See http://worldpress.org/Africa/1499.cfm.

sion of the Jomo Kenyatta International Airport and corruption in the former prime minister's office in 2012, where Kenya lost approximately 23 billion Kenya shillings in subsidies and taxes.[56] There was also the free primary education scandal in the Ministry of Education in 2013, where through corrupt deals money meant to meet the international mandate of free education for all was looted by well-connected individuals.[57] The National Hospital Insurance Fund (NHIF) scandal will remain in the annals of Kenyan history (running to 2019), perhaps the greatest attempt by people in power to loot not only funds meant for health but also the health of the nation itself. According to media reports, a scrutiny of the NHIF scheme revealed a curious decision in which some private and unscrupulous medical facilities received the bulk of the first-quarter disbursement of the new civil servants' out-patient medical cover rollout.[58]

The list continues to date, and by the time this book is published other scandals will have emerged unless something radical is done. Such cartels of well-connected people trying to further marginalize the Kenyan subaltern through corruption fund expansionist schemes that end up undermining the very life of the nation. The tentacles of such corrupt industry permeate almost every sector. It is a total corruption empire, complete with systems, its own law, and its own judiciary; the official law and judiciary are circumvented by perpetrators of such crimes. It is no wonder that their activities are likened to terrorism in the manner in which both compromise peace for abundant life. Unless this is stopped, the country may end up in the category of failed states.

---

56. *The Standard*, accessed June 8, 2018, http://www.standardmedia.co.ke/?id=11440 30785&cid=4&articleID=1144030785. According to Sam Ongeri, the original plan was an initiative to cushion the poor by selling maize directly to millers at below-market prices. The National Cereals and Produce Board (NCPB), which determines the producer price of maize by intervening to buy on behalf of the government in times of surplus harvest and selling when supply is low, chose to sell maize to brokers, who sold it to millers at a profit, which created conduits for corruption. In business deals involving politicians and businessmen, brokers—who sometimes doubled as millers—exploited the loophole and bought maize from NCPB, and later sold the consignments to millers at a profit, pushing maize prices to double that of international prices. While enriching a few rich tycoons, this move affected the urban poor, who are mainly net buyers, and the landless and subsistence farmers, who at some point in the growing cycle have to buy maize.

57. *The Standard*, "Ongeri Silent over Sh1.3b Book Scam," accessed June 8, 2018, http://www.standardmedia.co.ke/?articleID=1144025226&story_title=Ongeri-silent-over-Sh1.3b-book-scam.

58. See Peter Orengo, "How NHIF Plan May Have Been Turned into Cash Cow," accessed June 8, 2017, http://www.standardmedia.co.ke/?articleID=2000059152&story_title=How-NHIF-plan-may-have-been-turned-into-cash-cow 2012.

Corruption therefore not only robs the state of much-needed revenue through corrupt officials; it also ensures that the poor remain poor and have no chance of enjoying better services. The government of Kenya has admitted on several occasions that it had failed to tame corruption because the very institutions entrusted with this fight are fraught with corruption and political interference by interested parties bent on making their corrupt deals at the expense of the citizenry. Though the government exercised ingenuity in establishing the then Kenya Anti-Corruption Commission (KACC) in 2003, due to political interference by well-connected people, KACC and now the EACC have mainly functioned as public educators on corruption and not eradicators of the same.

Impunity and Connectedness

Impunity relies on networks for its continued spread in Kenya. These connections can be theorized using the term "individual connectedness." Connectedness, like imperialism, can be an expansionist ideology. It is subordinate to imperialism because it is a tool in empire building. Connectedness can be conceptualized in a spiral manner, whereby it is a sphere of influence. In this understanding, it stands for the ability of a person to wield power and influence at various levels of society. In Kenya, the main aim of connectedness is to spread tentacles far and wide, while ensuring those tentacles are anchored to the center.[59] Connectedness in Kenya is of a special type, and endemic because systems of governance are unreliable. Therefore, it is an attempt to fill the vacuums created by collapsed governance systems. Connectedness penetrates all sectors of a society, shattering all bureaucratic barriers, assuring, and delivering its services in record time.

Connectedness, when utilized for good purposes, can be useful in any society because it fosters communal integration and categorizes society in terms of expertise. However, when used by a few people in power, it can contribute to the worst form of othering in a society. For example, whereas tender rules require services to government to be advertised, on many occasions only those from connected or known people are shortlisted and finally approved for business. This phenomenon cuts

---

59. David Throup, "Elections and Political Legitimacy in Kenya," *AJIAI* 63, no. 3 (1993): 371–96.

across many counties and it becomes hard for first-time business owners and unconnected people to penetrate connection systems.

What is interesting about impunity and corruption in Kenya is the ability of the so-called "well-connected" people to circumvent the law. These are the people either at the bottom but connected, or those at the center of governance, but who are also connected to the masses. They are the decision makers, and wield influence on all or most law-enforcing agencies. According to Godwin Murunga, this problem stems from Kenya's centralization of power in the presidency that removes competition and benefits a few political actors.[60] Some of these are the people who represent the "others." Many of them bear Christian names and are also well connected in churches. They are the hegemonic powers that be and their hegemonic powers are represented from top to bottom in every sector of Kenyan society.

Their empires of corruption and impunity are sustained through connections. The police seem to know the perpetrators of economic and political crimes, but they are reluctant to arrest them. This is either because of bribery (corrupt police system), or inadequate evidence to link them to the offence, or their connections with the people in high places.[61] They are well-connected people, and for them impunity or life without legal consequences is a way of life. To break this cycle may require more than just constitutional dispensations.

Impunity and Postcolonial Identities in Kenya

Postcolonial identities emerge in Kenya in the discourse of tribe and ethnicity. Wanyonyi, a key writer on identities, begins his discourse on negative ethnicity in Kenya by borrowing from a newspaper article by the *Daily Nation* editor Philip Ochieng, which states that

> one word seems to drive our national fate; tribalism. If the December (27, 2007) elections were hijacked, we all blamed it confidently on tribalism. In any case, the most spectacular

---

60. Godwin R. Murunga, "Governance and the Politics of Structural Adjustment in Kenya," in *Kenya: The Struggle for Democracy*, eds. Godwin R. Murunga and Shadrack W. Nasong'o (London: Zed Books, 2007), 264.

61. Murunga, "Governance," 264.

consequences—the violence that rocked the entire country—seemed to pit certain tribes against others.[62]

Within the ambit of the 2007 postelection violence, Wanyonyi, like other writers, tries to conjure up the ghost of ethnicity into the widescale disregard of system authority in Kenya during that period. How much can tribalism and ethnicity be included in the definition of the impunity prevalent in Kenya? The answer to this question can only be determined by considering what tribe or ethnic identity means to the Kenyan.

TRIBE AND ETHNICITY

Although the terms "tribe" and "ethnicity" have related meanings, their definitions and usage may not be all that close. Various authorities have attempted to situate the origins of the two terms "tribe" and "ethnicity," and Wanyonyi argues for several possible ways in which the origin of tribe can be traced and understood.[63] First, he posits that "tribe" owes its origins to ancient Rome, getting its origins from the Latin word *tribus*, which originally signified each of the satellite regions into which Italian people were classified. He shows that with the expansion of the Roman Empire, the term later came to be applied to non-Italian people. Within this understanding, therefore, it stands to show that the meaning of tribe may not necessarily have been confined to blood, culture, or such related identities.

Second, Wanyonyi indicts the period fifteen hundred years ago when Western Europe began rising to the position of world hegemony. Under this stream, "tribe becomes a group of individuals with a common blood heritage, eking out a living at an exceptionally low level of socio-economic formation."[64] Wanyonyi further states that the word tribe can be identified with *trubutus*—"tributary," or third rate. In fact, he demonstrates that Julius Caesar, the first-century Roman emperor, used it when he conquered and colonized a people to distinguish his people from the conquered subjects. In the same understanding, it can be used to highlight the argument that the British after conquering Kenya classified the indigenous people as tribes and their languages as vernaculars.

---

62. See Pius Kakai Wanyonyi, "Historicizing Negative Ethnicity in Kenya," in *(Re)Membering Kenya; Identity, Culture and Freedom*, eds. Mbugua wa-Mungai and George Gona (Nairobi: Twaweza Communications, 2010), 118.

63. Wanyonyi, "Historicizing," 124.

64. Wanyonyi, "Historicizing," 124.

Therefore, within these two categories of origins, the terms *tribe* and *tribalism* are mostly pejorative and negative.

Turning to an understanding of "ethnicity" and following Wanyonyi, it can be noted that the term "ethnic" is derived from the Greek word *ethnikos* (ἐθνἱκος), which originally meant "nation." With time, it included meanings such as heathen, pagan, gentile, non-Jewish, and non-Christian. Over time, the pejorative overtones in the word have been minimized and in its application the term may not be as harsh as *tribe*. As such, the concept of ethnic identity is much less offensive or more acceptable to its composite term, *tribe*.

According to Ashcroft, *ethnicity* is a term that has been used increasingly since the 1960s to account for human variation in terms of culture, tradition, language, social patterns, and ancestry, rather than the discredited generalizations of race with its assumption of a humanity divided into fixed, genetically determined biological types.[65] Ethnicity refers to the fusion of many traits that belong to the nature of any ethnic group: a composite of shared values, beliefs, norms, tastes, behaviors, experiences, consciousness of kind, and loyalties.[66] A person's ethnic group is such a powerful identifier because, while he or she chooses to remain in it, it is an identity that cannot be denied, rejected, or taken away by others.

Whereas race emerges as a way of establishing a hierarchical division between Europe and its "others," identifying people according to fixed genetic criteria, ethnicity is usually deployed as an expression of a positive self-perception that offers certain advantages to its members. Membership of an ethnic group is shared according to certain agreed criteria, even though the nature, the combination, and the importance of those criteria may be debated or may change over time.[67] In addition to this, sociologists of race and ethnicity typically focus on the dynamics of racial and ethnic inequality, providing studies of income, education, discrimination, public opinion about race, and racially marked poor neighborhoods. They also concentrate on how people of various races and ethnicities adapt to life in their groupings.

In Ashcroft's view, the term *ethnicity* really only achieves wide currency when these "national" groups find themselves as minorities within

---

65. Ashcroft, *Post-Colonial Studies*, 89.

66. Rick Ash Schermerhorn, "Ethnicity in the Perspective of the Sociology of Knowledge," *Ethnicity* 1, no. 1 (1974): 23–39.

67. Schermerhorn, "Ethnicity," 23.

a larger national grouping, as occurs in the aftermath of colonization, either through immigration to settled colonies such as the USA, Canada, Australia, and New Zealand, or by the migration of colonized peoples to the colonizing center.[68] One further consequence of this movement is that older European nations can no longer claim to be coterminous with a particular ethnic group but are themselves heterogeneous and, in time, hybridized.

A feature of the use of the term is that the element of marginalization evident in the earliest uses of "ethnic" often seems to remain implied in contemporary usage. Where it originally referred to heathen nations, it now suggests groups that are not the mainstream—groups that are not traditionally identified with the dominant national mythology.

Thus, in settler colonies of the British Empire, the dominant Anglo-Saxon group was usually not seen as an ethnic group because its ethnicity constructed the mythology of national identity. Such identification is not limited to colonial experience, but does reveal the "imperialistic" nature of national mythology and the political implications of any link between ethnicity and nation. Given the fact that ethnicity comes into greatest contemporary currency in the context of immigration, Ashcroft views ethnicity as

> a group or category of persons who have a common ancestral origin and the same cultural traits, who have a sense of peoplehood and of group belonging, who are of immigrant background and have either minority or majority status within a larger society.[69]

He continues:

> Ethnic identities thus persist beyond cultural assimilation into the wider society and the persistence of ethnic identity is not necessarily related to the perpetuation of traditional cultures. In most cases, very few features of traditional culture need to be selected as 'symbolic elements' around which ethnic identity revolves, and individuals need experience very few of the defining criteria (e.g. common ancestry) to consider themselves members of the group. No ethnic group is completely unified or in complete agreement about

---

68. Ashcroft, *Post-Colonial Studies*, 78.
69. Ashcroft, *Post-Colonial Studies*, 77.

its own ethnicity and no one essential feature can ever be found in every member of the group. Nevertheless, this dynamic interweaving of identifying features has come to function as an increasingly potent locus of identity in an increasingly migratory, globalized, and hybridized world.[70]

The category of tribe and ethnicity in postcolonial discourse becomes an important category in othering. In the following section, I reveal how it is articulated and exploited in the Kenyan space, particularly by the hegemonizing class.

Tribe and Ethnicity in Kenya

According to Koigi Wamwere, tribe and ethnicity in Kenya are often not discussed the way postcolonial writers discuss them.[71] For Wamwere, they may mean the same, but "tribe" is often ascribed to Africans who are viewed by some as a lower class of people, while "ethnicity" tends to be ascribed to white people, who are viewed by some as higher class. According to Wamwere, "this distinction between intellectuals' ethnicity and ordinary folks' tribalism ensures that *wananchi*, or common people, are left out of scholarly discussions of ethnic hate."[72] In fact, Wamwere in many places uses the two terms interchangeably, although he reserves "tribalist" for anyone who harbors negative ethnicity.[73]

Notwithstanding this, tribe, and ethnicity in Kenya have a history, and not only in terms of origin but also in terms of prevalence. Tribe and ethnicity in Kenya can be discussed under four periods—namely, the colonial period, Jomo Kenyatta's regime (1963-1978), Daniel arap Moi's regime (1978-2002), and Mwai Kibaki's regime (2002-2012). These periods are markers of the four political transitions that Kenya has had

---

70. Ashcroft, *Post-Colonial Studies*, 92.

71. Theoretical studies have de-emphasized the positive aspects of the cross-cultural evolution of ethnic consciousness that had clear links to identify formation processes whose history predates the colonial period. Such cultural forces are usually conflated with the divisive forces of ethnicity and often projected as undermining the process of nation-state formation. The modernization theorists see cross-cultural linkages as anachronistic forms of ethnicity that were bound to disappear in the face of modernity of the new nation, Kenya. Dependency theories tend to concentrate on the external constraints on the Kenyan state, while neo-Marxist theories concentrate on the class structure of society, and often consign ethnicity to the realm of "false consciousness." In our brief sketch, we don't follow any of these particular theorists, but we highlight their usefulness in a triangulated manner.

72. Koigi Wamwere, *The Curse of Negative Ethnicity: Towards Genocide in Kenya* (Nairobi: Mvule Africa Publishers, 2008), 78.

73. Wamwere, *Negative Ethnicity*, 79.

in its journey to nationhood. This discussion can be held because the construction of tribe and ethnicity in Kenya is riddled with colonial bias and a craving for power and domination. To understand fully the effects of the application of tribe and ethnicity in Kenya, "postcolonial theory becomes a profitable alternative theory to uncover colonial domination in all its forms."[74]

COLONIAL PERIOD (1895-1963)

If ethnicity is taken to incorporate the non-pejorative meaning of what is tribe in Kenya, then several things can be noted. Among these is the picture of ethnic identities in Kenya before and after colonialism. According to Wanyonyi, precolonial people of Kenya existed in porous boundaries separating members of different communities. People intermingled freely, and it is possible that dominant groups assimilated the minor groups.[75] To affirm this, he further notes that colonialism for long periods of time created systems of production, exchange, and redistribution, which were predicated on local identities rather than specific Bantu or Nilotic identities. To demonstrate this, Muriuki observes that the Agikuyu, for example, represent a fusion of many different ethnic elements, including the Gumba, Maasai, Athi, and Okiek.[76] This can be construed as true of every other community in Kenya, such that "one cannot talk about a pure ethnic group."[77]

When the colonialists arrived in Kenya, this picture was completely altered. Upon establishing authority over their subjects, the colonial administration radically transformed interethnic relations, including interactions and mingling. This ushered in a quite different social milieu, with its hallmark the curtailed freedom of association among the colonized. Within this agenda of the colonialist, Wanyonyi observes that "colonial forces achieved this by introducing new authoritarian policies, administrative values and practices, all of which aimed at benefiting colonialists to the disadvantage of the colonized people."[78] In colonial worlding, eth-

---

74. R. S. Sugirtharajah, *The Postcolonial Biblical Reader* (Oxford: Blackwell, 2006), 64.

75. Wanyonyi, "Historicizing," 35.

76. Godfrey Muriuki, *A History of the Kikuyu*—1500–1900 (Nairobi: Oxford University Press, 1974), 89.

77. Wanyonyi, "Historicizing," 35.

78. Wanyonyi, "Historicizing," 36.

nic identities were of paramount importance, for part of colonial scheme as empire ideology is "divide and rule."

Within this ideology, Wanyonyi further notes that the introduction of the *kipande* (identity card) in colonial Kenya was primarily to help rigidify ethnicity. In carving Kenya into zones and provinces for different ethnic groups, the colonialists were thereby able to create what Wanyonyi terms "segregation boundaries."[79] Wanyonyi reserves uncharitable words for this accomplishment when he observes that "the strategy also helped to intensify and fossilize ethnic consciousness amongst the different communities and ended up promoting the feeling of exclusiveness and eventually planted the seeds of ethnocentrism and the urge for ethnocracy."[80] As Kenyan Nobel laureate Wangari Maathai observes, these "segregation boundaries" existed even in colonial "owned" spaces and in settler farms.[81] Maathai gives the example of settler Neylan's farm, where the labor force was drawn from different local ethnic groups. However, she notes that these communities could not live in close proximity to each other, even within Neylan's farm. She observes that

> Each community kept to the category of jobs assigned to it. The Kikuyu worked in the fields, the Luo labored around the homestead as domestic workers and the Kipsigis took care of the livestock and milking. These workers also lived separately. Thus, a Kikuyu village was separate from a Luo one which was in turn separate from a Kipsigis counterpart.[82]

What is noted is that this practice contributed to the emergence of specific ethnic stereotypes and at the same time perpetuated interethnic exclusivity. These in turn were to be the seedbeds of impunity along tribal lines.

---

79. Wanyonyi, "Historicizing," 37.
80. Wanyonyi, "Historicizing," 37.
81. Wangari Maathai, *Unbowed: A Memoir* (New York: Anchor Books, 2006), 120.
82. Maathai, *Unbowed*, 22.

JOMO KENYATTA PERIOD (1963-1978)

Having fossilized ethnicity in Kenya, the exit of the colonialists never marked the end of negative ethnicity.[83] In fact, ethnic othering blossomed like a kindled fire. To briefly illustrate this, it can be noted that the ideological differences between Jomo Kenyatta (Kikuyu tribe) and Oginga Odinga (Luo tribe) in post-independence Kenya were taken by many of their followers as ethnic differences.[84] This not only led to ethnic suspicion from time to time between Jomo Kenyatta and Oginga Odinga, but also between the Kikuyus and Luos whom they represented. Following Wanyonyi, it is observed that ethnic animosity between the Kikuyus and the Luos took a violent turn in 1969 with the assassination of Tom Mboya.[85] With the allegation that Tom Mboya (a Luo), was assassinated by Nahashon Njenga Njoroge (a Kikuyu), ethnic emotions rose to a crescendo in Nairobi and Nyanza (Kikuyus were more concentrated in Nairobi while the Luos were more to be found in Nyanza).[86]

Many commentators agree that the assassination of Mboya on July 5, 1969, was a significant moment that further divided the young republic along ethnic lines.[87] According to Bethuel Ogot, Mboya's death united the Luo under the leadership of Oginga Odinga and the Kikuyu under

---

83. In his article "Ethnicity and the Challenge of Nationhood in Kenya," in *Kenya: The Making of a Nation*, eds. Bethuel Ogot and W. Ochieng (Maseno, Kenya: Desktop Publishing Unit, 2000), 173–75, Nathan Kundu observes that the British froze interactions between Kenyan communities in order to perpetuate their philosophy of divide and rule. In doing so, they discouraged interethnic rural interactions and migrations. As a result, the various ethnic communities were kept apart in suspicion and prejudice. Even their education and religious policies were meant to be ethnic in orientation. Subsequently, ethnic groups began to be identified as predominantly Methodists in Meru, Anglicans in Western Kenya, Presbyterians in Central Kenya, Seventh Day Adventists in Kisii, Catholics in Ukambani, and so on.

84. Oginga Odinga was independent Kenya's first vice president.

85. Wanyonyi, "Historicizing," 128. Tom Mboya was a politician during Jomo Kenyatta's government, the founder of Nairobi People's Congress Party, and a key figure in the formation of Kenya National African Union (KANU). He was the Minister of Economic Planning and Development at the time of his death.

86. He was the only man arrested for the killing of Tom Mboya. He was a former waiter and watchmaker, and was later employed as a KANU activist and errand boy for various politicians. See www.tommboya.org. Accessed May 22, 2017.

87. Edwin Gimode, "The Role of Police in Kenya's Democratic Process," in *Kenya: The Struggle for Democracy*, eds. Godwin R. Murunga and Shadrack W. Nasong'o (Dakar: Codseria Books, 2007), 237.

Jomo Kenyatta. In retrospect, this death is also seen as having divided the nation along ethnic lines.[88]

Although there were other political assassinations during Kenyatta's time, which involved the death of fellow Kikuyus, consequential evidence can point to the fact that these assassinations happened to Kikuyus who aligned themselves with Kenyatta's dissidents.[89] Assassinations of dissidents and the economic balkanization of opposing "tribes" marked Kenyatta's way of polarizing Kenya along ethnic lines.[90] The foregoing and many other examples during this time show that Jomo Kenyatta's tenure was marked with tensions among the bulk of the Luo and Kikuyu populations. Other small ethnic groups were also inclined to align themselves with the bigger ethnic groups. Kenyatta's period was one of heightened ethnic conscientization, where the prevalent language of the day became which ethnic group was against which other.

DANIEL ARAP MOI PERIOD (1978-2002)

Daniel arap Moi's tenure proved difficult, and took ethnicity to a different level altogether. Perhaps ethnicity took its ugly and unique twist during Moi's regime because of his limited education and a kind of inferiority complex.[91] Upon ascending to the throne after the demise of Jomo Kenyatta, Moi gradually but systematically entrenched himself. By use of the slogan *nyayo* (footsteps), Moi promised the nation to follow in the footsteps of Jomo Kenyatta.[92] However, as came to be evident, Moi

---

88. Bethuel Ogot, "Boundary Changes and Invention of Tribes," in *Kenya: The Making of a Nation 1895–1995*, eds. Bethuel Ogot and William Ochieng (Kisumu, Kenya: Maseno University, 2000), 233.

89. Wamwere does not see this angle to Jomo Kenyatta's history. In fact, he reads against the grid and sees Kenyatta as having been totally against his Kikuyu kin, and he enumerates possible injustices that Kenyatta meted out against the Kikuyus (p. 41).

90. Gecaga, *Religious Movements and Democratization in Kenya*, 73.

91. Unlike Kenyatta, who had a high-level modern education, Gimode observes that Moi had a limited education. He also had a rather permanently hoarse voice, was a poor public speaker, and was from a less-esteemed ethnic background. This created his inferiority complex, which made him loathe academicians and other seemingly esteemed tribes.

92. Many scholars have theorized about the *nyayo* philosophy and what it meant. Augustine Haugerud, in *The Culture of Politics in Modern Kenya* (London: Cambridge University Press, 1997), consolidates several scholarly views and observes that the *nyayo* slogan drifted from its initial conceptualization. What was meant to be a continuation of Jomo Kenyatta's legacy or footsteps soon became "follow my footsteps." Later it became the footsteps of universal African spirit or the spirits of the ancestors.

meant something different, and his *nyayo* slogan became another way of perpetuating ethnicity.

For example, after he took over power, Moi appointed members of his ethnic group to key positions in government previously held by the Kikuyus.[93] He used state power to not only consolidate his power but also to destroy the Kikuyu economic base.[94] Although Moi initially attempted to stamp out ethnicity by outlawing ethnic groups such as Gikuyu, Embu, Meru Association (GEMA), the Luo Union, the New Akamba Union, and the Abaluhia Welfare Association, as well as ethnically based soccer clubs, it is evident that ethnically based practices in government offices never disappeared. In fact, to counter the GEMA movement that was proving to be an enigma during this period, Moi allowed the formation of the Kalenjin, Maasai, Turkana and Samburu (KAMATUSA), and the Luhya communities.

One of the key elements of Moi's governance that perpetrated ethnicity was his policy on District Focus for Rural Development. District Focus aimed at transferring development strategies from provincial to district level, but given that many districts in Kenya are constituted around ethnic communities, one might conclude that District Focus for Rural Development further reinforced negative ethnicity. Although Morton rather inadequately tries to defend Moi's scheme of District Focus for Rural Development, it can be noted that districts inhabited by ethnic communities favorable to Moi's regime benefited from allocation of resources from the national coffers.[95] What was meant to be district focus actually ended up being "Moi's selective focus." This heightened tribal suspicion and animosity, especially from ethnic groups that were oppressed by Moi's regime. If Kenyatta's regime pitted the Kikuyu against the Luo, Moi's regime pitted the Kikuyu against the Kalenjin.[96] Note-

---

93. Gecaga, "Religious Movements," 56.

94. Gecaga, "Religious Movements," 69.

95. Moi's biographer, Andrew Morton (*Moi: The Making of an African Statesman* [Nairobi: Michael Omara, 1999], 210), inadequately tries to argue that District Focus for Rural Development helped switch Kenya from tribal to political economics. According to him, it was an attempt to develop from the bottom rather than from the top. His arguments lack merit at the point he invokes Dr. Eshiwani, who at that time was a political crony of Moi's regime. Furthermore, Morton fails to state which districts were meant by "focus" and which districts actually benefited from Moi's selective focus.

96. Moses Amutabi, "Intellectuals and the Democratization Process in Kenya," in *Kenya: The Struggle for Democracy*, eds. G. R. Murunga and S. W. Nasong'o (London: Zed Books, 2000), 209.

worthy is that the Luos were also marginalized during Moi's time. The animosities between the Kikuyu and Kalenjin ethnic groups were to have their full expression in the 2008 postelection violence (although this was not the full cause of the postelection violence in 2008).

Although ethnicity and the poor education sector cannot wholly be blamed on Moi's regime, he used the education sector to propel ethnicity, hence contributing to ethnic consciousness in Kenya.[97] Moi introduced the quota system of admission into high schools. The quota system was meant to give opportunities to students from around the school locality and allowed admission of only a portion of students who hailed from outside the province. As Wanyonyi argues, this system, while meant to encourage communities to invest more in constructing new and better-equipped schools, adversely affected the nation-building approach.[98] Indeed, many undeveloped communities saw the quota system as a way of restricting certain ethnic identities to keep them from benefiting from national schools, many of which were located within the jurisdiction of the majority ethnic groups. This again contributed to ethnic suspicion and political unrest around ethnicity.

MWAI KIBAKI PERIOD (2002-2013)

To have a balanced view of negative ethnicity under all the presidents of Kenya, writers in Kenya history give fitting examples of how Kibaki's regime perpetuated ethnic biases. Wanyonyi argues that Kibaki's entry into State House exploited ethnic structures in the name of political parties that Moi had built around him for political security.[99] Under Moi, various political parties, though claiming to be national, were actually ethnic caucuses.[100] The Kenya National African Union (KANU) had largely become a Kalenjin party; Ford-Kenya was mainly comprised of Luo, while Ford-Asili and DP were mainly GEMA outfits.[101, 102] Every major political

---

97. Kundu, "Ethnicity," 45.

98. Wanyonyi, "Historicizing," 46.

99. Wanyonyi, "Historicizing," 53.

100. Macharia Munene, *Historical Reflections: Intellectual Adventurism, Politics and International Relations* (Nairobi: University of Nairobi Press, 2012), 131–7.

101. Forum for Restoration of Democracy (FORD)—a political party that split into two: Ford-Kenya and Ford-Asili. Ford-Kenya was a political outfit allied to ethnic groups residing in western Kenya, while Ford-Asili was mainly allied to Central Kenyan people.

102. Achieng Oloo, ed., *The Contemporary Opposition in Kenya: Between Internal Traits and State Manipulation* (London: Zed Books, 2007), 117.

party received its greatest support from the ethnic community its leader came from. Due to the democratic space offered and liberalism achieved by advent of multiparty politics, more ethnic parties were formed.[103] In the case of small ethnic groups, the era of tribal party alliances was inaugurated. When Moi's KANU made alliances with Raila's NDP (National Development Party), Kibaki's DP (Democratic Party) made similar alliances with Charity Ngilu's SDP and Kijana Wamalwa's Ford-Kenya to form the huge infamous ethnic stream that was the National Alliance Party of Kenya (NAK). It was to NAK that Raila Odinga and his allies decamped to when his alliance with Moi could not be sustained, but not without forming a loose alliance known as the Liberal Democratic Party (LDP) in 2002, which was comprised mainly of KANU dissidents.[104]

The marriage of NAK and LDP gave birth to NARC (National Alliance Rainbow Coalition) in 2002, which could have been viewed as a huge ethnic mainstream. Though many commentators view NARC as a viable model that could have downplayed ethnicity in Kenya, they fail to consider the othering it has done to the Kalenjins and affiliate identities.[105] NARC should be seen for what it was: a loose combination of groups by ethnic leaders for short-term political gains. This is the NARC that brought Kibaki to power in 2002, but not without a memorandum of understanding (MOU) as a pledge for ethnic balance.

Just like Jomo Kenyatta and Daniel arap Moi, Mwai Kibaki was unable to sing eloquently the song of tribal balance. In the initial years of his rule, Kibaki reneged upon the MOU that was signed in 2002 and marginalized the LDP allies. This kindled the wrath of Western Kenyan ethnic groups, who were sympathizers of LDP. This further raised animosity between these groups and the Central Kenyan groups. According to Mwangola, the trashing of the MOU became just another example of the Kibaki administration's determination to retain power along tribal ranks. On account of this, it can be argued that the 2005 national referendum on the so-called Wako Draft of the constitution was in many ways a contest between the Central Kenyan ethnicities and other ethnic groups.[106] In fact, "the overwhelming majority voted for 'NO' [orange] in the referen-

---

103. Munene, *Historical Reflections*, 137.
104. Oloo, *Contemporary Opposition*, 23.
105. Wanyonyi, "Historicizing," 14.
106. Mshai Mwangola, "Leaders of Tomorrow? The Youth and Democratization in Kenya," in *The Struggle for Democracy*, eds. Shadrack W. Nasong'o and Godwin R. Murunga (London: Zed Books, 2013), 157.

dum not to the constitution but to an ideology of anti-Kikuyuism that had coalesced amongst the 'YES' [banana] supporters."[107]

The picture that comes up in this work attempts to show that Kenya has become a center stage for negative ethnic theatrics, with politics being the main catalyst. Each political leadership, including the colonial, has never been able to completely remove Kenyans from an ethnic outfit and place them into "Kenyanness" or national identity. Ethnicity in Kenya is about transacted and perceived power and authority.[108] Negative ethnicity in Kenya is almost another way of life, and leads to power over and othering. Just as the story of Mark is sustained through Christ power, so is the story of Kenyan life sustained through tribal power. In fact, ethnic identity in Kenya has been "commodified" to the extent that it is the news that sells, just as soccer sells in England. If ethnic identity remains characterized by economic well-being and political favoritism, negative ethnicity will remain a major source of impunity in Kenya as groups use the political and economic arenas to outdo each other. It remains to be seen what the Uhuru Kenyatta presidency coupled with the current constitution will do to bring Kenyans to another experience of Kenyanness altogether.

ETHNIC IDENTITIES AND IMPUNITY IN KENYA

Negative ethnicity is so entrenched in the Kenyan fiber that you have not introduced yourself properly until you have answered the question "Where are you from?" in terms of ethnic identity. While it is certain that people can be born and married in areas where their parents did not come from, the fact that they bear certain names confines them to belong to where their names originated from. Even families who have been resident in an area for generations, perhaps with younger members who have never even set foot in their rural "home" of origin, are still subject to immigrant status.[109]

---

107. During the 2005 referendum on the constitution, the symbols "orange" for those against the constitution and "banana" for those favoring the constitution were used. Most "orange" supporters came from Western Kenyan ethnic groupings. Later, "orange" was used as a symbol for a political party. This party had support from the same tribes. See also Wanyonyi, "Historicizing," 18.

108. Wanyonyi, "Historicizing," 51.

109. S. Jenkins, "Ethnicity, Violence and the Immigrant-Guest Metaphor in Kenya," *AA* 111, no. 445 (2012): 576–96.

Because of such ingrained tribal differentiations, various atrocities in Kenya have been perpetrated in the name of tribal and ethnic identities. Impunity is meted out through zoning of areas to be tribal zones and no-go zones for members of other ethnicities. During the 2008 postelection violence, for example, parts of the Rift Valley, parts of Central Kenya, Western Kenya, Kenya's Coast, and Nairobi were no-go zones for other tribes.[110] Members of other ethnic groups who were found there were either killed, maimed, or forcefully evicted. Tribal gangs and illegal outfits ensured that this was accomplished in the name of tribe.[111] In spite of the fact that the former and current constitutions declared Kenya a land for all Kenyans, on account of tribal consciousness and impunity, these groups disregarded the law to behave the way they did.

Impunity in Kenya is vented through ethnic identity in times of unrest and when the law seems to be crippled. In view of the *kipande* that is noted as a powerful colonial tool, which continues today in the form of legally mandated national identity cards in Kenya, it can be argued that in postcolonial Kenya ethnic identity in times of turmoil was betrayed by the *kipande*. A case in point is the postelection violence that rocked Kenya in the wake of December 2007 and parts of January 2008. According to the state-sponsored Waki report, goons used the *kipande* to identify individuals' ethnic identity and either vented violence on them or spared them as the case demanded.[112] In this case, the goons in the Rift Valley were under instruction to remove all *madoadoa*s (literally "stains"—meaning those deemed as non-natives, even though they may have resided in the location for over half a century) from the Rift Valley province of Kenya.

Beyond the postelection violence, it is no wonder that in general circumstances, when it is business as usual, many Kenyans prefer introducing themselves to others using the Western or baptismal or other names, in order to disguise their tribal identity.[113] This concealment of identity cuts across all sectors, from business to employment to security. For example, even during the contextual Bible studies, it was noticed that in many instances in the purchase of bargainable items, the ethnic name of the seller and that of the buyer would determine the pricing of the item

---

110. J. K. Chelanga, J. K. Ndege, and S. M. Singo, eds., *The Crisis of Governance: Politics and Ethnic Conflicts in Kenya* (Eldoret: Moi University Press, 2009), 35.

111. P. N. Waki, *Report of the Commission of Inquiry in Post-Election Violence* (Nairobi: Government of Kenya, 2008), 1–124.

112. Waki, *Post-Election Violence*, 95.

113. Jenkins, "Immigrant-Guest Metaphor," 576–96.

in question.¹¹⁴ In such cases, ethnic group A would sell fruits to ethnic group B at an inflated price, while ethnic group B would repair ethnic group A's vehicle at an inflated price.

Though ethnic identity is a valued concept in postcolonial studies as a recovery of the subaltern identity erased from the mainstream memory by colonial narratives, engrossment with tribal identity in Kenya more often than not yields negative phenomena.¹¹⁵ Nevertheless, Kenyans, like others, must celebrate their ethnicity with ease, without fear of being victimized. The celebration of the ethnicity without resorting to impunity must be a task that postcolonial scholars in Kenya should endeavor to enable. This can be attested by sentiments of many contextual Bible study respondents and interviewees, the full findings of which will be incorporated in chapter three.

POVERTY, SUBALTERNITY, AND IMPUNITY

Poverty in Kenya has many dimensions that interlink with impunity. Ethnic politics in Kenya have a lot to do with ethnic ascendency on the economic ladder. Wrong argues that when used in a political campaign program, the slogan "it is our turn to eat" elicits a lot of support; and of course it leads to othering of those not "eating."¹¹⁶ Kenya, which was once a steadily growing economy, where all had something to eat, but later termed a "man eat man" society, has slowly become a "man eat nothing" society.¹¹⁷ Poverty in Kenya is a serious problem. If poverty has lines, many people live below the so-called poverty line. Many Kenyans are not poor per se; they have been made poorer.¹¹⁸

---

114. Interviewee #1. (The opinions of respondents in this book have been coded in such a manner. Research ethics in Kenya require that identities and actual names of respondents be concealed. This not only adheres to requirements and assurances enshrined in ethical consent forms but also shields their ethnicity and their comments from ethnic biases.)

115. R. S. Sugirtharajah, *The Bible and the Third World: Precolonial, Colonial and Postcolonial Encounters* (Cambridge: Cambridge University Press, 2001), 178.

116. Wrong, *Our Turn to Eat*, 76.

117. It may seem like ages since the late president Julius Kabarage Nyerere of Tanzania declared Kenya to be a "man eat man" society, meaning poor people were taxed heavily in order to keep the rich people alive. In response, the then attorney general Charles Mugane Njonjo quipped that Tanzania was a "man eat nothing" state due to its socialist "ujamaa" economic policy.
   http://nationofafrica.blogspot.com/2011/08/man-eat-man-society.html. Accessed June 7, 2017.

118. Munene, *Historical Reflections*, 79–80.

Poverty in Kenya can be termed systemic, and it is not by default that many Kenyans are poor, but by design.[119] I have in other studies traced the problem of poverty in Kenya to organizing principles of hegemony, which lead to an ever-widening gap between the rich and the poor at the center and the margins.[120] In my view, part of its genesis stems from Jomo Kenyatta's regime, which drafted the initial organizing principle upon attainment of independence. In line with this thinking, Norman Miller notes that Jomo Kenyatta's family had within the first years of independence transformed and entrenched itself into a famous political and economic power.[121] In fact, "the wife of the first president, Mama Ngina had acquired a substantial economic domain and was actively expanding to include large tracts of uncultivated land and working farms, plus businesses involving transport, ivory, wildlife trophies and mining."[122] This was tantamount to building an economic empire fashioned after and transcending that of the colonialists.

In constituting the picture of the rich and the poor in Kenya by "othering," Miller revealed that in the building of the Kenyan class empire, "nepotism was common place" and a large number of extended family members and others profited by their favored positions.[123] Furthermore, "in Jomo Kenyatta's regime, all major decisions flowed from the top to the bottom and were taken by Jomo Kenyatta or by his close lieutenants. The inner circle that held real power was the family," and apart from governing, "capital accumulation was the basic objective of the people close to the regime."[124] As a result, Miller, like Mwangola, observes that the private business and private wealth of the inner circle grew to astounding levels. This means that prosperity was directly or indirectly tied to connections to the first family.[125] Therefore, a class of the extraordinarily rich was in the making, and in retrospect another class of the poor. Just as it is noted

---

119. UNDP. "UNDP Kenya Annual Report 2011," accessed April 20, 2017, http://www.ke.undp.org.

120. Julius Kiambi, *Postcolonial "Redaction" of Social-economic Parables in Luke's Gospel* (Berlin: Lambert Academic Publishing, 2011), 64.

121. Miller, *Quest for Prosperity*, 50.

122. Miller, *Quest for Prosperity*, 50.

123. Miller, *Quest for Prosperity*, 51.

124. Miller, *Quest for Prosperity*, 50.

125. Mwangola, "Leaders of Tomorrow?," 14.

in Cassidy's *Politics and Society*,[126] so it can be noted of Jomo Kenyatta's time that "a clear patron client relationship existed between Kenyatta's cabinet members and a network of supporters in their home areas who benefited or hoped to benefit by their ties to those in power."[127]

This shows that at an early stage following Kenya's independence from Britain, poverty became a class issue. Those who were poor, but who knew somebody in power and were well connected, could get out of poverty. When those in power only "lift" those they know, it in essence results in a relatively stable lower middle economic class and a recognizable class of poor people, while others go ahead and obtain exceptional wealth.[128] Therefore, it can be noted that under Jomo Kenyatta, and even subsequent regimes, it is the wealthy black elite who govern the nation with an entrenched hegemony.

It is also important to point out that among these wealthy in the ruling class are the clergy. In essence, Kenya can further be regrouped into two distinct groups: the tiny minority *wenyenchi* ("those who own the nation," "the powerful and wealthy") and the masses, *wananchi* ("common citizenry," "children of the nation"). In postcolonial terminology, these translate to "the center" and "the margin," respectively. Oscillating between them, perhaps, are the middle (upper or lower) classes.

The systemic marginalization of the poor in Kenya can further be seen through an analysis of hybridity, which is an enticing idea in current postcolonial studies. As has been noted, the concept of hybridity helps explain marginalization by examining and unpacking societal configurations that enable and officiate stark obfuscated inequalities. Hybridity provides a way out of binary thinking, allowing the inscription of the agency of the subaltern, and permitting a restructuring and destabilizing of power.

Examined through this concept, the situation that created most of the marginalized in Kenya immediately after independence can best be described by Miller.[129]

> The elite began to regard themselves as a cohesive group that deserved prestige and economic wellbeing. There

---

126. Richard J. Cassidy, *Jesus, Politics and Society: A Study of Luke's Gospel* (Maryknoll, NY: Orbis Books, 1978), 45.

127. Miller, *Quest for Prosperity*, 62.

128. Munene, *Historical Reflections*, 83.

129. Miller, *Quest for Prosperity*, 78.

> were variations in income, but members of this elite were clearly distinguished from the poor and the lower middle class not only in income but in style. They adopted British styles in clothing, housing, furniture, and entertainment. They lived in red brick tiled bungalows with well-tended gardens in Nairobi's residential sections. They played tennis, drank whiskey, and owned well priced cars. In fact, the new African elite who had joined or replaced the white elite not only copied their lifestyle but often adopted their outlook. They would still help their poor relatives, in conformity with traditional African values, but many of them tended to keep aloof from less favored citizens. They were accused especially by university students of perpetrating dualistic social system of colonial days and of favoring a system of mutual accommodation with the remaining whites. They did not yet constitute a hereditary upper class...[130]

This argument that I quote from Miller illustrates how a hybrid generation that was a result of colonial mimicry was on its way and constituting itself in post independence Kenya. Thus, hybridity and mimicry played a big role in the stratification of Kenyan society between the poor and the rich.[131] The black elite who had wholeheartedly embraced Western values alienated themselves from their mother culture. This situation also highly contributed to the gap between the rich and the poor.[132] They did not believe that Kenyan cultural values were the key to development. Western religion (Westernized Christianity in particular), Western medicine, and free enterprise were each emphasized over indigenous systems. Due to this, Haugerud rightly sees modern politicians in Kenya not only as bypassing indigenous values, but also openly using Western

---

130. Miller, *Quest for Prosperity*, 72.

131. Even though Robert C. Young explains hybridity and mimicry as Bhabhan concepts that are used to show how the colonized resist colonial authorities by copying it, the Kenyan elites engage mimicry of a special type. They copy colonial identity and ideology when it aids them in colonizing the Kenyan subaltern, but they resist it when it threatens to shutter their hybrid identities. They hoodwink the Kenyan subaltern into believing that colonial power is over with the exit of colonial masters, yet they duplicate a subtle neocolonial rule in Kenya. See, Young, *Colonial Desire*, 67.

132. Munene, *Historical Reflections*, 81–86.

dress, automobiles, and forms of entertainment as status symbols, particularly as a way of distinguishing themselves from the subalterns.[133]

POVERTY REALITIES AND MARKERS OF IMPUNITY

Even though the gap between the rich and the poor in Kenya is read from a postcolonial angle of hybridity, poverty in Kenya is viewed from within the wider matrix of the poor nation itself. The state of official poverty in Kenya can best be described by using Webner and Rangers, who note that

> exports have declined in relative and absolute terms. Food production has declined. Imports of food and other necessities have risen greatly. Import-substitution industries have not lived up to expectations. Industrialization has, with some exceptions, failed to materialize. Borrowing and debt have soured. Currencies have weakened or collapsed. State revenues have plummeted. State controlled economic activities have foundered. State funded services have declined or disintegrated. Official economies have shrunk, and parallel economies have grown.[134]

Given this picture of poverty in Kenya and the potential representation of inequality in a mature class society, it can be expected that pockets of resistance and violence must result from time to time, especially from the submerged classes.

The reality of poverty in Kenya is also seen through the eyes of the United Nations Development Program (UNDP) report.[135] As noted on the front page of its website, the UNDP is the United Nations' global development network. It is the organization that advocates for change and connects countries to knowledge, experience, and resources to help people build a better life. The UNDP is on the ground in 166 countries, one of which is Kenya, working with them on their own solutions to global and national development challenges. The UNDP produced the first *Human Development Report* for Kenya in 1999 with an aim of assessing human development. Subsequent reports have followed annually, and in

---

133. D. Nyaga, *Customs and Traditions of the Ameru* (Nairobi: East African Educational Publishers, 1997), 149.
134. R. Werbner and T. Ranger, eds., *Postcolonial Identities in Africa* (London: Zed Books, 1996), 31.
135. UNDP Kenya, accessed April 20, 2017, http://www.ke.undp.org/.

many of them, human development in Kenya linked to issues of unequal distribution of resources has been a key concern. The *UNDP Kenya National Human Development Report 2006*, with its theme, "Human Security and Human Development: A Deliberate Choice," particularly dwells on how a secure environment enhances human development, and deals with issues of the gap between the rich and the poor in Kenya.

One of the key observations the report makes is that poverty in Kenya is systemic, partly due to deliberate marginalization of some areas. The sentiments of the report can be further buttressed by Munene's argument that creation of poverty is used as a control mechanism.[136] Poverty becomes a tool to be employed by those in power against those who would challenge the status quo. Although recent UNDP *Human Development Reports* testify to a profound shift in global dynamics, driven by fast-rising powers of the developing world, human poverty appears to have deepened. This can be attributed to the growing structural inequalities in the Human Poverty Index (HPI) components (access to health, water, and doctors, and the nutritional status of children).[137]

Analysis from HPI distribution per county, for example, shows that those without representation in the ruling class are the most affected by poverty levels, while those from where most of the ruling class hail attain relatively rich indexes. The rich index attained by the poor near the centers of power can be explained as benefit by default—that is, the benefits are not intended for the poor in the first place, but as the rich bring services closer to their localities, the poor who are close to them and mostly from their communities end up benefiting. Therefore, counties like Kiambu and Muranga (which are in central Kenya) have a lower HPI compared to Vihiga (located in western parts of Kenya) and Marsabit (located in remote northeastern parts of Kenya), which have a relatively high index. The same applies to counties within the central areas compared to those in the northern areas and coastal areas. The point is, even collective wealth in Kenya is unequally distributed and its distribution follows the patterns of poor and rich classifications, whereby the rich are typified by the elites who are colonial hybridists and mimics, while the poor are lower middle class and the general masses.

---

136. Munene, *Historical Reflections*, 82.

137. *UNDP Kenya Annual Report 2011*, accessed April 20, 2017, http://www.ke.undp.org.

Poverty and its creation in Kenya is a contrived process that has long historical roots.[138] As a contrived process, it is deliberate and manipulated by some people in power for the purposes of favoring or victimizing persons or groups of people. Those who believe they are victimized become resentful, believing their perceived poverty is due to those in authority. In the long run, the victimized encourage a disregard of the authority of those in power. Some of them nurture feelings of betrayal, which in the long run become justifications for full-blown impunity.

Economic inequalities in Kenyan society can be attributed to a schemed or deliberate imbalance.[139] As famed Kenyan novelist and activist Ngũgĩ wa Thiong'o argues, when the colonialists left Kenya, they only took away their physical presence, but they left behind their ideologies.[140] In turn, a breed of neocolonialists who were willing to foster the interests of the colonialists and their own interests connived to create poverty by amassing wealth for themselves. Githiga corroborates this:

> Since independence, there had been known cases where people in authority had accumulated property without thinking of the plight of the poor and the marginalized ... this grabbing of economic opportunities by a few Kenyans created a wide gap between the rich and the poor.[141]

What can be argued is that this phenomenon is a direct import from the colonial experience through interaction with the colonialists.

According to Horsley, the agenda of postcolonial discourse is to give voice in the central sites to subjects from previously colonized areas.[142] A postcolonial reading of impunity and poverty in Kenya must aim to emancipate previously submerged histories and identities in the process of revealing complex hybridity and contingencies in the contemporary world. Postcolonial discourse must reveal that conventional poverty and marginalization in Kenya contribute to the prevailing culture of impunity. Seen in this way, two strands of impunity begin to emerge: impunity as

---

138. Murungi, *In the Mad of Politics* (Nairobi: Acacia Stantex Publishers, 2000), 87.

139. See Munene, *Historical Reflections*, 87.

140. Ngũgĩ wa Thiong'o, *Devil on the Cross*, 216.

141. Gideon G. Githiga, "The Church as the Bulwark Against Authoritarianism: Development of Church-State Relations in Kenya, with Particular Reference to the Years after Political Independence 1963–1992,"
Transformation: An International Journal of Holistic Mission Studies 16, no. 2 (1991): 71–72, 89.

142. Horsley, "Submerged Biblical Histories and Imperial Biblical Studies," 158.

exercised by the ruling class and impunity as enjoined by the subaltern in their own struggles.

Impunity of the empire becomes the tool by the ruling class to maintain their status quo, while impunity by the subaltern becomes a tool of resistance. Impunity becomes an attempt by the subaltern to redefine authority, hence redefining self. Impunity of the subaltern stems from an awareness that resisting laws that be amounts to rejecting hegemonic or normative worlding that ensures the subaltern will never achieve economic freedom. Under postcolonial thinking, perhaps, rejecting the laws of the dominant is no longer impunity. It is an emancipatory quest for life that can provide a basis for political challenges to regnant or prevailing forms of domination.

IMPUNITY AND THE LAW

Before the advent of colonialism, many Kenyan communities were governed through unwritten and social rules and society customs and norms.[143] However, colonial agents and missionaries destroyed most outward manifestation of the old tradition; at the same time, they first built their own cognitive view of rural African society and then imposed it on daily life before or during the 1920s.[144] The colonialists also erected a structure called customary law, which was utterly foreign to the spirit of the former tradition. Customary law was the headstone on the grave of traditional legal structures.[145] The familiar old ways of life were reeling, and there was a tragic chasm between the physical and cognitive realities.

According to Wanyonyi, during this period variants of neo-African traditions were gestating in cities and the countryside, replacing the real identities of the Kenyan communities. The elites were left to shape the contours of Kenyan identity after the exit of the imperialists. They prevented the postcolonial Kenyan from inventing new structures to cope with new situations. Instead, the elites mimicked colonial structures, preferred to "Pan-Africanize" structures, and enforced them. These structures of perceiving life and reality made sense only to the elites,

---

143. Bethwell A. Ogot, "Boundary Changes and Invention of Tribes," in *Kenya: The Making of a Nation: A Hundred Years of Kenya's History, 1895–1995* (Maseno, Kenya: Maseno University, 2000), 23.

144. Wanyonyi, "Historicizing," 35–38.

145. Richard Werbner and Terence Ranger, eds., *Postcolonial Identities in Africa* (London: Zed Books, 1996), 275.

and so they created the need for the so-called civic education on how to live in the postcolonial country. The Kenyan was in an irreversible cultural crisis, and was being turned into something resembling a cultural schizophrenic.[146]

Law in Kenya today is a representation of mimicked colonial worlding. It is caught up in a capitalistic world, which Kenya copied from the colonial masters. It is the tool of the dominant meant to control the masses. When present-day Kenyan law and penal institutions are read through a Marxist lens, they can be viewed as being caught up in class relations and economic structures.[147]

Accordingly, David Garland argues that in a capitalist society, law evolves to produce categories that are legal expressions of bourgeois values. For him, law materializes and universalizes categories that are specific to a particular class-based mode of production.[148] Therefore, law provides a powerful ideology that helps legitimize these relations by phrasing economic interests in a vocabulary of universal right. Furthermore, Garland shows that law is an instrument of class domination and occasionally of class terror.[149] It protects the worldview of the dominant, as well as the social and moral structures that support that worldview, while excluding that of the subaltern. It is chiefly directed against those elements who have "lost their position" in society.

Postcolonial Marxism helps us to see law in a country like Kenya for what it really is: an ideological vehicle of the dominant class for social and economic control. Studies that fail to recognize and identify this class dimension and ordering of society by the dominant merely reproduce the ideological effect that law seeks to promote. The practice of law is thus a mechanism of class rule embodied in a legal form that seeks to disguise its class content. Law therefore is a weapon in immediate class struggles and not a guarantor of individual freedoms as it purports to be.[150] When the subalterns realize this, a revolution in social structures can bring about the conditions needed to dislodge the hegemonic class.

Law seen in this way becomes the vehicle for organized state terror. Conversely, this becomes inverted impunity because it is only permitted

---

146. Werbner and Ranger, *Identities*, 276.

147. David Garland, *Punishment and Modern Society: A Study in Social Theory* (Oxford: Oxford University Press, 1990), 111.

148. Garland and Ranger, *Punishment*, 112.

149. Garland and Ranger, *Punishment*, 113.

150. Garland and Ranger, *Punishment*, 114.

by a worldview that is sympathetic to the hegemonic class. For example, it is important to note that law in a dominant class serves that class's purpose in a way that also enlists support from the subaltern class. In such a situation, the law that protects everyone, at one level, also legalizes the basis whereby one class exploits another. Therefore, seen in another way, "impunity" becomes the subaltern's response to hegemonic worlding. In its performative aspect, impunity becomes an ideological counter-structure by which the subaltern cries out for an inclusive interpretation of the society. Seen in this way, law becomes a corrupt class instrument. Accordingly, law is all about social authority (ἐξουσία) and the governing claims of those in power. In this view, then, it becomes right to argue with Garland that law "reinforces these claims by means of coercive sanctions as well as symbolic displays."[151]

In Kenya, impunity by use of the law is perpetrated in many instances when the application of law tends to favor those in power or when structures of authority organize in view of the dominant class. For example, on May 30, 2012, Kenya's parliament approved a bill to control opinion polls. Part of the parliamentary debate noted that opinion polls in Kenya disregard many laws and are tools for popularity through impunity. Debaters argued that pollsters in Kenya disregard all law to manipulate or declare their kings as the most popular. In passing the bill, parliament noted this and included stiff penalties for those found flouting control laws governing opinion polls. How easy it is for the dominant powers to circumvent the consequences and intention of the law is shrouded in the words of one of the debaters, Hon. Boni Khalwale, as he argued for stiffer penalties: "If we don't enhance the punishment for breaking the law, then those who do it can ignore the law because they can afford the fine."[152]

This only illustrates part of what the dominant class can do when the law is legislated in their favor. It also illustrates that in Kenya it is easy to break the law willingly and use class position and money to settle the offense and escape punishment. To shed more light on this, during the contextual Bible studies, participants noted that law in Kenya is intended to favor the powerful and torment the powerless. For them, impunity thrives in an atmosphere where there is no fair playground.

In Kenya, the judiciary, which is supposed to act as the beacon of the rule of law, has to a great extent been marred by allegations of lack of

---

151. Garland and Ranger, *Punishment*, 123.
152. Eugene N. Shiundu and A. C. Wafula. "MPs Approve Bill to Control Opinion Polls," *Daily Nation*, May 31, 2012, 36.

transparency, inefficiency, and corruption among its members. This can be illustrated by the backlog of cases that have in the past filled the court system because, on many occasions, trials fail to commence within a reasonable time, and cases are not concluded expeditiously. Sometimes cases dismissed in Kenya for lack of evidence have been successfully concluded in other judicial systems, e.g., the drugs case of the Akasha family.[153] The cumulative effect of delayed and flawed prosecutions is the erosion of faith in the law on the part of the people and the undermining of the rule of law. When "justice delayed becomes justice denied," this provides little or no incentive to the citizen to obey and respect the law, as it is viewed as retrogressive. The interference of the judiciary by the political elites, legislature, and executives further undermines the due process of the law, thus promoting impunity.[154] It is no wonder that, during the contextual Bible studies, members noted interference with the judiciary by the powerful as one of the major contributing factors to impunity in Kenya.[155]

Impunity as Empire Resistance

Postcolonialism puts emphasis on the economic, material, and cultural conditions that determine the global systems in which postcolonial nations are required to operate. As Robert J. C. Young indicates, resistance must be registered often since there is no "postcolonial condition" outside of specific instances of complex intermingling of structural forces with local and personal experiences.[156] Postcolonialism must be both confrontational and committed to political ideals of a transnational social justice. It must attack the status quo of hegemonic economic imperialism, and do so with active engagement, as do Marxism and feminism. Drawing on these resources, postcolonialism must invite the subaltern other to some sort of interventionist methodology to combat

---

153. There was insufficient evidence to convict the Akashas in Kenya. However, when the case was prosecuted in the USA, the judicial system was able to successfully put them to trial after they pleaded guilty. Reuters, accessed November 20, 2019, https://af.reuters.com/article/topNews/idAFKCN1N00TN-OZATP.

154. International Commission of Jurists (ICJ), "Kenya Judicial Independence Corruption and Reform" (2005), accessed June 6, 2012, http://www.icj.org/news.php3?id_article=3663&lang=en.

155. Interviewee #2 (male).

156. Robert J. C. Young, *Postcolonialism: An Historical Introduction* (Oxford: Wiley-Blackwell, 2001), 57.

the continuing, often covert, operation of an imperialist system of economic, political, religious, and cultural domination.[157] A change of the prevailing conditions exerted by the empire upon its subjects must first attract critique and resistance from the position of its victims and not its perpetrators. As such, the empire must be resisted.

According to Young, the postcolonial era in its name pays tribute to the great historical achievements of resistance against colonial power, while paradoxically it also describes the conditions of existence that have followed in which many basic power structures have yet to change in any substantive way.[158] What Young explains is a condition of complacency immediately after many countries attained their political independence; a condition that ushered in new forms of colonial domination perpetrated by a "native bourgeois elite" produced during colonial times, and that took on board many Western presuppositions, including the idea of the nation-state itself.[159]

In Kenya, this is the group that superintends over hegemonic power. According to G. Magaga, it is the one that has overseen many violations of human rights.[160] Impunity through human rights violations and economic crimes that have occurred in Kenya over the years has left in its wake countless victims unheard, denied justice, their grievances and injuries having no redress. The victims and survivors include individuals and families of political assassinations and killings, torture, inhuman and degrading treatment, arbitrary arrest and detention, disappearances, abductions, and extrajudicial killings.[161]

Added to this group is an even larger number of victims of conflict, insecurity, civil strife, and internal displacements resulting from politically instigated clashes. Grand corruption and theft of public resources result in marginalized groups and countless numbers of landless poor, while the culture of impunity continues to breed lawlessness.[162] Pockets

---

157. Young, *Postcolonialism*, 58.

158. Young, *Postcolonialism*, 60.

159. Young, *Postcolonialism*, 59.

160. G. O. Magaga, "The African Dream: 1920–1963," in *Kenya: The Making of a Nation 1895–1995*, 23–45.

161. Some of these are discussed under various political eras of the presidents mentioned in this chapter. A catalogue of social injustices meted out to individual citizens and citizen groups can be constructed from the writings of Mwakikagile, Lumumba, Njoya, and others.

162. P. L. O. Lumumba, *A Call for Hygiene in Kenya Politics* (Nairobi: Mvule Africa Publishers, 2008), 4.

of violence and mass violence all point to some sort of fatigue and impatience with the hegemonic powers that be. In Kenya, despite a change of regime, it is difficult to trust the hegemonic powers that be to offer tools of resistance to the subaltern other. The *wanjiku*-driven constitutionalism seems to be the best moment for empire resistance.[163] However, this period in which the country stands also presents many challenges. Some of the challenges include undue delays in implementing the *wanjiku* constitution, and the desire by the hegemonic powers to amend *wanjiku* clauses that do not favor the status quo.

Resistance through Violence

According to L. Kurtz, violence has for centuries been a commonplace feature of social life, with its causes embedded in the sociocultural, historical, and economic contexts.[164] It can take varied forms, including physical, economic, political, ethnic, religious, or linguistic. Among other factors, violence resulting from conflict can be fueled by the institutionalization of difference whereby exclusion and inclusion are easily discernible.[165]

Writing in search of answers for the violence in Kenya that emanated from the contested presidential results of the December 2007 general elections, R. W. Ndüng'ü observes that the Kenyan "socializes into violence through multifaceted ideas and practices; economic, politics and culture all have something to do with this socialization."[166] Ndüng'ü arrives at this conclusion because, as she argues, in the case of the postelection violence, everyone who followed the events prior to the elections knew that trouble was brewing and was at some point inevitable.

Socialization to violence in Kenya cannot just be pegged to the 2007–2008 postelection violence; many Kenyans are quite socialized to

---

163. Wanjiku is a common Kikuyu female name. Wanjiku was one of the nine daughters of Gikuyu and Mumbi. It was coined during the making of the new constitution as a concept to represent the subaltern, the grassroots people or, said succinctly, the common *mwananchi*. It was President Moi who popularized the name during that time. When dismissing calls for a new constitution, he said, "Do you think Wanjiku understands what a constitution is?" People started to use the name in different forums and the name has stuck.

164. L. Kurtz, *The Language of War and Peace* (San Diego, Academic Press, 1999), 23.

165. R. W. Ndüng'ü, "Socialization and Violence: Ideas and Practices in Kenya," in *(Re) Membering Kenya; Identity, Culture and Freedom*, eds. wa-Mungai and Gona (Nairobi: Twaweza Communications, 2010), 112.

166. Ndüng'ü, "Socialization and Violence," 111.

violence, and this is illustrated on several fronts.[167] According to Fairclough, language is the chief tool for the socialization and institutionalization of violence.[168] Following Fairclough's model of Critical Discourse Analysis (CDA) Ndüng'ü argues that Kenyans have mainly been socialized to violence through language.[169] Maintaining that "human beings cannot claim their humanity in exclusion of the language that carries their culture because there is a very strong symbiotic relation between culture and language," she goes on to show how Kenyans are affected by violence markers in language.[170]

Accordingly, one of the ways in which Kenyans are socialized to violence is through the religious sphere. Religious language pictures the creator versus the creature. In doing so, it creates a hegemonic ideal that must be subscribed to without question. Employment of militant language in religious discourse encourages violence in subtle and blatant ways.[171] For example, it can be noted that many Christian songs of British origin embody combative metaphors, such as "Stand Up, Stand Up for Jesus" and "Onward Christian Soldiers." According to her, Kenya has similarly witnessed gospel songs that are reworked during times of agitation—for example, "Yote Yawezekana bila Moi" ("Everything is possible without Moi") and "Wakenya Msilale, Bado Mapambano" ("Kenyans do not resign to sleep, the struggle continues")—to give credibility to a violent struggle.[172]

Because of Christianity's central message that pictures Christians in constant battle with the devil, sermons from the pulpit have also been known to use combative language and metaphor. So have prophecies, which have also been used to achieve goals. This comports with Ndüng'ü's argument that "violence that is presented in religious con-

---

167. According to Jenkins, "Immigrant-Guest Metaphor," the 2008 violence was not an isolated incidence in Kenya's political history. Episodes of ethnic violence have characterized Kenyan elections since the transition to multiparty politics in 1992.

168. Fairclough, *Organization Studies*, 45.

169. Ndüng'ü, "Socialization and Violence," 113.

170. Ndüng'ü, "Socialization and Violence," 112.

171. Ndüng'ü, "Socialization and Violence," 143.

172. Gimode, "The Role of Police in Kenya's Democratic Process," 245.

texts and philosophies is volatile since the divine aspect is considered unquestionable."[173]

What all of this illustrates is that violence can become official and institutionalizing (as it has in Kenya) to the extent of becoming the inevitable way of achieving that which cannot be achieved in normal ways. The "might is right" mentality epitomized in the Swahili saying "*Mwenye nguvu mpishe*" ("Give way for the strong to pass") seems to propel the culture of impunity in Kenya. Violence breeds violence where there is a gap, and so impunity in Kenya takes the form of violence, which is given impetus by language. Therefore, in Kenya, the empire has become the most powerful domain; the one who can silence all others with whatever means; more so, the one who can silence the law with whatever means. When impunity is countered by impunity, then a society is on its knees and ready for imminent breakdown.

Conclusion

In this chapter I have assessed the situation of impunity in Kenya. I began by sketching a brief narrative of Kenya's history and linking the history of impunity to the history of colonialism in Kenya. I have developed the faces of impunity in Kenya and, through a postcolonial lens, explained how impunity is given impetus by ethnicity, colonialism, and a weak judicial system. Toward the end, I revealed the thin tension that exists between violence as a tool for resisting the empire and other ideological options available to a people in struggle.

My argument is that a world that does not exist sociologically but has always been present must be named. This world is the world of impunity that slowly seems to be forming itself as the official and unofficial world of Kenya. Given impetus by the craving for a Kenyan ἐξουσία, empty religion, eroded culture, and the hopelessness that is the hallmark of today, this world seems to threaten all by replacing the reason for being in the normative world. New concepts must be developed in which this world can be resisted and its ideology disentangled from the ideal world. By rereading Mark 1:21-28, the next chapter begins as an attempt to map how this disentangling can be conceptualized.

---

173. Ndüng'ü, "Socialization and Violence," 116.

CHAPTER THREE

Reading Otherwise: Mark's Ἐξουσία and Kenyan Impunity

Introduction

Much of my discussion so far has been based on the interpretive work of academic readers. Their questions and concerns have shaped most of the discussion, and yet the ordinary nonacademic readers, though present, are usually backgrounded. Quite a while ago, Spivak raised the need to be aware of the ordinary readers by asking the question, "Can the subaltern speak?" On the basic level, what Spivak intended, though with caution, was to raise awareness of the issue of representation by noting that mainstream scholars have always "pretended" to represent the subaltern.[1] Her argument was that the subalterns have a mind and a voice, and therefore academic readers should no longer represent them because they can speak for themselves.[2] Through a "reading with"

---

1. Spivak, *Subaltern Studies*, 113.

2. In "Can the Subaltern Speak?" Spivak encourages but also criticizes the efforts of the subaltern studies group, a project led by Ranajit Guha that has re-appropriated Gramsci's term "subaltern" (the economically dispossessed) in order to locate and re-establish a "voice" or collective locus of agency in postcolonial India. Although Spivak acknowledges the "epistemic violence" done upon Indian subalterns, she suggests that any attempt from the outside to ameliorate their condition by granting them collective speech will invariably encounter the following problems: (1) a logocentric assumption of cultural solidarity among a heterogeneous people, and (2) a dependence upon Western intellectuals to "speak for" the subaltern condition rather than allowing them to speak for themselves. As Spivak argues, by speaking out and reclaiming a collective cultural identity, subalterns will in fact reinscribe their subordinate position in society. The academic assumption of a subaltern collectivity becomes akin to an ethnocentric extension of Western logos—a totalizing, essentialist "mythology" as Derrida might describe it—that does not account for the heterogeneity of the colonized body politic. Postcolonial Web, accessed September 12, 2012, http://www.postcolonialweb.org/poldiscourse/spivak/spivak2.html.

approach, Spivak foregrounded and encouraged the voices of the subalterns to the level of celebration.

Sugirtharajah, in a similar venture, edited the seminal book *Voices from the Margins: Interpreting the Bible in the Third World* and brought out reading resources from the third world.[3, 4] Within a postcolonial framework, which problematizes the center and the margins, Sugirtharajah noted that "struggles and exegetical concerns of those who are on the periphery of the society must be foregrounded."[5] This was also in recognition of the fact that dominant biblical scholarship had elided the needs of the nonacademic readers in the society. As such, dominant Bible readings and interpretations had rarely focused on people's experience of hunger, sickness, and exploitation.

It is important to note that Spivak's and Sugirtharajah's criticisms were labeled against the hegemonic West and its attempt to dominate the rest in biblical scholarship.[6] The dichotomy of their argument was between dominant Western readers and third world readers in Asia, Africa, and Latin America. It should be noted that, for Sugirtharajah especially, third world did not mean a perception of geography but "a designation for a people who had and have been excluded from power ... a people who face harassment and exploitation wherever they are."[7]

In paying attention to this awareness raised by both Spivak and Sugirtharajah (among others), and as a celebration of the context that this volume foregrounds, I in this chapter aim to give the Kenyan subaltern a voice in the discourse of Bible and impunity. In doing this, I use Kenyan subaltern resources (through a contextual Bible study) to show the relationship between Mark's ἐξουσία and Kenyan impunity. In this chapter I cede my voice to a certain extent. I do this to demonstrate that impunity is not a matter of personal scholarly opinion, but pervades and affects the Kenyan masses, as demonstrated in the reading approaches of the

---

3. Sugirtharajah, *Voices*, 19.

4. Textual politics also recognize the use of the terms "Majority World" and "Two Thirds World" to refer to Africa, Asia, and Latin America, which were previously referred to as the third world.

5. Sugirtharajah, *Voices*, 109.

6. Sugirtharajah gives an example of the famous "Dictionary of Biblical Interpretation," whereby he notes that it is proudly presented as a work of distinguished scholars, yet it does not carry a single entry by an Asian, Latin American, or Black biblical interpreter. More revealingly, it has only one reference to the work of a non-Euro-American scholar.

7. Patrick A. Kalilombe, "The Bible and Non-Literate Communities," in *Voices from the Margin*, 397.

contextual Bible studies. This approach is made more obvious when I consider views from the contextual Bible study and bring them to the fore by integrating them into "mainstream" Kenyan readings of the Bible.

Why "Read with" the Ordinary?

Before presenting my view on how I read the Bible with the "ordinary reader," let me first underscore the necessity of reading the Bible with others and why it makes a difference with whom we read. Why should we read together? In general terms, the issue of impunity in relation to the Bible must be seen not merely as a matter of scholarly opinion but as emanating from a people's context. For this reason, the usually suppressed voices from the margins become a more authoritative hermeneutical key than mere scholarly analysis, and this is my posture in this chapter. So, why do we read with the "ordinary"? Part of the reason for "reading with" is because, as I noted in chapter one, the boundary between the classroom (or academy), and the village (the non-academy) must be strategically blurred and, if possible, eliminated. I see the need to close this boundary as an attempt to foster liberative readings as opposed to oppressive readings. Kalilombe has rightly noted that

> in the past, the Bible has often been invoked in such a way as to legitimize the most obvious social, economic, or political injustices, to discourage stirrings of revolt against oppressive or discriminatory practices and to promote attitudes of resignation and compliance in the face of exploitive manipulations of power-holders.[8]

Even today, there seems to be an intensified invasion of certain types of biblical interpretation that can only be characterized as simplistic and distracting in the way that they tend to whitewash the problems of a people in struggle. Such interpretations seem to center on the spiritual and interior needs of the people such that the connection between the Word of God and the realities of everyday life become secondary; almost irrelevant. This can be blamed on representative readings of the Bible that have been fostered by the "missionary" type of reading of the Bible. Now more than ever, there is a need for people from all walks of life to read and interpret the Bible for themselves.[9] Academic readers must

---

8. Kalilombe, "The Bible and Non-Literate Communities," 397.

9. Humphrey Waweru, *The Bible and African Culture: Mapping Transactional Inroads* (Eldoret, Kenya: Zapf Chancery, 2011): 83.

allow nonacademic readers a voice in biblical interpretation, or what this chapter terms "reading with."[10]

Within postcolonial biblical criticism, however, "reading with" the ordinary readers is done in recognition of the relationship between the center and the margins, or as West puts it, the "socially engaged biblical readers and ordinary readers."[11] The interface between academic readers of the Bible and ordinary readers of the Bible ("reading with") aims at deconstructing the traditional and hegemonic top-to-bottom approach to knowledge, or the so-called Freirean "banking method" of epistemology.[12] In retrospect, "reading with" promotes a mutual and shared learning as the basis of approach to knowledge.[13] It produces new energy as it opens up new horizons for repackaging liberative biblical concepts.

This approach recognizes that grand narratives, often, mirror the voices of the dominant while muting or abolishing the voices of the marginal. Constantly, Spivak's question "Can the subaltern speak?" becomes the urgent and haunting voice in this quest.[14] The disquiet produced by the urgency and the haunting voice, in turn, helps shutter the assumed correctness and appropriateness of the academic readers (though not for all times). "Reading with" also recognizes that the ordinary readers have hermeneutics, and though these hermeneutics are not mainstreamed in academic practices, they retain their interpretative potential.

"Reading with" the ordinary readers is subversive in that it brings down the "epistemological privilege of the ordained."[15] It brings it down to what can be termed a democratized knowledge, where it is no longer the teacher who has a monopoly on knowledge, but knowledge is constructed in the interface between the ordinary reader and academic reader. Within this mode of reading, there has been a rediscovery of the role of the ordinary reader in biblical interpretation. There is a need now more than ever for an active and transformative solidarity with ordinary

---

10. G. West, *The Academy of the Poor: Towards a Dialogical Reading of the Bible* (Sheffield, UK: Sheffield Academic Press, 1999), 21. This does not preclude the fact that academic readers can listen to and theorize the reading strategies of the ordinary.

11. West, *Academy*, 24.

12. Paulo Freire, *Pedagogy of the Oppressed*, trans. Myra Bergman Ramos (London: Penguin Books, 1972), 69.

13. Sarojini Nadar, "Sacred Stories as Theological Pedagogy," *JCTGRRA* 14, nos. 2 and 15 (2009): 9–23.

14. Spivak, *Can the Subaltern Speak?*, 12.

15. Nadar, "Sacred Stories," 13.

readers, and particularly in this study, the *wanjiku*s: oppressed and marginalized Kenyans who in, Spivak's terminology, are the subalterns.[16]

More pragmatic factors have played a role in foregrounding the ordinary reader in relation to the Bible. A factor that has relevance for the Kenyan context is the growing recognition that "we are the people" and that *wanjiku*s must be allowed to speak for themselves. For too long, the dominant in society have spoken on behalf of the suppressed or, worse, prescribed for the other. So, one of things I do in this chapter is allow the ordinary readers to speak for themselves in matters of biblical interpretation in relation to their own contexts. In doing this, interaction with views from church groups and key informants that I selected for the study will suffice for the greater part of the discussion. This journey begins with an examination of the difference it makes with whom we read and what this kind of unrepresentative reading entails.

Bible Reading in "Ordinary" Readers' Terms

Although African Bible readings have been indelibly marked by the missionary and colonial encounters and mediated by a crop of readers trained in imperial contexts, it is now more urgent that the Bible must be read in ordinary Africans' terms. An epistemological shift for reading the Bible in ordinary terms must be sought. As such, Africans must become their own primary dialogue partners. The reading practices of the ordinary I present in this chapter reveal that the African context as the object of interpretation is becoming increasingly stronger and gradually assuming the primary position with respect to the dialogue between the original meaning of the text and its meaning for the African people. It is for this reason that I urge ordinary readers to emerge from the shadows of their academically trained comrades and take a more prominent place in the process of biblical interpretation because it makes a difference with whom we read.

My point of inquiry for this section is: What difference does it make with whom we read the Bible? It is common knowledge that there is no innocent reading of the Bible because different people approach the text from their own vantage points and with many presuppositions. These vantages and presuppositions are informed by contexts, socializations,

---

16. The Kenyan subalterns, *wanjiku*, denotes the ordinary Kenyans, the lay, the untrained readers, but also the socially deprived, and economically and politically marginalized, members of society.

and aspirations of the readers, among other factors. Therefore, it becomes apparent that reading the Bible can never be a neutral enterprise and hence it matters with whom we read. Honestly said, a whole range of difference is experienced when we read with the "other." For this reason, to read the Bible with the ordinary reader means several things, as explained below.

FOREGROUNDING CONTEXTUAL ISSUES

To read the Bible with ordinary readers means that the views and concerns of ordinary readers are placed at the center of biblical interpretation. This means that the Bible is freed from preconceived interpretation and opened or allowed to take on new interpretations that are meaningful for readers. If freeing the Bible from previous interpretative entanglements can be imagined, then reading with the ordinary is tantamount to reading the Bible ideologically; that is the "point of view"[17] of the reader, and his or her *sitz-im-leben* is "importanced" in the meaning of the reading.[18] The "point of view" critique is introduced by Gary Yamasaki, who notes that in the context of literary analysis, the concept of "point of view" relates to the position held by the teller of a story vis-à-vis the elements of the story itself.[19] Yamasaki makes a comparison with cinema, showing that, in a movie, the story is filtered through the perspective of the camera's eye. In this way, and due to the preferences of the director, the viewer's perspective is both expanded and controlled by the camera; he or she can see the action from many directions and perspectives but can only see what the camera shows him or her. Likewise, Yamasaki observes that "biblical narratives like modern prose narratives, narrate like film. The narrator is the camera's eye; we see the story from what he [or she] presents."[20] For Africans, and othered world readers, this is crucial because the views about the Bible assert themselves in almost any discussion of the Bible.

Viewed in this light, biblical readings allow the interpretive interests and strategies of ordinary readers to permeate the meaning of the Bible.

---

17. Gary Yamasaki, *Watching a Biblical Narrative: Point of View in Biblical Exegesis* (London: T&T Clark, 2008), 90. That means that the audience sees the events of the biblical story, and in particular the parable, from various camera angles that are chosen for them by the director or narrator.

18. In biblical scholarship, *sitz-im-leben* is a German word that means "setting in life."

19. Yamasaki, *Watching*, 90.

20. Yamasaki, *Watching*, 90.

That is, instead of talking about the meaning of the text, ordinary reading explicates meaning in terms of interpretive interests.²¹ Interpretive interests in ordinary reading stand for the dimensions and contours of the text that readers privilege as the location of meaning, whether this be "in front of the text," "in the text" itself, or "behind the text."²²

In the end, this means that there is no precise or fixed meaning of the Bible when reading in ordinary terms. As in all postcolonial biblical readings, "when reading with," it becomes apparent that it may not be texts that contain meaning, as though waiting to be discovered, "but meaning is properly viewed as being construed in the text-reader interaction."²³ Therefore, the meaning of the Bible is construed in the interface between the particular reader and the particular context of the ordinary reader, showing that another meaning for the same text may be achieved in another reading of that text such that same text may mean different things when read each time. Clearly, ordinary readers recreate the biblical meaning guided by their peculiar contexts and experiences, and this is the main reason why with whom we read is of such importance.

SELECTIVE READINGS

Bible reading with the ordinary reveals that the Bible is read selectively. Although South African theologian Tinyiko Maluleke is much more attuned to liberation hermeneutics than the broader postcolonial criticism, he nevertheless rightly observes that ordinary readers are creatively pragmatic and selective in their use of the Bible so that the Bible may enhance rather than frustrate their life struggles.²⁴ In this mode, the Bible is read with a looseness toward the text, revealing an inter-

---

21. Alpheus Masoga, "Redefining Power: Reading the Bible in Africa from the Peripheral and Central Positions," in *Reading the Bible in the Global Village: Cape Town*, Justin S. Ukpong et al. (Atlanta: Society for Biblical Literature, 2002), 98.

22. See Gerald West, "African Biblical Scholarship as Post-Colonial, Tri-Polar, and a Site-of-

Struggle," in *Present and Future of Biblical Studies Celebrating 25 Years of Brill's Biblical Interpretation*, ed. Tat-Siong Benny Liew (Leiden, Netherlands: Brill, 2018) and J. Draper, "African Contextual Hermeneutics Readers: Reading Communities, and Their Options between Text and Context," *Religion and Theology* 22 (2015): 3–15 for a tripolar exegetical model. In Draper's tripolar exegetical model, the three processes of distantiation, contextualization, and appropriation are advocated.

23. Jeremy Punt, "Postcolonial Biblical Criticism in South Africa: Some Mind and Road Mapping," *Neotestamentica* 37, no. 1 (2003): 59–85.

24. Tinyiko Maluleke, "Black and African Theologies in New World Order: A Time to Drink from Our Own Wells," *JTSA* 96, no. 6 (1996): 3–19, 13.

pretation that is not so much controlled by the words of the "text" as by the reader's social experience. Therefore, just as in Black theology and liberation theology, reading strategies of the ordinary readers involve smoothening the Bible and aligning it with the aspirations of a people in struggle.

RETRIEVING SUBMERGED ORDINARY RESOURCES

Bible reading with the ordinary in retrospect reveals that "academic readers recognize that there remain elements of ordinary reading in their own 'scholarly' reading process."[25] This is not an attempt to recover a primary naïveté, but is a recognition that academic readers remain in some sense ordinary readers, especially when they don't give prominence to the systematized and structured interpretive processes they learn in their seminaries. This revelation means that biblical scholarship becomes more inclusive of scholars, non-scholars, the rich, and the poor.[26] Consequently, ordinary readers may not be featured as mere informants for the enterprise of academic readers, but they rightfully become part of constituting the meaning of the Bible.

Fourth, Bible reading in ordinary terms means that the voice and interpretive understandings of the hegemonic class are shuttered, while those of the ordinary are acknowledged and celebrated. For example, if in reading the biblical story of the conquest of Canaan (with the eyes of the Canaanites) from the vantage of the marginalized victims of land grabbing in Kenya, then questions would probably be raised as to whether God sides with the land grabbers as he did with the tribe of Israel.[27] This reading would see the story of the conquest of Canaan as a potentially dangerous story in the Kenyan context, where land is a volatile issue. Bible reading in ordinary terms enables the reader to understand the meaning of the Bible differently, especially when that

---

25. G. West, "Unpacking the Package That Is the Bible in African Biblical Scholarship," in *Reading the Bible in the Global Village*, Justin Ukpong et al., 72.

26. Teresa Okure, "Feminist Interpretation in Africa," in *Searching the Scriptures: A Feminist Interpretation*, ed. Fiorenza Elizabeth Schüssler (New York: Crossroads, 1993): 77.

27. Michael Prior, *The Bible and Colonialism: A Moral Critique* (Sheffield, UK: Sheffield Academic Press, 1997), views a consistent reading of the biblical text as requiring the liberating God of the exodus to become the oppressive God of the occupation of Canaan. This reading requires the Bible to be read with the eyes of the Canaanites inasmuch as it is read with the eyes of the Israelites. The Bible provides the title deed for the establishment of the state of Israel in a land held by another community in trust. This is an act of impunity and provides the basis for potential community conflict.

reading is enabled by the resources of the subaltern. This understanding means that ordinary readers are forced to see the meaning of the Bible within overturned structures of the dominant and are called upon to participate in the re-worlding of the world in ordinary terms.

Fifth and finally, Bible reading in ordinary terms not only identifies the utopian character to which academic reading succumbs by merely moralizing the prophetic message into a well-meaning admonition for those in power to repent and put an end to injustice; it also calls upon those in power to account for their deeds. The checks and balances involved in this mode of reading become the primary role of the ordinary readers for challenging the status quo. This mode of reading also reveals that there are good and pragmatic reasons for continuing to read the Bible in ordinary terms and with the ordinary. Therefore, so long as the Bible remains the church's most readily available resource for social transformation, then it must be read with all and by all. This is particularly so in reading beyond Mark 1:21–28.

Ordinary Readers' Analysis within Contextual Bible Studies

As explained in chapter one, a total of six church groups from within the Kenyan capital city of Nairobi, comprising twelve participants, were involved in contextual Bible studies. The groups were comprised of Bible readers who were mainly ordinary, nonacademic, and untrained readers of the Bible—that is, those who had no formal training in reading the Bible. The participants were confirmed members of the sampled churches and had some ordinary knowledge of the Bible. Respondents read Mark 1:21–28 within an understanding that they were sniffing for ways in which sections of the text can inform impunity; what one might term a "framework of impunity." Several questions were presented to the respondents to this effect, and their responses are presented below.

Q1. Read Mark 1:21–28. What is the text about?

During the contextual Bible study sessions, participants read Mark 1:21–28 and came up with their own views concerning the main theme of the text. The most frequent responses were as follows: All the six groups pointed out that the text was about the authority of Jesus. Five groups also mentioned that the text was about representation of authority of men. All the groups also pointed out that the text had something to do with the power of Jesus. On the same theme, four groups said that the text was about the power of Jesus, while two groups saw the text as being about the display and interpretation of the power of Jesus. Five groups reported that the text was about the defeat of Satan. Two groups maintained that the text was also about Jesus's teaching. From the findings, it stands out that power and authority were the dominant theme of the text.

> Q2. Now read Mark 1:14–20, the text that immediately precedes Mark 1:21–28. Are there connections between 1:14–20 and 1:21–28? If so, what are they?

Under this question, participants read Mark 1:14–20 as part of the main pericope and brought out the connections between it and the key text that is Mark 1:21–28. All the groups saw the supremacy of Jesus as the main connection between the two readings. They pointed out that Jesus was acting and was not being acted upon; his presence was active not passive. To arrive at this, four groups pointed out that in both texts, there was respect for authority. For two groups, it seemed that the theme of restoration of new authority was a connection between the two readings; that in both readings Jesus is seen as instituting a new form of authority. All six groups maintained that Jesus's authority over nature and the spiritual world was the main connection between the two readings.

It is important to note that two groups out of six mentioned that obedience to Christ was a major connection between the two readings. The groups pointed out that Jesus is a commander in the two readings, and especially that the disciples are coerced to follow Jesus and they abandon their careers without serious questioning. At this point, though not overtly, the groups seemed to admit that this was being done against their wish—which can be a seedbed for impunity.

> Q3. Now also read Mark 1:29–45, the text that immediately follows Mark 1:21–28. Are there connections between 1:21–28 and 1:29–45? If so, what are they?

To place the key text that is Mark 1:21–28 within its proper context in the continuing pericope, the contextual Bible study groups further read Mark 1:29–45 and sought lines of connection between the two texts. All six groups saw the continuing supremacy and dominance of Jesus as the main connection between the texts. The groups mentioned issues to do with the power and authority Jesus was wielding. Four out of six groups pointed out issues to do with Jesus's identity as the main connection.

They particularly mentioned the reluctance of Jesus to reveal his identity as the main connection. In addition, the groups noted the onerous tension between the desire Jesus had to display his power and need to conceal his identity. All six groups pointed to the healing power of Jesus as the main connection between the two texts—that is, in the two texts Jesus is seen as having power over sickness.

> Q4. In the first part of his ministry at Galilee, Jesus enters the scene (Capernaum) at 1:21 and leaves the temple at 1:45. In this continuing passage, who are the main characters or groups of characters? What do we know about them, and what are the relationships between them?

This question was meant to let the groups scrutinize the role of the characters and how authority influences their relationships in the entire section in Mark's gospel. All six groups repeated the role of each character as spelt out in the text. Concerning authority, all the groups noted that authority is hierarchically stratified, with Jesus at the top of the echelon. From these relationships, all six groups conceived a top-to-bottom model of authority. Several groups debated on how the demon's power and authority can be understood. Most of the groups agreed that demons are only more powerful than human beings when the latter have lost their godliness.

Power and authority as conceived in the contextual Bible studies was mirroring power as it was construed in the world of first-century Palestine. According to Waetjen, the distribution of power and authority is pictured as a pyramid in which much of the power is concentrated in a relatively small group of people at the pinnacle, while most of the people at the bottom held little or no power.[28]

> Q5. Based on this passage, how did the synagogue function during the time of Jesus (first-century Palestine), and what authoritative role does Jesus play in the synagogue?

Many groups did not understand the exact distinction between the functions of the temple and the synagogue in first-century Palestine. However, based on the text, respondents agreed that the synagogue acted as place of prayer (προσέυχη—house of prayer) in the same way a modern-day church building functions. They especially noted that both acted as places for practicing power; the power stage.[29] For them, the

---

28. Waetjen, *A Reordering of Power*, 6–11.
29. CBS: All Saints Cathedral, June 21, 2012.

temple was a place for religious and Jewish cultural bureaucracy,[30] while the synagogue was a place for healing. It was a place for linking God and humanity; a religious center.[31] The respondents noted that in Mark 1:21–28, the synagogue was used as a place where Jesus exercised authority. It was also used as a place for teaching and receiving religious instruction. It was a place for rubberstamping authority. It can be noted that the respondents understood the two places to stand for a place of prayer. Jesus chose a place of prayer as his performance stage because his authority would be enhanced by it.[32]

> Q6. Do you think the political leaders of his day were comfortable with his authority? In your own opinion, what are some of the factors that could have contributed to the underlying comfort or discomfort?

During the study, the respondents noted that it was highly probable that many of the leaders in Jesus's day were uncomfortable with his authority. They explained that the text was clear that Jesus's authority was favored by the audience, and this could have created rancor and tension with other groups or power players.[33] On the question of the factors that could have contributed to acrimony and uneasiness with other power players, respondents noted (among other things) envy, as it was seen as if Jesus's authority was out to replace theirs.[34] For some respondents, it was because Jesus is presented as attracting more power from the people.[35] Other respondents mentioned that Jesus was spiritual and the other people were carnal, and they were envious of his spirituality. Some groups argued that the would-be powers of his day also had demons and that was why they were reluctant to appreciate Jesus's power as emanating from above. Additionally, some groups brought out the fact that the political and religious powers of his day felt threatened that Jesus was out to make them irrelevant.

---

30. CBS: International Christian Centre, Mombasa Road, July 24, 2012.
31. CBS: African Independent Pentecostal Church of Africa, October 11, 2012.
32. CBS: Holy Family Basilica, August 1, 2012.
33. CBS: Holy Family Basilica, August 1, 2012.
34. CBS: Nairobi Pentecostal Church, October 23, 2012.
35. CBS: Kariokor Methodist Church, July 7, 2012.

CHAPTER THREE: READING OTHERWISE: MARK'S ἘΞΟΥΣΙΑ AND KENYAN IMPUNITY

> **Q7. With respect to disregard of the rule of the law being experienced in Kenya (impunity), how would this text speak about the exercise of authority in our respective context?**

According to the respondents, power and authority are being misused in our country.[36] The respondents noted that in Kenya many people desired power to overpower others. Moreover, those entrusted with power misused it for personal advantage. Respondents noted that Mark 1:21–28 was instructive to our context on how power should be construed. One group pointed out that people entrusted with authority must look to God for guidance on how to exercise their authority, for God is the absolute authority and the source of all authority.[37] It was particularly noted that Jesus should be allowed to heal our nation and cast out demons, as he did with the sick man. The groups commented that Jesus should be recognized as the ultimate authority and be submitted to.

Other groups, noting the progressive dictatorial posture of Jesus in the passage, argued that Kenya needed someone like Jesus, who had different power and authority, and would subdue all the impunity being currently experienced in Kenya. However, some groups noted that Jesus's action in disregarding the authorities of the day and displaying himself as the most powerful was tantamount to impunity.[38] They pointed out that in other gospel passages, Jesus is seen as disobeying the laws of the day and replacing them with his own laws. Some respondents pointed out that, coming from a savior and divine person, such an action could be copied and misused by many Kenyan leaders and justified using scripture to oppress others.[39] This posture taken by Jesus could further be taken as the main interface between authority and impunity.

> **Q8. Do you have any comments to make concerning the relationship between authority in this text and the presence of impunity in our context?**

In response to the above question, several important comments were offered by the groups. Some argued that impunity in Kenya was indirectly a result of some biblical interpretation. People in authority could use (or misuse) the Bible to justify their acts. They argued that those who know

---

36. CBS: Kariokor Methodist Church, July 7, 2012.
37. CBS: All Saints Cathedral, June 21, 2013.
38. CBS: Kariokor Methodist Church, July 7, 2012, and CBS: Nairobi Pentecostal Church, October 23, 2012.
39. CBS: Kariokor Methodist Church, July 7, 2012.

the law are the ones who are breaking it. To end impunity in Kenya today, those who are not in power must be able to respect the authorities; at the same time, those in power must use authority in the right way. The law must be strengthened and respected. Many leaders are driven by self-interest and not the interests of the majority, as Jesus was.

It was remarked that charismatic leaders should not be apologetic; rather, they should be like Jesus when championing causes that benefit the majority and when rescuing people from oppressive powers. Respondents noted that, in his day, Jesus did not keep quiet in the face of impunity, and neither should Kenyans. In the face of impunity in Kenya, respondents noted that "with God all things are possible," a direct reference to Jesus's own teaching in Mark 10:27: "Jesus looked at them and said, 'With man this is impossible, but not with God; all things are possible with God.'" They expressed optimism that God would one day change the status quo of impunity in Kenya. Some respondents, however, showed some form of critical thinking and noted that though the gospel passage displays Jesus in favorable light, it is possible to copy his style of leadership but use it to oppress others.[40] The groups that thought this way remarked that Jesus was so authoritative that he could be questioned. He does things single-handedly, as he alone sees fit. Therefore, Jesus's style of leadership cannot fit in a working democracy.

Q9. What actions will you take in response to this contextual Bible study?

In line with James 1:22 ("be doers of the word and not hearers only"), the goal of every contextual Bible study was action. Contextual Bible studies require participants to respond to the study with creative points of action in the respective societies. Owing to this, and in response to the question, respondents mentioned several actions that would be planned in response to the study. Most groups responded that they would act on whatever scale they could to change the face of impunity in Kenya. All six groups said they would run a program in their respective churches to sensitize people to the need to stop impunity. All groups said that they would conduct a contextual Bible study session to sensitize their members on the need to speak out and reduce impunity. The groups expressed their willingness to have personnel facilitate the sessions. All

---

40. CBS: All Saints Cathedral, June 21, 2012.

the participants agreed to take personal responsibility, speak about it, and condemn it openly in all available forums.

Reading Mark 1:21–28 for Impunity: Reading with the Key Respondents

To bring out more precisely the connections between Kenyan impunity and the text of Mark 1:21–28, twelve key informants were interviewed. Their mode of study was through interviews, and they also read Mark 1:21–28 within a framework of impunity. Some of the interviewees were trained biblical readers and they held specific viewpoints in line with the interests of the study. However, none of them was trained in postcolonial criticism. Six of them were clergy and six of them were laypersons but holding leadership roles in their various churches. Section by section, their responses are analyzed below.

SECTION A

Q1. In your opinion, what is impunity?

Respondents defined impunity in various ways. Impunity was defined as a culture of irresponsibility and "don't- carism."[41] It was mentioned as a lack of respect for law or recognition of authority reflected in people's behavior.[42] Impunity was also defined as behavior that arises from the knowledge of the possibility to get away with offences without any repercussions.[43] Impunity was further defined as the total disregard for the rule of the law: "Life goes on as if there is no law." It is harmful actions propelled by a "nothing will happen to me mentality."[44] It was doing wrong without caring about the consequences. Most respondents believed impunity entailed a deliberate lack of accountability. It was also seen as wrongdoing because of the ability to circumvent justice. These definitions were generally in agreement with the study's definition and revealed that the respondents understood the topic, but were also delimited by the culture.

---

41. Interviewee #1.
42. Interviewee #3 (female).
43. Interviewee #4 (male).
44. Interviewee #4.

Q2. What are your thoughts about impunity in Kenya?

The respondents felt that the levels of impunity in Kenya were extremely high. They used words such as "prevalent," "rampant," and "excessive." Respondents noted that impunity as experienced in Kenya today is of the highest order: "It is the life of Kenyans and levels are growing higher even with a new constitution."[45] They also noted that the presence of impunity in the life of Kenyans was a serious indictment for a people who are 82 percent Christian; that people do not care anymore because of selfishness coupled with a weak moral fiber. Some noted that impunity was "common practice"[46] in Kenya and Kenyans have come to a point where they care less about laws. It was noted that impunity was practiced everywhere and that there was low and high impunity; impunity practiced by both the elites and the poor citizens. Another respondent noted that impunity as exercised in Kenya today was because Kenyans had lost the moral responsibility to look to law for guidance.[47] With regard to the prevalence of the culture of impunity, the respondents added that the country had never come to such a point before.

Q3. What are your thoughts about impunity and the church?

This question was meant to enlighten the study of the impunity practiced in the church (if any), and the nature it took. One of the frequent answers given was that the church in Kenya today is compromised and lacks the moral authority to condemn impunity. Some respondents reserved harsh comments for the church. One stated that "the architects of impunity are found in the church."[48] The church was accused of directing the gospel but refusing to be directed by the gospel.

One respondent noted that some Christians would use the Bible to justify their acts of impunity, for example during the postelection violence of 2007. During this time, some Christians justified fighting for land in the same way that the Israelites justified fighting for land in Canaan.[49] Another frequent response that came up was that church leaders were seen to be above the church law and seriously abused the goodwill of the congregants. Impunity in the church was cited as cover-up of scandals

---

45. Interviewee #2 (female).
46. Interviewee #3.
47. Interviewee #6 (female).
48. Interviewee #7 (male).
49. Interviewee #7.

committed by the leadership in the church.[50] The church was also indicted as being a beneficiary of impunity—for example, corruption and land grabbing. This respondent also frequently noted that preaching against impunity was weakened because the church had failed to set a good example. In addition, this respondent maintained that church members were practicing impunity and getting away with it without any discipline. Christians wore a "do it now and repent later" mentality, whereby repentance meant a sentimentalization of a God who overlooks impunity.

Q4. What should be the Christian response to impunity?

According to the respondents, Christians should set a good example. They should fight impunity and stand against it even if it is practiced by the people they love. Another response, repeated several times, was that Christians should speak against it, shun it, and eradicate it. Christians should be on the front line in eradicating impunity by following the commands of God. Christians should be law-abiding citizens.

Q5. What should be done to people who get involved in acts of impunity?

During the interview, most of the respondents noted that people still practicing impunity should be brought to book. They should bear individual responsibility and be punished for their deeds. One of the respondents, however, argued that they should be forgiven but allowed to bear the consequences.[51] The respondent added that there is a need to know "which vengeance belongs to God" so that people can be held accountable for their deeds. Most respondents said that if people guilty of impunity are Christians, they should be excluded from the fellowship. Respondents, expressing the mission of the church, noted that such people should be warned and forgiven.[52]

---

50. Interviewee #4.
51. Interviewee #3.
52. Interviewee #8 (male).

SECTION B

Q1. If you are employed, what time are you meant to report for work?

Most questions in this section were meant to measure the personal accountability of each respondent. Some respondents were not in formal employment and they had no answers to give. However, most of the respondents who were employed mentioned that under the Kenyan labor laws, they were meant to report to work at eight in the morning. A few respondents who were self-employed observed that their schedule operated differently based on the nature of the business they had for each day.[53]

Q2. What time do you report for work?

Respondents who had jobs noted that they reported to work before eight in the morning.

Q3. If you report late, what action is taken by the management?

Although this question did not apply to all the respondents, it was meant to show what organizations were doing to stem the rise of impunity. Applicable respondents noted that they are mainly reprimanded and warned about repeating the mistake. Other respondents noted that they are required by the management to explain the causes for their lateness.[54] One respondent noted that the management is also usually late and is not very keen to follow up on punctuality.

Q4. What would be your general comment about the action?

This question did not apply to all the respondents. Applicable respondents noted that most of the actions taken by the management were fair; they deterred future lateness and mediocrity in the organization.[55]

---

53. For example, Interviewee #12 (female).
54. Interviewee #8 (male).
55. Interviewee #9 (female).

CHAPTER THREE: READING OTHERWISE: MARK'S ἘΞΟΥΣΙΑ AND KENYAN IMPUNITY

SECTION C

Q1. What are your comments about church attendance in terms of regularity and punctuality?

Questions under this section were meant to link the church with impunity. This question attracted a myriad of responses from the interviewees. One respondent noted that it was not a major problem in their denomination: "Catholics don't have a major problem here."[56] Several respondents noted that it was a major problem but beyond their sphere of influence. Other respondents noted that it depended on what programs were being run in the church: "Some programs are more attractive."[57] One respondent noted that the weather was a determining factor, because in times of unfavorable weather, regularity and punctuality were always an issue of concern. Another respondent noted that this was a serious problem in their denomination, and was an indication of impunity. This respondent also reported that "the pastor always reprimands the congregation because they report to their offices punctually, yet they always come to church late. They respect their employers more than God."[58]

Q2. What in your view should be done to members who miss church or who come late?

Most of the respondents noted that church is a voluntary society and people cannot be punished or excluded for missing it or coming late. They responded that people should be encouraged to improve their standards. They should be taught the importance of taking church seriously. They should be followed up by the pastors.

Q3. Is there any action you are aware of that is taken against people who miss church or come to church late?

Most respondents were not aware of any action. Other respondents said, "Not anymore,"[59] insinuating that something used to be done, but which they were not privy to. One respondent answered that as pertains

---

56. Interviewee #9.
57. Interviewee #4.
58. Interviewee #6.
59. Interviewee #11 (male).

to lateness, the church's main door would be closed when important activities were going on, such as prayers, sermons, or Holy Communion.[60]

Q4. Is there any need in your church to address attendance and punctuality? What do you think should be done?

In response to the above question, most of the respondents felt that there was a need to address the issue of attendance in terms of punctuality and regularity. Again, most of the respondents pointed to teaching as the main action that should change the behavior of the congregants. Moreover, some added that people should be encouraged, and church attendance publicized, in every event. Other respondents noted that the church should be made lively and relevant so that it can attract some level of seriousness. Some respondents were of the view that people's personal walk with God should be encouraged so that members can be accountable in their own ways.

SECTION D

Q1. Why do you think there is impunity in Kenya, yet the Christian population is well over 82 percent?

Questions in this section were meant to help decipher the relationship between Christianity and impunity. For this question, respondents gave varied answers. There were some who felt that the 82 percent statistic of Christians in Kenya only reflected religious affiliations and not Christianity as lifestyle.[61] Respondents argued that people in Kenya were only Christian in name and that Christianity had not "sunk"—that is, Christians had not allowed the gospel to transform them. Many other respondents gave answers that reflected this view. In line with this thinking, respondents noted that Christianity in Kenya was compromised. Others felt that Christians were beneficiaries of impunity and were living double-standard lives.

According to some respondents, people in Kenya are suffering from colonial hangover, because "African culture had no impunity."[62] Colonial laws were against the Blacks. African leaders have copied their lifestyles, and impunity is one of them. Some respondents also saw lack of models

---

60. Interviewee #9.
61. Interviewee #2.
62. Interviewee #3.

as the reason why the some Christians were drawn to act with impunity.[63] Others said that it is because impunity is a culture, and many have been born into it.

Q2. What do you think are some of the factors that have led to high impunity levels in Kenya?

Most of these factors are directly or indirectly addressed in the Bible. Those which were repeated and again included selfishness, poor parenting, greed, materialism, impatience, unhealthy competition, negative ethnicity, slow or absent justice, and injustice. One respondent noted that "society that rewards wrong and basis success on might and power" is the root cause of impunity.[64] Another respondent commented that "frustrations by political powers" poor leadership, inequality in society, and ability to purchase (in)justice" were root causes.[65] In the debate, another respondent went further:

> If you see what time it takes to conclude a simple case for the poor person, while the rich go about justice in a short time. How long will the poor person wait? When you catch a thief and take him or her to the police, the same person is released to steal and torment you again. Next time the person is caught, *wananchi* will not consult the police; they will mete instant justice on the person.[66]

During the interviews, most respondents pointed out that many governance systems in Kenya are dysfunctional and create a climate where impunity can thrive.

Q3. As per your definition of impunity in Section 1 above, what form (if any) do you think it would take in the following institutions in Kenya:

Family: In the institution of the family, the frequency of forms of impunity revolved around rebellion in children, lateness at home, disregard of family rules, spousal abuse, verbal, and nonverbal violence, underpayment of domestic workers, and dictatorship.

---

63. For example, Interviewee #5 (male).
64. Interviewee #4.
65. Interviewee #7.
66. Interviewee #4.

Police: In the police sector, respondents frequently mentioned brutality, bribery, corruption, negligence of duty, favoritism, and police executions.

Judiciary: Bribery was the most frequent form of impunity mentioned under this category. Other forms frequently mentioned were delayed judgment, corruption, and unfair judgments.

Public Transport: Regarding the transportation sector, respondents maintained that public transport was the home of impunity. Frequently mentioned forms of impunity in this category were disrespect for traffic rules, disrespect for passengers and pedestrians, and extortion by hiking fares at will. Other forms of impunity in this sector include careless driving, bribery, speeding, obstruction, and reckless overtaking.

The Executive: Respondents maintained that disregard of the law—for example, "unclear appointment of county commissioners"—was the main form of impunity experienced by the executive arm of government.[67] Dictatorship was also mentioned, with the example of the late Hon. John Michuki and the KTN saga.[68]

> When [Michuki] was minister for internal security, the Kenya Television Network (KTN) was raided by alleged government mercenaries. When the minister was questioned by journalists about it, he had retorted, "If you rattle a snake be ready to be bitten," insinuating that the government had actually raided the station because it was "a snake that had been rattled."

Church Institutions: Frequently mentioned forms of impunity under this category included dictatorship by bishops and clergy, corruption, manipulation of worshippers, high-handedness in the administration of justice, cover-up of scandals, and abuse of goodwill.

The Legislature: Corruption in the legislature took the form of grand corruption, theft of national coffers (for example, CDF money), and bribery.[69]

---

67. Interviewee #2.
68. Interviewee #9.
69. Interviewee #7.

CHAPTER THREE: READING OTHERWISE: MARK'S ἘΞΟΥΣΙΑ AND KENYAN IMPUNITY

SECTION E

Q1. From your interactions with the Bible, do you think in any way that there is any condition of impunity in Mark 1:21–28?

This section was important because it was meant to highlight the connection between Mark's gospel and impunity. During the interviews, respondents argued that there was no impunity or condition for impunity in Mark's gospel.[70] The rest agreed in various ways that there was impunity and there were conditions for impunity in Mark 1:21–28. Of these, one respondent said, "Yes, Jesus came to set liberty of the oppressed; if there was no impunity, Jesus would not have come."[71] Another respondent calmly put it this way:

> Is Mark perpetuating impunity? Is he a child of impunity? Look at the "don't-care" spirit he portrays Jesus with. Mark cultivates a culture of non-questioning. Mark's disciples are puppets; they do not engage logic.[72]

A respondent cited Jesus's power over the scribes as impunity. This respondent also mentioned the time when Jesus's disciples did not fast as expected; that it was tantamount to impunity.

Q2. How does impunity (if present) in the Bible affect the hearing, reading, and interpretation of Mark's gospel in Kenya?

With regard to this question, those who had admitted that there were conditions for impunity in Mark's gospel also maintained that this can affect the reception and interpretation of the gospel in Kenya. Respondent interviewee #12 mentioned that it was likely that those in power would mimic Jesus's authority and use the law for their own benefit. This respondent maintained that Mark's gospel invites those oppressed to retaliate in the name of liberating themselves. Another respondent[73] seriously criticized Jesus's action of breaking the law and stated:

> Authority that breaks the law encourages breaking the law.... Yes, images are powerful.... People can copy Jesus and become unquestionable like Jesus, such as pastors who do things in the name of Jesus and cannot be questioned.

---

70. Interviewees #10, 2, 7, and 9.
71. Interviewee #6.
72. Interviewee #3.
73. Interviewee #9.

> Q3. Think about any situation of impunity in Kenya, such as during the postelection violence: Do you think authority as constructed in Mark's gospel would be used or misused to justify any facet of the same?

This question was meant to ascertain if Kenyans invoked the Bible to act as they did in times of turmoil. Insofar as this question was concerned, most of the respondents did not think that anybody can use the Bible to justify irrational violence. A few respondents thought some portions of the Bible can be "twisted" to justify violence—for example, portions of the book of Joshua.[74]

> Q4. Read Mark 1:21-28. What are your general comments on the exercise of authority by Jesus in Mark 1:21-28?

The primary intention of this question was to help analyze Jesus's use of power and authority. In the opinion of many respondents, Jesus is portrayed as a firm leader; he spoke the truth and stood for justice. Additionally, many respondents saw Jesus as an uncompromising leader. Although he was extremely authoritative, he was genuine in his concern for the people. He had the interests of the people at heart. In explaining this further, interviewee #8 pointed out that Jesus's authority was recognized and accepted in that it was associated with God. He added that Jesus was aware of who he was and what his mission entailed. Therefore, the exercise of authority by Jesus set him above other authorities. It is important to consider interviewee #3, who argued that Jesus was God and it was Mark's authorial intention to build Jesus in such a manner in view of other conflicts in the gospel.

> Q5. (a) From your knowledge of the Bible, and in particular Mark's gospel, how would you describe the exercise of authority by Jesus? (b) On the same terms, how would you describe the exercise of authority by the following actors in Mark's gospel?

In response to this question, most of the respondents described the exercise of authority by Jesus in the following terms: authoritarian, absolute, and final, leading and not misleading, godly, and just. In the second part of the same question, respondents pointed out the following concerning the exercise of authority by other actors in Mark's gospel.

Judiciary and the Trial of Jesus: In general, respondents touched on Pilate as a representative of the judiciary. They responded that he did not make the right decisions; he acted according to the wishes of the

---

74. For example, Interviewee #9.

CHAPTER THREE: READING OTHERWISE: MARK'S ἘΞΟΥΣΙΑ AND KENYAN IMPUNITY

Jews and not according to the law. Pilate avoided using his authority by not scrutinizing the witnesses who spoke untruth. The judiciary was compromised.

The Synagogue System: Respondents mentioned that the way they understood it from the Bible, the synagogue (not to be confused with προσέυχη—the place of worship) was already a corrupt place: It was not spiritual, it was a symbol of prestige, it was conservative, it was questionable, it had authority but was not committed to justice, and it was not democratic. Many respondents did not differentiate between the synagogue and the temple. Therefore, in the study, other NT portions that referred to the temple were quoted as if they referred to the synagogue. Two references stood out: Matthew 21:20, when the temple was used as a "forex bureau," and Matthew 12:41, where rich people are mentioned as giving large sums of money in the temple.[75]

The Disciples: Most of the respondents saw the disciples as powerless puppets: They were "docile and confused about their authority."[76]

> Q6. In your own opinion, can authority as expressed in Mark's gospel be used to solve contextual and other situations of impunity in Kenya?

This was the last question. It sought to establish if the Bible could be endorsed as a text with solutions for addressing impunity in Kenya. All the respondents agreed that authority as expressed in Mark's gospel can be used to solve contextual and other situations of impunity in Kenya. The respondents did not show how, but they gave several reasons to explain their opinion. Respondent interviewee #4 observed that

> people in authority should be cautious; totalitarian authority can be used positively. During the PEV [postelection violence], Kenya lacked a person with authority who could quieten the nation.... When late Hon. Michuki used totalitarian authority, order was restored on our roads. Authority can end impunity.[77]

Other respondents, including Interviewee #2, also responded by saying that

---

75. Interviewee #3.

76. Interviewee #8.

77. Late Hon. Michuki was Minister for Transport and later Minister for Internal Security and Environment. During his tenure as Minister for Transport, Hon. Michuki was acclaimed for restoring order and discipline on the Kenyan roads through the famous "Michuki rules."

we must learn from the way Jesus exercised power and authority in Mark's gospel; he did it with skill and ability. Every leader is given authority; it is a trust and not a right and should be used for the benefit of the people and not for self. Christ models how to exercise power and authority.

In answer to the same question, some respondents, such as Interviewee #9, put it this way: "Yes, Christ is exercising real authority in that he is genuine and pays attention to the context. We must assert authority to end impunity." However, others, like Interviewee #1, cautioned that if authority as exercised by Jesus is not interpreted correctly by human beings, it cannot be used to end impunity; instead, it can be misinterpreted to promote impunity. To this end, respondents noted that to end impunity, power and authority must be used correctly by somebody "bigger." Good authority should be respected and submitted to. According to Interviewee #1, democracy should indulge some dictatorial powers.

Restating Ordinary Voices

Within a postcolonial framework, we now turn to decrypting what the respondents said. In order to do this, it is important to bear in mind key postcolonial concerns, particularly those of prioritizing the margins at the expense of the center.[78] Postcolonial criticism is a critical sensibility acutely attuned to a specific range of interrelated historical and social phenomena.[79] It provides the grounds for mounting serious challenges against reigning forms of hegemony. Furthermore, it functions as an anamnestic and heuristic framework within which to engage the biblical texts.[80] From the responses of the contextual Bible studies, Mark 1:21-28 seemed a logical place from which to launch a postcolonial reading of Mark's gospel, centered on the issues of power, empire, and representation.

---

78. J. Punt, "Why Not Postcolonial Biblical Criticism in (South) Africa: Stating the Obvious or Looking for the Impossible?" *Scriptura* 91 (2006): 63–82, 67.

79. Moore, *Empire and Apocalypse*, 7.

80. Horsley, "Submerged," 170.

CHAPTER THREE: READING OTHERWISE: MARK'S ἘΞΟΥΣΙΑ AND KENYAN IMPUNITY

AUTHORITY IN KENYA AS DERIVED FROM MARK'S ἘΞΟΥΣΙΑ

In the contextual Bible study discussions (section A, question two), the groups validated the claim that Jesus had absolute ἐξουσία and that authority in Mark 1:21–28 is hierarchically structured. It was clear from the respondents that, despite a stance of anti-authority rhetoric in Mark, he is concerned with replacing one authority with another.[81] In Mark, there is a discernible hierarchy of authority, with the elites always on top. This authority always involves the representation of the rest by the "Other." The views from the respondents point to the fact that this is Mark's way of conceiving reality in the realm of power. In other words, Mark enjoins an ideology of absolutism to portray that power must always be wielded from the top and by those at the top. In effect, theorized from a postcolonial perspective, by reporting that Mark conceives a very powerful Jesus the respondents were endorsing the view that Mark mimics the Roman colonial discourse and structures of power.[82] In the view of Liew, Jesus's absolute tyrannical authority is evident in the way he is represented in categories of authority in relational, hierarchical terms. Thus, in Mark 1:21–28, the representative voice of the colonialist Jesus has just begun to emerge.

Although some respondents tried to excuse Jesus from the portrait of a tyrant (section A, question two) that clearly protrudes from the reading, by ascribing "God" to him, they could not deny that Mark's Jesus disrupts all other authorities to reinstate his own. Jesus becomes extremely powerful and thus patronizes all other powers. In Jesus, Mark is guilty of "othering"; he creates a "them" versus "me" binary in power relations. In the end, his power becomes more attractive than repellent, and especially to would-be rulers.

KENYAN AUTHORITY AS MIMICKED AND HYBRIDIZED POWER

As has already been demonstrated, key respondents described Kenyan authority in the following terms: authoritative, colonial, absolutes, authority that pleases the West, selfish authority, and inconsiderate (section D, question three). According to them, those who wield power and authority in Kenya do so for their own benefit. In the view of Interviewee #7, "they always want to be on top and practice impunity at the top and even use the Bible to justify some of their actions." Key respondents

---

81. Liew, "Tyranny," 13.
82. Liew, "Tyranny," 23.

highlighted the following forms of impunity by those wielding power and authority: bribery, corruption, brutality, lack of performance, and justice on sale (Section D, question three). In relation to postcolonial categories of mimicry and hybridity, what the respondents attested to is that much of Kenyan power and authority that relates to impunity is mimicked in the way it is hybridized. Since, according to Bhabha, "colonial mimicry is a strategy of the colonizers that backfires," Kenyan authority enjoins both mimicry and hybridity.[83]

Kenyan authority mimics in the way it desires a reformed recognizable other. In doing this, it copies the colonialists in order to disrupt colonialism, but unfortunately the gaze remains, thus alienating Kenyans from their cultural "purity or essence," and shifting them into the cultural regimes of their colonial masters.[84] What can be said is that power and authority in Kenya are overpowering. They are the products of the Bible and of the colonialists. Thus, power and authority in Kenya become a blurred copy of the original power and authority, producing many misrepresentations of the same. These misrepresentations bring forth offshoots of distorted power, including the rise of impunity. Such views can be supported by the answers given in section E, question two.

Within the thinking of the key respondents (section E, question four), power and authority in Kenya can be construed as hybridized in the way they condone an "in-betweenness"[85] They are a mixture of the traditional, the colonial, and the biblical. What it means for this study is that power and authority in Kenya are a concoction of all, and conscious of none. They bring forth new signs of identity of a people and innovative sites of collaboration, while at the same time inviting contestation of this hybrid identity. In hybridized societies, the struggle to become breeds all sorts of power struggles. In such situations, impunity emerges as a language of struggle. It becomes both a way of taking advantage by the elite and a way of self-redefinition by the subaltern. Impunity in such sites thus becomes complex, a vice that needs to be rooted out, and at the same time an ongoing negotiation with the powers that be, demanding an all-inclusive interpretation of what it means to be in authority.

One more thing needs to be said about the way the respondents understood power and authority. Most contextual Bible study groups

---

83. Bhabha, *Location*, 212.

84. Simon Samuel, *A Postcolonial Reading of Mark's Story of Jesus* (London: T&T Clark, 2007), 27.

85. Samuel, *Postcolonial*, 29.

construed power as hierarchical. The idea of a "sovereign power" was not elided.[86] Traditionally, power has been understood as being at the top of a pyramid, and that was all it was understood to be. Although this was the mainline thinking of the respondents, there were indications that power can be understood otherwise, and within a fuller understanding. Some respondents, for example interviewee #1, believed power arises in all kinds of relationships (although, in Mark's gospel, it was noted that it is the pen of the narrator that assigns this power depending on the character he wants to build) (section B, question one).

For the contextual Bible study participants, power was seen to be in Jesus, in the venue (synagogue), in the evil spirit, the possessed man, the teachers of the law, and the people. In this way, the views of the respondents can be aligned to key readers in power, for example, Lynch, who notes that "power is omnipresent, that is, power is found in all social interactions."[87] This means that power is always there and that no one is outside of power.[88] What Foucault has in mind is the accidental feature of power in particular contexts and that power has an essential characteristic that allows it in all spheres of interactions. Therefore, in constituting the picture of impunity in Kenya, it is all these dimensions of power that are considered.

Impunity, if it is seen as negative power, thrives at all levels in Kenyan society. This can best be illustrated by how the respondents handled the question of impunity in the family (section D, question three). To quote one respondent: "Impunity in the family is not just a top–bottom issue; on the contrary, it goes back and forth, drawing its synergy from all players, such as children, parents, and others."[89] Similarly, impunity in the public-transport sector goes back and forth, and involves "our" national participation: pedestrians, *matatu*s, and personal vehicles.

EMPIRE AND IMPUNITY IN MARK 1:21–28

According to Richard Horsley, "postcolonial criticism of prevailing political-economic and cultural relations in the modern world makes it possible to discern the concrete ways in which various layers of biblical

---

86. Lynch, "Foucault's Power," 13.
87. Lynch, "Foucault's Power," 15.
88. Michel Foucault, *Power/Knowledge: Selected Writings and Other Interviews* (New York: Pantheon, 1980), 141.
89. Interviewee #11.

literature are the products of the very emergence of domination and authority."[90] This domination took form in the empire's power to overwrite various traditions, creating a version authorized by its own. Now more than ever, it is the task of modern colonized readers to unearth previously submerged biblical voices and histories that undermine self-authorization to represent others by the empire, as well as the current beneficiaries of that hegemonizing posture of the empire.

In thinking about empire in Mark's gospel, one need go no further than Horsley to see Mark as adapting the distinctively Israelite script of a popular messiah, acclaimed by the people as the leader of their independence from human rulers, but then captured and executed by the imperial rulers.[91] What Horsley attests to is that Mark's gospel is fully aware of the empire. It is aware of a people who have become creatures of the empire, and the empire can be termed the backdrop of the stage on which Mark's gospel is performed.[92] Mark nurtures this notion of empire, and knowingly or unknowingly intermingles the character of his Jesus within the confines of empire.

In thinking about empire and impunity in Mark 1:21–28 and Kenya, various views were provided by the respondents during the study. First, empire can be seen in the expansion program that Jesus inaugurates.[93] He comes to the fore, whether by narrator's intent or by imposing himself upon others. Put in postcolonial terms, respondents mentioned that Jesus overwrites the rules of the teachers of the law, the people, and the evil spirit to institute his own.[94] Many respondents agreed that Jesus represented the interests of the heavenly kingdom (empire) in his mission. In other words, Jesus's empire now replaced the Roman Empire. More pertinent is the way he did this: He "taught with authority" (Mark 1:22) and replaced other empires by force. He was intolerant, and never gave the evil spirit a chance to express its point of view fully, but forced the evil spirit to "be quiet" (Mark 1:25). In Mark 1:21–28, Jesus is the dominant voice; for him, might is right, and this is another definition of impunity.[95]

---

90. Horsley, "Submerged Histories,"153.
91. Horsley, "Submerged Histories," 153.
92. Horsley, "Submerged Histories," 158.
93. CBS: AIPCA, October 11, 2012.
94. Interviewee #11.
95. Interviewee #3.

As Horsley notes, "power to narrate or to block other narratives from forming and emerging, is very important to culture and imperialism and constitutes one of the major connections between them."[96] Equally, the power to be on top of everybody, as it is in Kenya by way of silencing and violating others, is very important to the culture of impunity. It constitutes part of what Jesus is seen to be doing in Mark 1:21–28, and it forms the road that impunity treads in Kenya.

POSTCOLONIAL FEMINIST CONCERNS IN MARK 1:21–28

Where are women in Mark's text? Are they learning in silence, as Paul instructs them in 1 Timothy 2:11–14? On the question of what Mark 1:21–28 was all about, many female respondents pointed out that the text was about male exercise of authority.[97] This point that was raised by some respondents further highlights the difference it makes with whom we read. Without serious scrutiny, a male reader might not notice that the characters enjoined by Mark in this episode presuppose a male cast. If the episode is historical, one could ask if it was a true reflection of the *sitz-im-leben*. If it was not so, then why are women absent or silenced in Mark 1:21–28? Why are they sometimes constituted where they are not for the sake of the narrative? According to Musa Dube, the challenge posed by imperializing texts that silence the participation of women calls for a feminist reading that reads to recover or reconstruct women's participation in the biblical narrative.[98]

Therefore, Mark 1:21–28 should be investigated for patriarchy and be decolonized from its male-centered presentation of life. This male-centered presentation of life enables Mark to pen a narrative involving the whole community, while still silencing women. Reading Mark's gospel (and not just 1:21–28) as a postcolonial feminist reader involves paying attention to those intricate details that render women able to deconstruct gendered imperialistic narratives.

When postcolonial feminist readers read this way, they notice that, often, female characters are presented as being of questionable moral character (e.g., Mark 14:3–9). An ideology of subjugation begins to emerge as female gender is used to articulate relations of subordination and

---

96. Horsley, "Submerged Biblical Histories and Imperial Biblical Studies," 161.
97. CBS: All Saints Cathedral, June 21, 2012.
98. Dube, "Toward," 20.

insubordination.[99] So, in Mark 1:21–28, women need to be foregrounded, known, and represented. But how can they be known and represented in a state of utter silencing? Isn't this also in the culture of impunity that women can be silenced deliberately? If patriarchy is enjoining impunity in its project, then the answer to this question is yes.

Dube proposes that it is only in imagining and retelling the biblical narrative that women can come alive again and be liberated. Doing this will form part of the task of the next chapter. Nevertheless, at this stage, a postcolonial feminist reader is invited to notice those texts and life situations that tell women they are not part of the human journey and that, if they are, they only exist in roles dictated by men.

Conclusion

In this chapter, particular attention has been paid to the reading resources of the ordinary or nonacademic readers, including what this process entails. A presentation of what transpired during the "reading with" process is analyzed. Succinctly said, field data have been presented and analyzed in this chapter. This effort was aimed at laying the ground for a reading from the Kenyan space and to offer an interpretation of the interface between Mark's ἐξουσία and Kenyan impunity within a postcolonial framework.

In reading with ordinary and nonacademic readers of the Bible in Kenya, several points emerge. Major conclusions must now be drawn on the findings that have emerged in this interface:

> 1. Ordinary readers as referred to in the study have something to offer insofar as biblical interpretation is concerned. This "something" has to do with their situations and contexts. Meaningful Bible reading should not therefore exclude the interpretations of those whom the Bible was meant to liberate. To do this, a hermeneutical key that irons out and incorporates a reinterpretation of eisegesis needs to be sought.
>
> 2. If read within a postcolonial framework, ἐξουσία in Mark 1:21–28 constitutes grounds for impunity as experienced in Kenya. There is an obvious relationship between ἐξουσία in Mark 1:21–28 and impunity in Kenya. The text offers

---

99. Dube, "Toward," 19.

grounds for othering, patriarchal impunity, representation of the other, mimicking impunity, authorizing impunity, and hybridized impunity. The text not only presents power in its most absolute form but also celebrates overpowering. Ἐξουσία is understood hierarchically, and it remains a device for the center and not for the periphery.

3. Impunity as experienced in Kenya today is a result of long-standing history with colonialism and cultural exchanges with colonial masters. The Bible, which is a product of an imperial culture, is part of that exchange. It enjoins motives, images, language, and attitudes that are intended to serve the interests of the empire. It therefore needs to be read for decolonization.

Since many biblical narratives are imperializing texts insofar as they use history to propound power relations, "it is imperative that biblical scholars take cognizance of the world that is wedged between imperial domination, collaboration and resistance."[100] As Dube further explains:

It is also imperative that biblical scholars take cognizance of texts that, more often than not offer models of internal relationships which are less than liberating; which have served in different imperializing projects and lift up writing-reading communities which are calling for decolonization.[101]

In the chapter that follows, a postcolonial liberative reading is espoused, together with its ramifications for othered worlds.

---

100. Dube, "Reading for Decolonization (John 4:1–42)," 314.
101. Dube, "Reading for Decolonization (John 4:1–42)," 314.

CHAPTER FOUR

Dethroning Empires of Impunity

Introduction

The first task of this chapter is to offer alternative hermeneutics for reading Mark 1:21–28 while pointing out the major implications for dethroning empires of impunity. What follows is a brief explanation of how I accomplish such a reading. Since in the previous chapter I dealt at length with issues of "reading with" the ordinary readers, in this chapter I introduce the debate on a search for an alternative hermeneutic that is suitable for dethroning impunity, not only in Kenya, but also in othered worlds. In this chapter, therefore, I bring out postcolonial readings that situate Mark 1:21–28 in the sphere of literature that would help address impunity.

The second task of the chapter is to show the effects that reading Mark for impunity will have on its readers. Within the mandate of the first task (situating Mark 1:21–28 in the sphere of literature that would help address impunity), this chapter begins by considering Mark 1:21–28 within the scope of two postcolonial reading resources proposed by two African readers. These are a contrapuntal reading by Humphrey Waweru and divining by Musa Dube.[1] Later on in this chapter I bring out a hermeneutics for reading impunity in the context of Kenyan spaces.[2]

---

1. Musa W. Dube, *Other Ways of Reading: African Women and the Bible* (Atlanta, GA: Society of Biblical Literature, 2001), 34.
2. H. Waweru, *Bible and African Culture*, 12.

Contrapuntalism and Mark 1:21–28

The concept of contrapuntalism was first used by Edward Said in the essay "Reflections on Exile" and then developed in more detail in *Culture and Imperialism*.[3] Said was responding to critics of his earlier work *Orientalism* (1978), who argued that in *Orientalism*, he had focused more on European culture than on the voices and agency of former colonized peoples. Although I note that the work of Edward Said was largely ignored by mainstream studies, postcolonial scholarship was a notable exception to this trend.[4]

The main contribution of Said in his contrapuntal reading is that he engages in a reading back that uncovers the submerged but crucial presence of empire in canonical texts.[5] Bayani and Rubi also demonstrate that, unlike univocal readings in which the stories told by dominant powers become naturalized and acquire the status of "common sense," Said's contrapuntal reading demonstrates a simultaneous awareness both of the metropolitan history and of those other histories against which (and together with which) the dominating discourse acts.[6] Since this concept is borrowed from Said's love of Western classical music, the concept borrows heavily from musicality.

What Said sought in a contrapuntal reading was a simultaneous interpretation of discrepant experiences to a point of achieving coherence, and this is what should be sought for in Mark's ἐξουσία. Humphrey Waweru's application of Said's method in interpreting experiences that are fundamentally relational, coherent but separate, and comprehensible to particular traditions reveals a counterpoint.[7] In music, a counterpoint is the result of two voices and rhythms being played independently, but that nevertheless end up creating a harmony. Said himself shows that

> in the counterpoint of western classical music, various themes play off one another, with only a provisional privilege being given to any one; yet in the resulting polyphony there is concert and order, an organized interplay that

---

3. Edward Said, *Culture and Imperialism*, 165.

4. Geeta Chowdhry, "Edward Said and Contrapuntal Reading: Implications for Critical Interventions in International Relations," *Millennium: Journal of International Studies* 36, no. 101 (2007): 1–17, 3.

5. Chowdhry, "Contrapuntal Reading," 5.

6. M. Bayani and A. Rubin, eds., *The Edward Said Reader* (New York, Vintage Books, 2000), 23.

7. Waweru, *Bible and African Culture*, 84.

derives from the themes, not from a rigorous melodic or formal principle outside the work.⁸

The goal of a contrapuntal reading is thus not to privilege any narrative but to reveal the wholeness of the text: the intermeshed, overlapping, and mutually embedded histories of metropolitan and colonized societies, and of the elite and subaltern. Accordingly, contrapuntal reading is like a fugue, which can contain two, three, four, or five voices; they are all part of the same composition, but are each distinct.

Contrapuntalism is taken up more eloquently, and in an African setting, by Humphrey Waweru, who proposes contrapuntalism as a category for reading the Bible in Africa.⁹ Though Waweru sees similarity with comparative studies and inculturation in this approach, he nevertheless argues that as a "profoundly ideological model," contrapuntal reading is one mode of approach among others.¹⁰ Within this understanding, Waweru uses the contrapuntal model to read the book of Revelation alongside the Kikuyu culture. The issue is to understand what John in the book of Revelation says about the future in the Apocalypse, and to understand how Kikuyu myths about the past can influence how we interpret John's view of the future and access its meaning in the "Apocalypse community."¹¹ In a broader sense, Waweru's contrapuntalism is attuned to reading the entire Bible. In Waweru's contrapuntalism, therefore, it can be observed that meaning or the counterpoint becomes the interface between the reading and the reader of the Bible.

Within the parameters of an African contrapuntal transaction that Waweru champions, Mark's ἐξουσία can be read (or sung) alongside the Kenyan context to achieve its counterpoint. This would be done in view of Said's plea for a contrapuntal reading. On this point, Said is best explained by Chowdhry when she observes that

> a contrapuntal reading is not meant to valorize plurality, rather it is a plea for worlding the texts, institutions and practices, for historicizing them, for interrogating their sociality and materiality, for paying attention to the hierar-

---

8. Said, *Culture and Imperialism*, 208.

9. Waweru, *Bible and African Culture*, 89.

10. Waweru, *Bible and African Culture*, 85. In this article, Waweru regards Johannine community as an apocalyptic community, meaning that they regarded themselves as a "last days" community.

11. Waweru, *Bible and African Culture*, 86.

chies and the power-knowledge nexus embedded in them, and for recuperating a non-coercive and non-dominating knowledge.[12]

Therefore, and within the confines of Mark 1:21–28, Mark when assigning ἐξουσία to Jesus creates a stage that venerates a Jesus (person) who is above all preexisting laws—one who makes, interprets, and applies the law as he goes and as is suitable for him. Similarly, in many political and ecclesiastical spheres in the third world, the public perceives leadership or power in persons who are reminiscent of dictators (whether progressive or retrogressive), who mess up and fix society at their own prerogative.[13] Even under the dispensation of improved constitutions, this perception has not been minimized in the public sphere. It remains to be seen if what is occasionally put on paper will ever be actualized in real life.

When Mark 1:21–28, as a drum, is played on its own, the sound of an excess ἐξουσία is heard. Although ἐξουσία can be played out without impunity, and although Mark's ἐξουσία is divine, it cannot be acted out without connotations of impunity. If, on the other hand, the subaltern context as a drum is played on its own, the sound of dictatorial human authority is heard. Likewise, it creates room for impunity to thrive. When Mark and the othered world contexts are played together, the harmonious voice of power and authority is heard. Thus, to create not just a counterpoint but a beneficial counterpoint, I propose that a unique contrapuntal reading of the same needs to be sought for reading impunity and Mark in Kenya.

A unique contrapuntal reading involves a reading that incorporates the benefit of Mark's divine ἐξουσία in achieving the counterpoint. This means that Markan ἐξουσία, which mainly has divine elements, would inform authority in the othered world contexts and not vice versa. In such a reading, impunity can be addressed, for it is not the project of this study to do away with the Bible. If impunity can be "coerced" into a contrapuntal reading in that a counterpoint can be achieved through such a proposal, then the imagination of an impunity-free world can be achieved.

When advocating a contrapuntal reading of Mark and "othered" worlds' contexts, one needs to bear in mind that contrapuntalism remains primarily a Western category, and therefore needs to be used with caution

---

12. Chowdhry, "Contrapuntal," 6.
13. Interviewee #4.

in the Kenyan context. Unless it is used as a mimicked category—offering the gaze that disrupts the master's conceptualization—then contrapuntalism retains the mainstream and hegemonic elements postcolonialism loathes. However, safely used, it remains a suitable postcolonial category for addressing impunity.

Divination and Mark 1:21-28

In the wake of postcolonial readings, it has become apparent that it is no longer worthwhile to continue reading the Bible in Africa while guided by the contours and images of alien perspectives. The time has come for African biblical scholars to reimagine Western conceptualizations of truth, including the Bible itself. As Chris Manus notes, "for too long African theological education was integrated into the mainstream European and North American academic tradition, neglecting the norms, values principles and insights inherent in African culture."[14] Divination is introduced into postcolonialism by Dube as a way of transacting the Bible and the sacred oral "texts" of indigenous African religions.[15] It is also introduced as a way of launching the uniqueness of African biblical studies and as a way of balancing Bible readings inside and outside the academy.[16]

In an unmatched and groundbreaking paper, "Divining Ruth for International Relations," Musa Dube, within a Botswana socio-location, offers various ways in which the concept of divination can be used as a category for studying the Bible in Africa. Dube defines divination as the art employed by a divine healer to read books of social life, to diagnose problems and offer solutions to consulting readers. She notes in part:

> For Batswana and other South Africans, reading a divining set with a professional diviner-healer was, and still is tantamount to reading an authoritative book of social life. Diviner-healers read divining sets to diagnose problems and to offer solutions to consulting (nonprofessional) readers. Divining sets, which could be composed of carved bones,

---

14. Chris Ukachukwu Manus, *Intercultural Hermeneutics in Africa: Methods and Approaches* (Nairobi: Acton Publishers, 2003), 1.

15. Gerald West, "Mapping African Biblical Interpretation: A Tentative Sketch," in *The Bible in Africa: Transaction, Trajectories, and Trends*, ed. Musa W. Dube and Gerald O. West, (Leiden, Netherlands: Brill, 2000), 28–53, 96.

16. Dube, *Other Ways of Reading*, 194.

beans, beads, coins and so on are not fixed or closed canons or stories. Rather, each consulting reader writes and reads his/her own story with the diviner-healer in the reading session.[17]

Dube explains this concept as borrowed from the Batswana, and especially when the missionary Robert Moffat first read and interpreted the Bible to Batswana. During this memorable reading, their response was to regard the Bible as a talking book and as a divination set. According to Dube, with time the Bible became one of the divining sets among the Batswana, and especially those emanating from the African Independent Churches.[18] It was and is used for treating troubled relationships as well as physical ailments, for health among Africans, and is associated with healthy relationships.[19]

In divination (whether using the Bible or other divining sets), the professional healer reads to diagnose and heal distorted or broken relationships and to encourage homogeneity and life-affirming relations in society as therapy for hurting (submerged) bodies. Noting that with the coming of Christianity in Botswana, the Bible has extensively been used as one of the divining sets, Dube argues that divination as an art must be encouraged "as an ethical method of reading in ... Africa."[20] In this way, it can be shown that divining[21] entails production of new knowledge, for it requires "... substantial understanding of social relationships."[22]

It is important to note that reading a divining set is not as esoteric as many catechized African Christians may think. On the contrary, "it involves reading and rereading human stories and confirming them as the divining set progressively reveals."[23] It places demands upon the consulting reader to right the wrongs within their social relationships.

---

17. Dube, *Other Ways of Reading*, 194.

18. Melissa Browning, "Hanging out a Red Ribbon: Listening to Musa Dube's Postcolonial Feminist Theology," *JRER* 2, no. 13 (2011): 1–27.

19. Dube, *Other Ways of Reading*, 181.

20. Dube, *Other Ways of Reading*, 184.

21. T. Maluleke encourages further theorization of this category but cautions against the use of this category uncritically (though in a feminist sense), citing that divination procedures are situated within a patriarchal setting and have sometimes been used to foster violence against women. This taken care of, we should note that Dube's intention, within the broader postcolonial framework, is to resist Western categories by employing an African category to approach knowledge; or rather, to employ subaltern tools to demolish the master's house.

22. Dube, *Other Ways of Reading*, 190.

23. Browning, "Red Ribbon," 17.

Therefore, neither the diviner-healer nor the divining sets possess exclusive knowledge; nor does the consulting reader bring hidden knowledge. Divination, according to Browning, is thus a production of social knowledge that demands ethical commitment from all participating readers. Its hermeneutical turning point is given impetus in the way it always starts with the experience of the people.[24]

Divination in African societies, and in Kenyan society, was and is used to diagnose living texts for physical and social healing; although it is largely stigmatized and relegated to abstruse spaces. Divination was one of the practices that Christian missionaries and colonialists tarnished as backward and termed witchcraft or black magic. This body of knowledge that contributed healing to many African communities, families, and individuals was replaced by more Western Christian and colonial friendly methods of counseling and "modern" medicine. Though this die-hard practice continues, it has been highly stereotyped and is only practiced among a minority of Kenyans.

The precise link between divination and postcolonial criticism lies in the fact that divination as a subaltern category cannot only be used to deconstruct the master's house; it also paves the way for the use of other and similar categories—something of a subversive act of decolonizing. This category assists in placing the margins' reading resources at the center of biblical interpretation and without displacing the center's categories.

When divination is used as a category for reading the Bible, it opens many points of connection for relating the text to the African readers' context. According to Vincent Wimbush, divination offers the right to invade and disrupt the discursive world of Western academic biblical interpretation with an interpretation that is equally important and astounding.[25] The value of divination lies in the fact that it is a starting point for engaging other indigenous categories in doing biblical studies in othered contexts. What follows now is a demonstration of how a "divinized" reading of Mark 1:21-28 can be used to address impunity in Kenya and other contexts as well.

---

24. Browning, "Red Ribbon," 18.

25. Vincent L. Wimbush, "Other Ways of Reading (Book)," *Shofar: An Interdisciplinary Journal of Jewish Studies* 21, no. 167 (2003): 1–32.

DIVINING MARK 1:21-28 FOR IMPUNITY

One of the key aims of postcolonialism is to contest Eurocentric ways of thinking as the only ways of approaching knowledge. Using the divining technique is one such way that Eurocentric conceptions of knowledge can be contested. Therefore, in divining Mark 1:21-28 for impunity, consulting readers must first account for what makes the power relations in this text so predetermined. Again, in allowing this story to accompany his narration, what ideo-theological impact does Mark make on the part of the readers?[26] One of the noticeable things that is directly expressed in reading the Markan text is that "power is socially constructed and therefore ideological."[27]

When the divining set is opened within a literary framework and with this conscientization, it can be noticed that in Mark 1:21-28, Jesus is exposed as the over-towering and overpowering one. According to Samuel, the Markan Jesus embodies the "sultanate" of the son of humanity.[28] What is notable is that in this high and towering view of Jesus, Mark already creates a tension between Jesus and other religious leaders. This in turn creates possible tensions and divisions between him and other religious caregivers, whether they are right or wrong by their own standards. As Fernando Belo observes, "What attracts attention is the authority (ἐξουσία) with which he speaks, for it contrasts with the habitual teaching practice of the scribes."[29] Moreover, Mark heightens this tension by portraying Jesus as the one who wields authority and exercises a commanding vision and voice. He is the only one allowed to define reality and existence for others.

By allocating Jesus such a space, the divining set already reveals a stage set for religious conflict, which revolves around the issue of power and authority. Mark's Jesus is set to act with impunity if by use of this space he abrogates all other authorities. This can be expressed more freely if

---

26. Gerald West, "Interpreting 'the Exile' in African Biblical Scholarship, and "An Ideo-Theological Dilemma In Post-Colonial South Africa," in *Exile and Suffering: A Selection of Papers Read at the 50th Anniversary of the Old Testament Society of South Africa*, ed. Bob Becking and Dirk J. Human (Leiden, Netherlands: Brill, 2009): 247–68, 258.

27. George Shillington, *Reading the Sacred Text: An Introduction to Biblical Studies* (London: T&T Clark, 2002), 272.

28. Samuel, *Postcolonial*, 122.

29. Fernando Belo, *A Materialist Reading of the Gospel of Mark*, trans. Matthew J. O'Connell; Maryknoll, NY: Orbis, 1981), 103.

"judicial authority and military or political dominion"³⁰ is brought to bear upon the meaning of ἐξουσία.

Setting the stage for religious conflict in Kenya would rightly be setting up others for religious division. Denominationalism can be a major problem in Kenya. When missionaries first brought the gospel to Kenya, the various denominations competed for space among the Kenyan communities by dividing Kenyans along denominational lines.

In terms of the Kenyan context, many religion seekers would buy into the fallacy of who has "a new teaching and with authority" (ἐξουσία), creating a "them" versus "us" identity. Such communities need a diviner, a healer who shoots or waters down religious competition and fosters communal healing. The issue here is power games and ideology, coupled with the desire to maintain the most powerful religious system. Kenya, being a religious country, has many societies reordered by use of religion. That is why for many Kenyans, including their politicians, it is important to acquire religious power possible because it means access to control. Frequently, politicians have been known to camp around those "religious people" who, like Jesus, have some ἐξουσία.

It is best stated that several religious movements and denominations that exist because they have overpowered others need to be exorcised in Kenya. In line with this, the former archbishop of the Anglican Church of Kenya (ACK), David Gitari, gives an example of evangelism to the nomadic communities of northern Kenya. He cautions against religious movements that offer individualized or sectional salvation by stating that "we are convinced that in our primary evangelism among the nomadic [Kenyan] peoples, our approach must not be that of rescuing individuals from a sinking boat but rather winning communities to Jesus Christ."³¹ Gitari's argument is that religion among communities that have strong family ties should not be used to overpower "others" but to free and empower all of them.³² Divisive evangelism (binarism) not only causes tribal, family, and societal feuds and disintegration; it also fosters religious animosity. Texts like Mark 1:21–28, which tend to celebrate the one religious group overpowering others, need to be exorcised of imperial

---

30. Samuel, *Postcolonial*, 122.

31. David Gitari, *Responsible Church Leadership* (Nairobi: Acton Publishers, 2005), 112.

32. Gitari references the New Testament mandate for such evangelism when he notes that Paul baptized the household of Cornelius and of the Philippian jailer in Acts 16. Thereby, evangelism is not plucking individuals out of their communities but having communities turn to Christ.

binary traits and language that they enjoin because they become breeding points for chaos and impunity.

Second, the divining set notices that Mark is so engrossed with Jesus's power and superiority over and against the empires of this world that he makes Jesus deal only with personal issues at the expense of the communal. In the healing episode (Mark 1:26), Jesus should have concentrated on facing and addressing structures that make for individual infirmity and demon possession. On the contrary, Mark's Jesus concentrates on healing an individual and ignores structural sins that leave a whole community vulnerable to multiple possessions, including impunity.

The divining set focused on power relations reveals that Mark does one more thing: He pits Jesus and the evil spirit in a contest. For Mark, the greatness of Jesus lies not in the freedom of the healed man but in the defeat of the evil spirit. Jesus should have been more interested in dismantling the imperial and systemic spaces that are stubborn in the face of religion; that colonize the other.

Mark seems to accept the notion that defeat of the subject counts for more power and reputation than freedom of the object. Viewed in Walter Brueggemann's *Prophetic Imagination*, Mark's Jesus lacks a "prophetic ministry" fueled by a "prophetic imagination" that creates and nurtures an alternative consciousness, which in turn creates and nurtures an alternative community.[33] Thus, Jesus's action, however benevolent, lacks a critique that is centered on eliminating numbness to the death of the organizing principles of our world. Mark fails to present Jesus as God who accords freedom to all, who dismantles the structures of weariness and dethrones the powers of fatigue, declaring them incapable of offering what they claim to offer. If only for this text, the divining set must exorcise by decolonizing this individuated idol that Mark perceives for Jesus and replacing him with an almighty God who has all the dimensions of existence in his purview.

From the foregoing, it can be surmised that divination helps reveal the strongholds of impunity that are embedded in Mark's placement of ἐξουσία and resultant power plays. To address impunity in Kenya, divination becomes a useful category since it continually offers the possibility of speaking to unhealthy relationships.

---

33. Walter Brueggemann, *The Prophetic Imagination* (Minneapolis, MN: Fortress Press, 2001), 13–16.

Since biblical texts are social productions and emerge out of very particular social and material settings, it becomes important to reveal how they take sides in social debates; debates which usually revolve around issues of power that challenge or defend the way in which people are socially constituted. In Mark 1:21-28, for example, power relations are made to protrude by the author, and are both embedded and assumed in the text. The narrative of the confrontation between Jesus, the teachers of the law, and the man possessed by an evil spirit in Mark 1:21-28 not only preserves a memory of how these were socially constructed in the past; it also advocates for a similar or different social ranking of such in the present. This opens ways in which Mark 1:21-28 can yield "oppressive strands" and be construed as a "text of terror."[34]

Divining Mark 1:21-28 not only reveals social stratifications; it also yields ideological perspectives of power and authority that are inscribed in the text. Whose interests are being served in the preservation and commodification of ἐξουσία in this narrative? From whose point of view is the narrative told? Power in this narrative constitutes a dominant ideology, for without it, the whole logic of the narrative would collapse.

Power as Mark construes it in 1:21-28 is ideological because it has been accepted by the dominated segments of the society for what it is. The ideological creation of power subordinates presents two rival ideologies in the same narrative. Ἐξουσία requires subordinate subjects, and the Markan society can be construed to have constituted itself to fit the order. This is a tension that Mark maintains not only in 1:21-28, but throughout the gospel. In the end it is difficult to tell if Mark is a pro-subaltern text or a pro-empire text; but the counterpoint of ideological tension remains.

DIVINING APPLAUSE OF ΕΞΟΥΣΙΑ IN MARK 1:21-28

Whitney Shiner has ably placed Mark in the body of literature that enjoins applause as one of the elements (ideologies) in its formation.[35] For her, applause as a performance in Mark's gospel serves as an indicator of audience reaction not only to the gospel but also to the person of Jesus Christ and the way Mark makes his Jesus elicit such a reaction.

---

34. Phyllis Trible, *Texts of Terror: Literary-Feminist Readings of Biblical Narratives* (Philadelphia, PA: Fortress Press, 1984), 12.

35. Whitney Shiner, "Applause and Applause Lines in the Gospel of Mark," in *Rhetorics and Hermeneutics*, ed. James D. Hester (London: T&T Clark, 2004), 131.

According to Shiner, the public presentation of the gospel before it was written resembled that found in other sorts of oral performances in the ancient world.[36]

In line with this, Rhoads and Michie also suggest that "if the meaning of the gospel is found in the way it moves the emotions rather than in the facts that it presents, then applause, both as a marker of emotional reaction and as a factor inducing its own emotional response, is quite significant for our understanding of the gospel."[37] That Mark was fully aware of this element is attested not only in the way he brings it to bear upon the ἐξουσία of Jesus, but also in the way he enjoins applause throughout the gospel narrative.[38]

The ideology of applause is prominent in 1:27–28. In it, Mark records: "And they were all amazed, so that they kept on asking one another, saying, 'What is this? A new teaching—with authority! He commands even the unclean spirits, and they obey him.' And immediately his fame began to spread throughout the surrounding region of Galilee."

In this passage, it seems audience experience was part of the reception of the gospel: The performer must have tried to move and involve the audience during the recitation of the gospel. It is also imperative to think about the kind of response and applause the performer would expect during the performance. As Shiner further remarks, "We misunderstand the gospel in its first century context as long as we are thinking of it as a text on a page rather than words that are heard, gestures that are seen, and the response of those standing, sitting, or reclining around the listeners."[39] Was applause part of Mark's material for sewing the garment of his gospel, and what ideological import could it have had on his understanding of ἐξουσία?

According to Olbricht, applause was such an important factor in the impact made by an oration that it was not uncommon during the first century CE to find people hiring cheerers during orations.[40] This phenomenon of hired people indicates the extent to which applause was received as an important part of orations. Although Shiner points out that in religious gatherings applause could have been more restrained,

---

36. Shiner, "Applause," 130–136.

37. David Rhoads and Donald Michie, eds., *Mark as Story: An Introduction to the Narrative of a Gospel* (Philadelphia, PA: Fortress Press, 1982), 37.

38. Shiner, "Applause," 131.

39. Shiner, "Applause," 133.

40. Thomas Olbricht and Jerry L. Sumney, *Paul and Pathos* (Atlanta, GA: SBL, 2001), 17.

he underscores the strong emotional impact it had on religious orations.[41] It is therefore highly probable that the crowd in Mark 1:21–28 is to a large extent an applause crowd.

In Mark, the "audience is amazed at the authority of Jesus' teaching; one man, possessed by a demon, yells out disruptively, causing Jesus to seriously modify his presentation; and the audience discuss the meaning of Jesus and his teaching after the exorcism."[42] Besides, Mark's gospel has many places where the logic of any narrative would not make sense except that it gets endorsements from the constituted crowds. In view of this, and if Shiner's hypothesis is plausible, Mark can be construed as having used the ideology of applause to pamper the ἐξουσία of Jesus.

Thus, Mark lays the ground from which his Jesus can be viewed as practicing overall and imperial power using applause ideology. Although it is not worth painting the entire gospel as an applause gospel, it is possible to identify the reason why Mark's audience would be enjoined in applause and whose interests are being served; mainly the inscription of the difference. Just as early audiences were likely to do when their side defeated the opposition, Mark's audience applauds when Jesus silences the scribes and defeats the evil spirit.

Applied in conjunction with other methods of textual analysis, and in particular postcolonialism, applause can be construed as a tool of the hegemony if it is employed to keep the gaze of the subaltern at the center. Analysis of the text for expected applause lines can help us to establish the meaning of the text and the emotional impact it had on its readers. This is because emotional meaning is much the same as intellectual meaning. This may help explain why uncritical use of applause merely for indicating power in Mark's gospel may also be borrowed by its readers and applied to life situations. The question is whether it is possible for Kenyans to applaud impunity (probably!), and, more trenchantly, whether impunity is constituted by the hegemonic and the favorable side.

As an ideology, applause was used to account for "differences between people, differences that eventuate in stereotypes and differences that

---

41. Shiner, "Applause," 134.
42. Shiner, "Applause," 136.

manifest themselves in power relations."[43] Whether in the media, or in religious, political, or other gatherings, the ideology of applause in Kenya is used to recreate structures of the empire; structures that aid celebration of impunity and make it seemingly harmless, especially when it is practiced by those who have ἐξουσία and are applauded by the subaltern.

FINDING A POSTCOLONIAL HERMENEUTICAL KEY FOR MARK 1:21–28

There are many other holes in Mark 1:21–28 into which hermeneutical keys could be inserted. Bearing in mind that one of postcolonial criticism's interests is to critique travel narratives that end up celebrating the occupation of other peoples' land and spaces, then in Mark 1:21–28 the evil spirit becomes an important place to insert such a postcolonial hermeneutical key.

If the evil spirit in 1:21–28 is to be identified analogically with the Roman occupation, the man with the evil spirit may be identified in turn as the land and people under occupation and overpowered. The evil spirit claims to speak on behalf of the man and even to possess knowledge of the almighty, and entreats Jesus not to send the spirit away; but Jesus "rebuked" (Mark 1:25) the spirit and cast him out. Jesus's later proclamation that his plundering of the property of the "strong man" portends the end of Satan's empire (Mark 3:23–27) could then be read as equally portending the end of the Roman Empire in the life of this man.

Seen in this manner and in line with Moore's postulation, reading Mark in such a way uses "possession" as a hermeneutical key.[44] Such a hermeneutical key can tentatively be used to read the whole of Mark's gospel to unlock the wider implications of Mark's ἐξουσία. However, caution needs to be taken, for as Moore warns, "if such a hermeneutical key is overused it can easily break in the lock."[45] It is not surprising, therefore, to note that reading Mark within the framework of such a hermeneutical key is to read Mark within the confines of its major identity: as an allegory. This is to pay attention to the extent to which individual situations can

---

43. Renita Weems, "Ideological Criticism of Biblical Texts," *Semeia* 59, no. 3 (1992): 26–47.

44. Moore, *Empire and Apocalypse*, 27.
45. Moore, *Empire and Apocalypse*, 27.

be generalized to represent histories and destinies of most peoples, especially former colonial subjects like Kenyans.

Reading "Possession" in the Kenyan Context

Possession involves displacement, occupation, and settlement. In Mark 1:21-28, the evil spirit had made an abode of the possessed man. Most of the possessions are not symbiotic relationships, but are a result of empire building for economic reasons and for the benefit of the colonizer. Within this ambit, Kenya can symbolically be termed as possessed by an "evil spirit" of impunity that forms fertile ground for other forms of subalternization.

This evil spirit ravages and estranges the victim. Impunity thrives in impoverishing and marginalizing the other. It thrives in domination, and representation through hegemony; in the classification of the "other" in all forms of political and even ecclesial machinations. The "other" is totally overpowered and disempowered, mainly for economic reasons. In the example of Kenya, politics of impunity grip the nation mainly for economic reasons. The evil spirit that possesses Kenya can further be conceptualized through Munene's lens.[46]

According to Munene, this evil spirit cannot be fully understood without a clear grasp of the country's colonial history. Munene argues that many in the top echelon of the coalition government that was formed in 2008 are products of British norms and thinking. Some are the products of education at Mangu, Alliance, and Maseno, and later Makerere, in the 1950s and early 1960s. Others were junior officers in the British colonial service in the 1950s and 1960s. These are part of the group that inherited the colonial state as youth of the day, formed a new political class, and in many ways remain in charge of the country irrespective of the political party to which they claim to belong. The children of this political class are supposedly the younger generation of leaders and are likely to have attended academic institutions such as St. Mary's, Lenana, and Nairobi School. These ended up at the universities and training colleges. Some joined the elite in terms of wealth acquisition and the ability to manipulate the political climate.

---

46. Munene, *Historical Reflections*, 9.

What Munene construes is a "who's who" class structure that has evolved in Kenya over the years, which has its roots in the dominant families upon independence. Therefore, a spirit of neocolonialism is breathed on Kenyans by the second generation of neocolonialists. The spirit presents itself in othering, representation, hegemony, and the empire. This is the spirit that grips Kenya and needs a "new teaching" with ἐξουσία to cast it out. This is the spirit of the empire, and when threatened, it occasionally finds ways of assuaging the ego of the subalterns. It does so by incorporating a few leaders of the subalterns into the empire club or by mounting temporary diversions such as drumming up ethnic hostility. Like a vicious cycle, the "evil spirit" generates and domesticates impunity, and the grips of both the spirit and impunity become tighter with every passing year.

"POSSESSED" BY IMPUNITY

The spirit that possesses Kenyans is that of impunity. Impunity often manifests and thrives amid poverty. Poverty in Kenya is systemic and endemic, partly due to the deliberate marginalization of some peoples and regions. The Human Poverty Index (HPI) in Kenya continues to rise with every passing year. The HPI value for Kenya is lower than the income poverty level. Despite rapid economic growth in the last few years, human poverty appears to continue deepening. According to the UNDP, this can be attributed to the growing structural inequalities that thrive in a climate of impunity.[47]

In an impunity-possessed society, poverty or the subaltern other in Kenya continues to be created; it is not natural, and it is relative rather than absolute. Impunity and poverty in Kenya have different levels and dimensions, which end up complementing each other. Because of that complementary role, impunity, empire, and poverty form a dangerous triad. It should not be taken for granted that the empire enjoins poverty to sustain impunity. It follows then that the reason the empire goes out to create poverty is political, because "poverty is a controlling mechanism."[48] According to Munene, creating poverty was also a controlling mechanism, which colonialism ably applied to Africa.[49]

---

47. "UNDP Kenya Annual Report: 2011," accessed April 20, 2017, http://www.ke.undp.org, 17.
48. Kiraitu Murungi. *In the Mud of Politics* (Nairobi: Acacia Stantex Publishers, 2000), 58.
49. Murungi, *Politics*, 82.

Those who write on poverty have seen Kenya, like other African and majority world nations, as having been a victim of poverty creation by donor countries. The tragedy is that they do that with the full knowledge and support of the governments of the states whose peoples are being made poor. It is those governments that evict people from their land to make land available for the multinationals, and so on. Therefore, as Munene adds, poverty creation is a contrived process that has long historical roots.[50]

As mentioned before, much of the poverty experienced in Kenya is a result of a contrived process, and is deliberate and manipulated by people in authority. Church and political power are used for the purposes of favoring or victimizing particular groups of people.[51] Those who believe they are victimized become resentful, believing their poverty is due to those in authority.[52] Some nurture feelings of betrayal, which sometimes results in acts of impunity. Addressing systemic poverty, therefore, becomes an important step in the direction of reducing impunity levels in Kenya.

"POSSESSED" BY THE POWERFUL

Writers on power also depict Kenya as having been possessed by the powerful people. That Kenya is "possessed" by the powerful can be attested by the economic disparities that exist today: The rich get richer and the poor get poorer. In Kenya, many top spaces are dominated by the elites, hence it is the "boss" who matters. This cultural aspect of power is mainly an import from the colonialists. According to Norman Miller, the Kenyan elites who had direct or indirect contact with the colonialists have keenly followed in the *nyayo* (footsteps) of the colonialists.[53] Miller's argument is that in Kenya the black elites continue to wholeheartedly embrace all the power and overpowering traits that were reflected by

---

50. Murungi, *Politics*, 87.
51. Murungi, *Politics*, 79.
52. Munene, *Historical Reflections*, 45.
53. "Nyayo philosophy," which was the brainchild of Daniel arap Moi, the second, and longest-serving, president of Kenya, meant that he would not depart from the footsteps of the first president, Jomo Kenyatta, for, so it was thought, Kenyatta had governed the country well. In our view, however, this is seen as a pledge to maintain the imperial dispositions of the former president, and as a way of maintaining the dictatorial status quo.

colonial lifestyles. Consequently, in status, symbols, and wealth, a brand of elites is possessed by power, and in turn they possess Kenya.[54]

In trying to maintain and sustain a power identity, and by mimicking the rule that the colonialists had on Kenyans, the dominant class has selectively used aspects of the British Empire that favor their lifestyles and economic dominance.[55] They have used the buildings, wealth, infrastructure, and political structures inherited from the Whites to entrench their hegemony. They have used Christianity and the Bible (and especially the language, images, and ideology) to provide a religious approval to this hegemony.

In their brand of leadership, they have neither governed in the same way as the British did, nor have they replicated colonial ideology in the same terms, but they have produced a more oppressive point and a worse rule than that of the colonizers. Since the power of the empire is the interlocutor of postcolonialism, it can be argued that their power dominance has been the recipe for the prevailing situation of impunity in Kenya. The Bible has provided images, language, and ideology for justifying the grounds of this dominance.

Kenyans as Reformists

During the 2012 general election campaigns in Kenya, one of the raging debates was about who the reformers were and who the conformists were. Unfortunately, the definition of these two categories was narrowed down to tribal affiliations. In whichever way it can be viewed, Kenyans can be ambivalent as reformists and conformists at the same time. The reality of who Kenyans are can be detrimental or useful in the fight against impunity. Kenyans boast success in resistance struggles. Kenyans battled the colonial masters through the Mau-Mau and won; Kenyans battled Moi's dictatorship under the single-party rule and ushered in democracy in style. Kenyans have recently battled Al-Shabaab

---

54. Miller, *Quest for Prosperity*, 84.

55. In reference to the mimicry and hybridity of this "comprador bourgeoisie," Ngũgĩ wa Thiong'o, in the novel *The Wizard and the Crow*, notes that "this class has incurable wish for permanent identification with the culture of the imperialists ... but to truly and really become an integral part of that culture, they would have to live and grow abroad. But to do so would remove the political base of their economic constitution as a class. So, this class can only admire that class from undesirable distance and try to ape it the best way they can within the severe limitations of territory and history" (56).

CHAPTER FOUR: DETHRONING EMPIRES OF IMPUNITY

under the Africa Mission in Somalia (AMISOM), and expelled vigilante and terrorist groups from Somalia.[56]

All these are visible enemies; however, enemies can sometimes be invisible. Kenya's history is dotted with stories of success so far as resistance and armed struggle are concerned; unfortunately, it could be possible that Kenyans are successful in fighting visible enemies and not invisible ones. It remains to be seen how Kenyans can handle ideological and invisible enemies. The shackles of impunity that bind Kenyans are more ideological and invisible than visible. Kenyans will need to think harder to liberate themselves from the ideological silo of impunity in which they have been entombed.

In view of this and the raging debates on impunity, Mark's gospel abounds with resources that could aid in triumphing over ideological foes. Although Mark has largely been read as a conformist gospel, it can also be read retrospectively as a resistant and reformist gospel. Read this way, Jesus in Mark 1:21-28 is seen as defeating his enemies ideologically through direct confrontation and through teaching; but more so using his ἐξουσία.

Can reading Mark within a postcolonial framework portray it as resistant literature and bring out these resources? In Horsley's view, Mark's good news is the (hi)story of a concrete renewal movement of a people in resistance to imperial domination.[57] In a similar manner, Samuel views Mark's story of Jesus as written from the periphery, from the perspective of the other, for the "out-of-the-way" people, the colonized of Galilee.[58] Seen in this way, Mark stands not in what the anthropologists have called the "great tradition" of the Judean scribes and their temple state sponsors, but in the "little" or popular tradition of Galilean peasantry. Therefore, Mark becomes the voice that speaks for the masses in opposition to institutions in an imperial order.[59] This aspect of resistance in Mark's gospel can be used to encourage ongoing resistance of naming and shaming impunity.

---

56. Etymologically, the Arabic word means "the youth." It has been picked up by terrorist groups as a brand name. It is an offshoot of the Islamic Courts Union, which seeks to extend Islamic rule in Somalia and wage war over "enemies of Islam." Kenya recognizes Al-Shabaab as a terrorist group and has waged war to uproot it from the vicinity of its border with Somalia.

57. Horsley, "Submerged Histories," 185.

58. Samuel, *Postcolonial*, 77.

59. Except for Ched Myers and Burton Mack, few scholars have seen in Mark the element of resistance; the majority of the myriad of scholarship and voices focused on Mark agree that Mark is conformist literature.

Kenyans as Conformists

Conformity arises when members of society accept how the oppressor applies it. On the other hand, conformity can be recognized as consensus for achievement of social goals; for any stability in a given social formation, there has to be consensus among its members over a given period.[60] In reading Kenyans as conformists, from the resources offered by Mark 1:21–28, and without lumping the entire population together as single-minded, one immediately recalls the αὐτοὺς (them/crowd) of 1:22. In 1:22, Mark paints the picture of a conformist followership that he exploits throughout the gospel in order to sustain his concept of authority. In Kierkegaard's school of thought, a conformist is a naïve follower.[61] It is anybody whose behavior borders on sycophancy or one who agrees to all things so long as they do not derail the treasures of a comfort zone. An age that does not develop critical thinkers breeds conformists.[62] By use of the word αὐτοὺς, Mark presents a highly compromised and conformist audience, or one that is "ambivalent" in postcolonial terminology. It is an audience that is willing to sacrifice its known authorial figure, the scribe, and subscribe itself to the authority of any new teacher that seems to possess greater authority. It becomes an audience that applauds power and impunity because it is committed by the mighty and not the Almighty. It is possible that the Markan crowd applauds the power exuded by Jesus but not the divinity of Jesus.

Kenyan society mirrors the crowd of Mark in that it tends to be ambivalent about impunity. Not many Kenyans seem ready to champion an uprising or reformist agenda against impunity, and the majority seem to prefer to mind their own business. Moreover, there is a gating community, many of whom are beneficiaries of a climate of impunity that loathes demonstrations, uprisings, and resistance. If the monster of impunity does not turn on them, this brand of Kenyans remains mum while the monster keeps on feeding and growing. So, a few Kenyans have become rich, "fat," patriotic, and comfortable with the present order of impunity, and other advantages that come with the power. There is an extreme captivity to capitalism, even in the churches, that conditions

---

60. Ndüng'ü, *Socialization and Violence*, 121.

61. Søren Kierkegaard, *Fear and Trembling*, trans. Alastair Hannay (London: Penguin Books, 2003), 111.

62. Neo-philosophy, accessed February 6, 2013, http://www.neo-philosophy.com/Phil101Week14.html.

the reading of the Bible in selective ways, and makes the present outlook of impunity seem ordained or even willed by God.

Therefore, impunity in Kenya becomes both a religious and a political issue. It is the trust in the legitimacy of the two systems (religion and politics) that gives rise to the political and economic conformity that has bankrupted Kenyan ethics.[63] Conformity to the inevitabilities of history has been a common and debilitating failure in the history of the church.[64] The distinctive and decisive witness to the word of God, and the uniquely crucial role that can be played by the gathered community of God's people, can become obscured or completely lost in that process of conformity. Although I am aware that many Kenyans trust in God, my proposal is that the entirety of Kenya ought to place its faith solely and completely in the efficacy of the word of God. It must hope in the gospel alone.[65] According to Wallis, "this is to establish an eternal revolutionary posture in the world which unceasingly and in every circumstance perpetually seeks justice, liberation and peace."[66] In Tutu's words, "it is never being satisfied to rest false hopes in the powers and idols and systems of the world that continually claims to be our salvation."[67]

Prophetically speaking, Kenyan Christians must come out of their comfort zones and engage the powers that be; the powers that make it possible for impunity to thrive and subdue an entire society. Kenyan Christians must liberate themselves from ideological silos[68] in which they have been caged by enjoining "reformist" talk in addressing impunity. When it comes to the use of the Bible, Kenyan Christians must read for decolonization, being wary of all attitudes and ideologies that directly or indirectly feed the monster of impunity.[69]

---

63. "Prosperity Gospel: An Experience at a Kenyan Church," accessed February 6, 2013, http://davidbawks.wordpress.com/2011/11/30/prosperity-gospel-an-experience-at-a-kenyan-church/.

64. Jim Wallis, "Liberation and Conformity," in *Mission Trends 4: Liberation Theologies*, ed. Gerald H. Anderson and Thomas F. Stransky (Grand Rapids, MI: William B. Eerdmans, 1979), 52.

65. Jim Wallis, "Liberation and Conformity," 52.

66. Jim Wallis, "Liberation and Conformity," 56.

67. Desmond Tutu, *No Future without Forgiveness* (New York: Hodder & Stoughton, 1999), 56.

68. Jose M. Bonino, "Marxist Critical Tools: Are They Helpful in Breaking the Stranglehold of Idealist Hermeneutics?" in *Voices from the Margin*, ed. R. S. Sugirtharajah, 42.

69. Dube, "Toward," 12.

A Hermeneutics of Impunity

If hermeneutics is the science and art of biblical interpretation, then this science must be brought to bear upon the reality of what it means to be a Kenyan Christian living in a context of impunity. For it is no longer sensible to continue reading the Bible from alien perspectives. So far, it is noted that impunity as a slippery subject can be conceptualized in two ways. It can be viewed as positive energy and as negative energy.

In the negative sense, people who practice impunity convince themselves that other human beings they are violating, and whose well-being they do not protect, are unworthy of something better. They entrench themselves as more powerful and important at the expense of the "other's" good. Impunity becomes an entrenched reality in society to the point that it takes the form of a "culture." It becomes part of the culture by wearing down its resistance, to the point that even its victims resign to "this is the way things are!" desolation.

Positively, impunit*ism* (henceforth) is seen as the desire for a better society, and taking charge in order to attain it. An old Swahili adage proclaims, *Dawa ya moto ni moto!* (Respond to fire with fire). The response to negative impunity needs to be positive impunity. In this way, impunitism is the desire to burst open existence in terms of what has been defined by hegemony. It is the determination to burst open the fallacy of social order by disorienting the establishment. Therefore, impunitism can be theorized as a "hermeneutic of dialogue." It involves a dialectical process that is a constant conversation between the Bible and the Kenyan context, challenging the established order of things and calling for action against those that are dehumanizing others.

Thus conceived, impunitism is the process of creating new horizons and connecting the disparate elements of our lives into a meaningful whole. In this way, it stands for deconstruction of power and reconstitution of the same, involving decentering the hegemonic understanding of power and instituting negotiated power. This happens especially in situations where power has been misused. Only in this sense can Jesus in Mark 1:21-28 be read as making use of positive impunity energy.

In the negative space, however, the constitution of impunity to make up another *ism* involves several attitudes that are aligned with it, including *don't-carism* and *overpowerism*. Impunitism understood in such a manner indicates the replacement of power by the powerful or resisting power by the powerless. This replacement is an inherent desire in human nature to ascend beyond, to stand above, and not to withstand or equalize or neutralize. Negative impunitism is the spirit behind competition and superpowerism. It is power leadership of a powerless followership. It is the disordering of society such that representation is inevitable. It is ascendency, domination, and domineering. This evokes resistance, which involves disregard of the rule of the law of laid-down systems, for as David Garland notes, these systems are suspected of hegemony laden with the ideology of class control.[70]

POSTCOLONIALISM AND IMPUNITISM

The past decade has witnessed the birth of a wide array of postcolonial readings of the Bible from a variety of postcolonial and Majority World contexts. Following this hermeneutical trend, an interface between postcolonialism and impunity becomes necessary. The cues for a postcolonial impunity hermeneutics are politically and ideologically drawn primarily from a myriad of other "grown-up" hermeneutical persuasions, including postcolonial feminist hermeneutics, liberation hermeneutics, cultural hermeneutics, and Marxist hermeneutics. Postcolonialism and impunitism raise the following question: To what extent does impunity become a tool of hegemony and empire analysis? And, as a counterpoint, to what extent does it become a tool for analyzing subaltern resistance?[71] In answer to the first question, two fronts are seen to emerge: the front that advocates impunity as a tool of the empire and the front that sees it as a subaltern tool for resisting impunity.

In thinking about impunity as a tool of the empire, postcolonial criticism scrutinizes and exposes how impunity is a form of colonial domination and power, and in particular how it is embodied in imperial texts, and in their interpretations and the Bible (such as Mark 1:21-28).[72] This tool aids in the imagination of how colonial perspectives riddled with imperialism can be overturned and dismantled. It fosters an active confrontation with the dominant system of thought, with its lopsidedness

---

70. David Garland, *Punishment and Modern Society: A Study in Social Theory* (Oxford, UK: Oxford University Press, 1990), 5.

71. David Jobling, *"Very Limited Ideological Options*: Marxism and Biblical Studies in Postcolonial Scenes," in *Postcolonial Biblical Criticism: Interdisciplinary Intersections*, ed. Stephen D. Moore and Fernando F. Segovia (London: T&T Clark, 2005), 122.

72. To study postcolonialism without taking into consideration the use of the Bible in informing and justifying colonialism and imperialism is useless. See Malebogo Kgalemang, "Ngũgĩ 's Postcolonial Bible: Devil on the Cross," *Scriptura* 92, no. 1 (2006): 218–24.

and inadequacies that permit impunity to thrive unchecked, and the declaration of its unsuitability for any community, and Kenyan society.

Although impunity is present across all cultures, cultural impunity that has its contents poured out on another culture is more intolerable than impunity imposed from within a culture. Therefore, impunity that is manufactured in imperial centers becomes more detrimental to Kenyan society than what can be termed "mother-tongue impunity." This is because imperialism proceeds by denying the validity of the other's values while it imposes its own "master values" on them. Therefore, impunitism is both a reconstruction of national impunity and an option for a counter memory for the same. As a hermeneutic, it seeks to state that society must be negotiated from both the center and the peripheral; the previous and the current spaces. Otherwise, there will be impunity and counter impunity unless a negotiated plan for a just society is put in place.

ANALYSIS OF IMPUNITISM AS A HERMENEUTICAL TOOL

As Kwok Pui-lan notes, biblical interpretation is never simply a religious matter, for the process of formation, canonization, and transmission of the Bible was imbued with issues of authority and power.[73] Within this understanding, there is a complex relationship of truth and power that needs to be taken into account when developing impunity as an orientation for reading the Bible. Impunitism can be developed as an analytical tool for biblical interpretation. Viewed in such a manner, it does not take a totally different contour from other prominent hermeneutics. Within postcolonialism, it would be picking up and foregrounding the peripheral, othered themes and texts of the Bible. Admittedly, there would be a creative tension that would begin to emerge when impunity is theorized as a hermeneutical tool. The tension would be between, on the one hand, its usefulness in overturning, rejecting, and disregarding bourgeois laws, and on the other, the call to maintain an orderly society. Viewed thus, impunity could serve both as a hermeneutic and a hermeneutical key.

As a hermeneutic, impunitism would be able to make the connections that are to view the entire Bible—whether reading "behind the text," "in the text," or "in front of the text"—within the grid of impunity. Equally, as a hermeneutical key, impunity would act as a key that would help unlock

---

[73]. Kwok Pui-lan, "Discovering the Bible in the Non-Biblical World," *Semeia* 47 (1989): 25–42, 26.

pericopes, narratives, and sections of the Bible using an impunity orientation. This would account for why the Bible advocates for acceptability of some ἐξουσία while openly calling for resistance and rejection of other forms of the same.

IMPUNITISM AND SERVICE TO GOD

Can acts of impunity be serving the cause of God? Is there progressive and retrogressive impunity? Can the impunity inscribed in the ἐξουσία of Mark 1:21-28 be termed entirely retrogressive? Not at all! A similar biblical illustration will suffice to answer this question. Exodus 1:15-22 introduces the narrative of the Hebrew midwives. The narrative can be read as celebrating acts of impunity since the Hebrew midwives reject the king's decree and replace it with their own actions. This is because, as the narrative progresses, it is noticeable that the midwives are commanded by the king to kill all male children born of Israelite women. These women conspire and, without excuse, reject the king's injunction. When these women are called upon to account for their actions, they are again involved in total disobedience by lying blatantly. The narrator adds that they do this in fear of God, and God in turn *rewards* their behavior "with good families."

Can God tolerate impunity when it seems to honor God? Does the honor and glory of God enjoin evil to add to a social mileage? Quite the contrary: The midwives do not lie; they simply do not tell what hegemony considers the whole truth. Truth is their definition. As Weems points out,

it is the conventional weapon of the powerless, especially women in the Old Testament, against those in power, to use the weapon of deception where "truth" is not defined by the powerful, but becomes the priority of the underclass to interpret and shape meaning according to their own reality.[74]

By rejecting the Pharaoh's "truth," the Hebrew women become a law unto themselves, or at least what they perceive to be a higher truth: fear of God. This refusal to obey Pharaoh is a refusal to adopt hegemonic assertions, and their "impunity" in turn becomes a most effective way to counter the authority of the empire. "Disobedience," or in this case impunitism, becomes a sure way in which service to God is rendered in

---

74. Weems, "Ideological Criticism," 29.

this narrative. The rejection of bourgeois laws becomes part of subaltern service to God.[75]

In exercising his ἐξουσία in Mark 1:21–28, Jesus is depicted as being caught up in impunity, and yet not many dare term it as such because of his messianic designation and mission. Impunity as service to God brings out a tension, especially when Jesus is viewed as enjoining impunity to achieve his divinely mandated mission. There is a need for biblical readers to work creatively with such a tension because it is not only necessary; it also cannot be easily resolved. This tension that emanates from enjoining some measure of impunity by invoking the divine requires understanding in all its parameters, for it can be used to liberate the oppressed.

Conclusion

In this chapter, I have addressed the issues of some postcolonial readings of Mark and exposed some implications for Kenyan readers. On the one hand, using a contrapuntal reading, the revelation is that Kenyan society must be brought into a counterpoint and dis-counterpoint with itself; a harmony of acting ἐξουσία with itself even in the face of the culture of impunity. On the other hand, using a divining category, I have noted that Kenyan society needs a diviner/healer with "a new teaching" and with "power and authority." This diviner/healer must open a radical set that reads the Bible for decolonization.

The meaning for Kenyan readers is that they must be willing to reshape or understand differently the truths of the Bible; an understanding that a postcolonial hermeneutic promises. In what I have theorized as impunitism, I have concluded by proposing an "impunitism hermeneutic"; one that reads ἐξουσία in Mark 1:21–28 by advocating proactivity. The benefit for this would be to decolonize and free Bible readings from ideological cover-ups of negative impunity. The question that this conclusion poses for the final chapter is: How can all the propositions raised in this chapter be made more practical for a context like Kenya?

---

75. In Romans 13, Paul advocates imperial obedience as obedience to God; however, in 2 Corinthians 11:32–33, Paul narrates how he "disobeyed" King Aretas in order to serve God. See Acts 4, Peter's and John's response to the Sanhedrin.

CHAPTER FIVE

Beyond Empires of Impunity

Introduction

My point of inquiry has been based on the observation that in Mark's gospel, Jesus is presented as the authoritative one in the sense that he exercises power and authority by virtue of his high position and relationship to God. It has further been noted that power and authority are concepts that Mark builds up in his gospel with the use of the word ἐξουσία, to distinguish Jesus's authority from that found in the rest of the world. Therefore, in view of postcolonial biblical criticism, I have in this study explored Mark's usage of ἐξουσία in 1:21–28, and my conclusion is that he has used this concept to create a space that can be exploited by those desiring to construct and contain an empire of impunity.

As already stated, the inquiry on the usage of ἐξουσία in Mark's gospel takes place against a background of an ever-growing culture of impunity in the Roman Empire, which can be juxtaposed with a culture of impunity in the predominantly Christian Kenyan society. Therefore, in this book I have dealt with the question of addressing the prevailing and ever-growing culture of impunity in Kenya through a postcolonial reading of the concept of ἐξουσία in Mark 1:21–28. To address this and other emergent questions, I have employed the postcolonial framework to argue that Mark is influenced by the imperial setting of his day to provide the images that he does in the concept of ἐξουσία. Therefore, my main objectives have been to offer an alternative and contextual reading of ἐξουσία in Mark's gospel, and to establish the need for postcolonial biblical criticism in Kenya.

The task of this chapter, therefore, is to build a vision of a world beyond "empires of impunity," through critical analysis and recommendations. In so doing, I propose in this chapter ways in which the Kenyan church can rally most of its adherents to address the issues of impunity. This is done in view of Mark 1:21–28's promise of "new" ἐξουσία and the space offered in postcolonial biblical interpretation.

Impunity and Mark's Legacy

The overall picture so far is that there is a cost of reading Mark's gospel and its legacy. Mark is not an innocent book. It is part of colonial literature through which Western cultures have viewed other worlds. Its imaginative scheme has formed part of the scheme through which categories of reality have been constructed, including ἐξουσία, which leads to impunity in the colonial enterprise. The legacy that remains, therefore, is that ideological imports into the post- or neocolonial Kenyan elite abound in the usage of ἐξουσία in terms found in Mark 1:21–28. As such, the usage of the concept of ἐξουσία in Mark's gospel is also not innocent.

This is to say that ἐξουσία is a concept that Mark employs ideologically in his gospel to make his Jesus stand out as being above all authority. The ἐξουσία of impunity in Mark 1:21–28 is best seen alongside Mark's wider scheme of mimicking Rome, and reproducing in his gospel a typology of Rome for his immediate and extended audience. Therefore, whenever Mark uses the concept of ἐξουσία, he maps out a space of a bigger Rome, inevitably allocating Roman impunity to his Jesus. To achieve this, Mark marshals all available literary tools just to make Jesus's authority stand out as absolute. As exemplified in verse 25, Jesus uses the word Φιμώθητι ("come out"), which was used in the ancient world in magic spells for binding people and demons.[1] In verse 27, the word ἐθαμβήθησαν (*to be amazed*) is not only used to express an escalation of astonishment among the audience but also to heighten Jesus's ἐξουσία.

I have constantly raised the question of why Mark cuts out a unique picture for the ἐξουσία that he assigns to his Jesus. My proposal is that it is because Mark's story of Jesus is couched in a multilayered imperial framework. Even so, Mark contains resistance of the existing colonial (dis)order, and at the same time traces of colonial "mimicry" that retain colonial domination. Therefore, Mark's Jesus is like the Roman emperor,

---

1. Compare also the conduct of Paul in reference to the girl possessed with the spirit of Apollo in Acts 16:16–18. See Hooker, *St. Mark*, 64.

but because of his divinity, he is more akin to a Roman god; reasoning this way, I see his ἐξουσία as a trajectory of Roman rule.

Through a postcolonial orientation, it can also be noted that contacts with the empire, and reading imperial literature, have evolved a residue of impunity in Kenya. Impunity in Kenya and othered worlds is more than behavior that is naturalized. As illustrated in this book, impunity is worse than corruption, for it breeds unjust rules, negative ethnicity, gender and economic profiling of people, and other ills in society. In Kenya, for example, impunity is like an ideology that has developed over time into a culture. In fact, it has become a tool of the ruling class for crippling and containing the "other" (political enemies, the poor and marginalized, and so on). Although there is a cultural dimension to impunity, most of the impunity practiced in Kenya and othered worlds is a by-product of colonial contact with the empire. However, this does not exonerate the neocolonialist practitioner in the elite and ruling classes in Kenya.

With illustrations from Kenya, I have argued that there is an economic dimension of impunity. This conclusion is drawn based on the fluidity of social structures and poor identities that impunity aims at recreating in Kenya each day. As a strategy of the empire, impunity is recognized for its residue of organizing principle and colonial "worlding." Whenever poverty has decreased in Kenya, impunity has often been used to recreate it as a means of social control. Furthermore, economic impunity is not devoid of a gender dimension, and the worst effects are borne by women. Women's experiences are varied depending on their social location and proximity to the empire. However, they bear the brunt of both impunity and patriarchy in Kenya even though their experience under any form of imperialism and patriarchy is one of second-class or lower citizen status. Therefore, gender perspectives become necessary in reading empire and impunity because of the importance of gender positions during the struggles for power.

On the issue of Christianity and "empires of impunity," it is alarming to note, for example, that though 82 percent of Kenyans identify themselves as Christians, many of these same Kenyans are the ones engaged in the practice of impunity. To this end, it can be concluded that Mark 1:21–28 enjoins a subtle ideology of power that in many ways informs Christian impunity in Kenya. Though all dimensions of Christianity are not encapsulated in this conclusion, this posture can be blamed on the Eurocentric modes of reading the Bible that do not permit decolonizing criticality.

The Bible, when read uncritically, endorses, and reinscribes both positive and negative sentiments, forms, and postures like impunity. The element of power in Christianity and the Christian church is such that many Christians still understand ἐξουσία as the ability to have one's commands obeyed and followed, or the power to wipe out those who do not obey. Many Kenyan churches and their brand of Christianity are overtly influenced by the Bible in the way they construe and construct power. Just as Mark's gospel mimics imperial Rome in its construction of ἐξουσία, Kenyan Christianity in many ways mimics the powers that be in the construction of ecclesiastical power.[2] This is true for Kenya and othered contexts, and a thin line separates power and impunity in contemporary Christianities.

To this end, therefore, there are implications of a postcolonial reading of Mark 1:21-28 within a climate of impunity. Although the Bible is by extension a text of the empire, it should be noted, first, that the Bible is not a text that can easily be dismissed in Kenya. It is central not just in defining their religious lives, but in all other segments of their lives. Thus, a postcolonial approach of regarding the Bible as a colonial artifact, while useful, may find it difficult to navigate in some Kenyan spaces because of the divine space that the Bible is accorded in Kenya, and because the postcolonial optic largely remains an academic category. Second, continued reading of the Bible from alien perspectives has multiplied impunity and other vices in the Kenyan Christian community. There is therefore the need to popularize the postcolonial hermeneutics so it can be grasped by both academia and the other readers of the Bible.

The Debate Goes On

Reading Mark as a solution center must involve what Brueggemann calls a dialogical imagination, which must bear in mind the consciousness of conflict that Mark presents.[3] This is the recognition that there is something not fitting about Mark and the entire Bible insofar as solutions to real-life conflicts are concerned. Dialogical imagination involves finding a new image, and patterning reality and interpretation according to that image.

---

2. For example, it is not unusual to see bishops with motorcades, bodyguards, and aides, which are symbols of mimicked power.

3. Brueggemann, *Hopeful Imagination*, 24.

Kenyan Christians are recognizing the dissonance between the kind of biblical interpretation they inherited from the empire and the realities they are now facing. Therefore, there is a need to find new images for realities of "othered worlds" and to make new connections between the Bible and contemporary African life. Again and again, the usefulness of postcolonialism as a tool for scrutinizing and exposing colonial "worlding" as embodied in biblical texts and in interpretations, and as a tool for fronting alternative hermeneutics while overturning and dismantling colonial perspectives, has been reiterated.

While noting that impunity often is multiplied in the public spaces, it is my recommendation that an approach that considers public participation needs to be incorporated in addressing the culture of impunity. While advocating for an application of cultural policy in the public sphere, Jim McGuigan informs us that the institutional core of the public sphere is to enable public stakeholding in the solution to social issues.[4] It comprises communicative networks that make it possible for the public to participate in the reproduction of a culture and "for a public of citizens of the state to participate in the social integration mediated by public opinion."[5] Though a public-sphere concept is not the pursuit of this study, a recommendation is made for its incorporation in creating the vision for a world beyond impunity.

Since impunity in many spaces remains mainly unconceptualized and abstractly mentioned in media and other spaces, and to compel analysis and critical judgment to address it, impunity needs to be taught directly from the subaltern spaces. Impunity issues should therefore be incorporated in the ethics committees and/or formation of national commissions for campaigning against impunity should be formed. The implication of this is that social issues, including impunity, are brought to public attention in a deliberate manner and with the permission of the public.

Addressing impunity through a postcolonial reading of ἐξουσία in Mark 1:21–28 in this study is not meant to be an arena for presenting grand theoretical plans. The aim is to identify and interrogate impunity as a social and religious issue from the point of view of emancipatory knowledge such as postcolonial biblical criticism. Impunity as treated here remains an ongoing concern. It remains an object of praxis, an object

---

4. Jim McGuigan, *Culture, and the Public Sphere* (London: Routledge, 1996), 176.
5. McGuigan, *Culture*, 176.

of theoretical interpretation and of public debate, and for this venture voices of future postcolonial readers are invited.

Within the scope of the findings, therefore, the following conclusions can be drawn. First, following Liew, a conclusion can be drawn that Mark is a gospel of "colonial mimicry of tyranny, boundary and might," in that it is a colonialist discourse that duplicates and internalizes the colonial ideology of the imperial (dis)order.[6] Through an ideologically caricatured Jesus, Mark's gospel extends its own brand of imperial tyranny, boundary, and might; in other words, it propagates an imperial regime of impunity. Mark 1:21–28 presents Jesus in categories of suppressive authority, not only in relational and hierarchical terms but also in terms of unilateral and absolute authority. Jesus in Mark enjoys "tyrannical" authority to interpret, change, or break scripture. Mark's gospel is irredeemably Roman in its imagery, and therefore this gospel is a source of impunity for its readers.

Second, the unilateral and absolute authority of Mark's Jesus is ideological. The conclusion I arrive at is that Jesus's claim to singularity is an effective ideological weapon that leads to absolutism by allowing no comparison or competition. If impunity is an imperial force with an accompanying domination strategy, then Mark's gospel sustains impunity in the strategy of authority that it employs for Jesus.[7] Under the guise of divinity, Mark maps a space of unquestioned authority, and through this he can allow instances of null expectation of punishment for any of Jesus's actions. This way, Mark reduplicates colonial ideology and presents an all-authoritative Jesus who will eventually annihilate all opponents and all other authorities. Therefore, Mark has recreated in his gospel a "hierarchical, punitive and tyrannical" concept of ruler and ruled, and has subtly weaved it in religious language and left it for his readers to emulate.[8]

Noting the imperial nature of the text of the Bible, it is plausible to conclude, as Dube would put it "there is need for revising that complex collection of texts that are brought, born and used in imperial setting to legitimate, resist, or collaborate with imperialism."[9] Attuned to this is acknowledgement that the general experience in Africa is that the

---

6. Liew, "Tyranny,"15
7. See also Samuel, *Postcolonial*, 297.
8. Samuel, *Postcolonial*, 297.
9. Dube, *Postcolonial Feminist*, 47.

traditional mode of the official Euro-linked church's reading of the Bible is not capable of responding adequately to the questions that Kenyan Christians are asking about their lives in Christ and their experience with the Bible. Therefore, Kenyan readers, and Africans in general, must start reading the Bible otherwise, even as they take charge of biblical interpretation.

While also noting the limitation of reading the Bible from alien perspectives, it is still possible to use the Bible to tackle the culture of impunity. For this to happen, Kenyan Bible readers must bear the progressive consequence of reading the Bible under postcolonial methodologies. This will mean using the Bible both as a text for retrieval of silenced voices and of subversive speech, directed to the prevailing imperial structures of oppression. The text of the Bible, even in its compromised state, helps to speak back to the empire, whereby world-organizing imperialistic principles are unmasked for what they are: messengers of the empire. Just as Jesus brings in new teaching, and with ἐξουσία in Mark 1:21–28, impunity must be addressed by a determination to replace the old order of things with a new order; old laws with new laws.

Although on several occasions in this study we have taken an extremely critical view of the Bible, and even considered it as colonial literature and a suspicious site of struggle, the conclusion is that the Bible is not a text that can easily be dismissed in Kenya. It is well embedded in the Kenyan imagination. Therefore, while the natural posture of the Bible is ambivalent, it remains the best tool for dismantling the master's house. The Bible can be read in energizing, imaginative, and attractive ways that help address imperial traits.

The promise of Mark's gospel in ending impunity lies in the fact that the text is so powerful and compelling, so passionate, and uncompromising in its anguish and hope, that it requires readers to submit their experience to it and thereby reenter their experience on new terms. Indeed, ending impunity in othered worlds depends on the reading and hearing of the text. If readers fail to hear the text, they may succumb to a fraudulent discernment of their situation.

Thus, everything depends on the Bible, for without this "transformative, critical, liberating, subversive speech, readers can live in a speechless, text-less world that is always misunderstood."[10] Therefore, without the Bible, people are at the mercy of powerful ideology of misrepresent-

---

10. Brueggemann, *Hopeful Imagination*, 21.

ing propaganda, of anxieties that make them conformists, and despair that drives them to impunity. It is precisely the Bible, in its colonial and imperial embeddedness, in its odd offer of holiness and pathos, rending and healing, that dismisses ideology, exposes propaganda, and offers the vision of life beyond the empires of impunity.

REFERENCES

Adeleye, Francis. "Prosperity Gospel: Walk in Simplicity, Rejecting the Idolatry of Greed." *The Standard*, 2012. Accessed October 4, 2012. www.standardmedia.co.ke/m/story.php?articleID=2000068727.

Aijaz, Ahmad. "The Politics of Literary Postcoloniality." In *Postcolonial Theory: A Reader*, edited by Padmini Mongia, 276–93. London: Arnold, 1996.

Alston, Philip. *Promotion and Protection of All Human Rights, Civil, Political, Economic, Social and Cultural Rights, Including the Right to Development: Report of the Special Rapporteur on Extrajudicial, Summary or Arbitrary Executions, Philip Alston—Mission to Kenya*, 1–45. Geneva: United Nations—Human Rights Council, 2009.

Ambetsa Oparanya, W. *Population and Census Report (2010)*. Accessed April 15, 2017. http://www.scribd.com/doc/36670466/Kenyan-Population-and-Housing-Census-PDF.

Anassi, Peter. *Corruption in Africa: The Kenyan Experience*. Nairobi: Trafford Publishing, 2004.

Ashcroft, Bill, Gareth Griffiths, and Helen Tiffin, eds. *Post-Colonial Studies: The Key Concepts*. 2nd ed. London: Routledge, 2007.

Bakhtin, M. *The Dialogic Imagination: Four Essays*. Edited by Michael Holquist. Austin, TX: University of Texas, 1990.

Bawks, Daniel. "Prosperity Gospel: An Experience at a Kenyan Church," 2011. Accessed February 6, 2017. http://davidbawks.wordpress.com/2011/11/30/prosperity-gospel-an-experience-at-a-kenyan-church/.

Bayani, Moustafa, and Andrew Rubin, eds. *The Edward Said Reader*. New York: Vintage Books, 2000.

Beavis, Mary Ann. *Mark*. Grand Rapids, MI: Baker Academic, 2011.

———. *Mark's Audience: The Literary and Social Setting of Mark 4:11–12*. Sheffield, UK: Sheffield Academic Press, 1989.

Belo, Fernando. *A Materialist Reading of the Gospel of Mark*. Translated by Mathew J. O'Connell. Maryknoll, NY: Orbis Book, 1981.

Boer, Roland. "Marx, Postcolonialism, and the Bible." In *Postcolonial Biblical Criticism: Interdisciplinary Intersections*, edited by Stephen D. Moore and Fernando F. Segovia, 167–199. London: T&T Clark, 2005.

Berger, Adriana. "Cultural Hermeneutics: The Concept of Imagination in the Phenomenological Approaches of Henry Corbin and Mircea Eliade." *The Journal of Religion* 66, no. 2 (1986): 141–56.

Berman, Bruce, and John Lonsdale. *Unhappy Valley: Conflict in Kenya and Africa.* Vol. 1, *State and Class.* Nairobi: Heinemann, 1992.

Berquist, Jon L. "Postcolonialism and Imperial Motives for Canonization." *Semeia* 75 (1996): 15–36.

Best, Ernest. *Following Jesus: Discipleship in the Gospel of Mark.* Sheffield, UK: Sheffield Academic Press, 1981.

———. *Mark: The Gospel as Story.* Edinburgh: T&T Clark, 1983.

Bhabha, Homi. *The Location of Culture.* 1st and 2nd eds. New York: Routledge, 1994 and 2004.

Bogdan, R. C., and S. K. Biklen. *Qualitative Research for Education: An Introduction to Theory and Methods.* 2nd ed. Needham Heights: Allyn & Bacon, 1992.

Boggs, Carl. *Gramsci's Marxism.* London: Pluto Press, 1976.

Bonino, José Miguez. "Marxist Critical Tools: Are They Helpful in Breaking the Stranglehold of Idealist Hermeneutics?" In *Voices from the Margin: Interpreting the Bible in the Third World*, edited by R. S. Sugirtharajah, 40–48. London: SPCK, 2006.

Boring, Eugene. *Mark: A Commentary.* Louisville, KY: Westminster John Knox Press, 2006.

Brantlinger, Patrick. *Rule of Darkness: British Literature and Imperialism, 1830–1914.* New York: Cornell University Press, 1988.

Bratcher, Robert G. *A Commentary on Mark's Gospel.* Michigan: United Bible Society, 1961.

Browning, Melissa D. "Hanging Out a Red Ribbon: Listening to Musa Dube's Postcolonial Feminist Theology." *Journal of Race, Ethnicity, and Religion* 2, no. 13 (2011): 1–27.

Brueggemann, Walter. *Commentary on Jeremiah: Exile and Homecoming.* Grand Rapids, MI: William B. Eerdmans, 1998.

———. *Hopeful Imagination: Prophetic Voices in Exile.* Philadelphia, PA: Fortress Press, 1986.

———. *The Prophetic Imagination.* 2nd ed. Minneapolis, MN: Fortress Press, 2001.

Carroll, Robert P. "Exile, Restoration and Colony: Judah in the Persian Empire." In *The Blackwell Companion to the Hebrew Bible*, edited by L. G. Perdue, 110–32. Oxford, UK: Blackwell Publishers, 2001.

Cassidy, Richard J. *Jesus, Politics and Society: A Study of Luke's Gospel.* Maryknoll, NY: Orbis Books, 1978.

Cassidy, Richard J., and Philip J. Scharper, eds. *Political Issues in Luke-Acts.* Maryknoll, NY: Orbis Books, 1983.

Cheney, Emily. *She Can Read: Feminist Reading Strategies for Biblical Narrative*. Valley Forge, PA: Trinity Press International, 1996.

Choi, Jin Young. *Postcolonial Discipleship of Embodiment: An Asian and Asian American Feminist Reading of the Gospel of Mark*. New York: Palgrave Macmillan, 2015.

Chowdhry, Geeta. "Edward Said and Contrapuntal Reading: Implications for Critical Interventions in International Relations." *Millennium: Journal of International Studies* 36, no. 101 (2007): 1–17.

Cline, Mark. "The Gospel of Mark and Authority" (2009). Accessed June 16, 2016. http://reclinerramblings.com/2009/03/gospel-of-mark-and-authority.html.

Cline, Michael. *The Gospel of Mark and Authority*. Aumsville, OR: n.p., 2009.

Cobb, Laurel K. *Mark and Empire: Feminist Reflections*. Maryknoll, NY: Orbis Books, 2013.

Crossan, John Dominic. *Four Other Gospels: Shadows on the Contours of Canon*. Minneapolis, MN: Winston Press, 1985.

Cuddy, Line. "Søren Kierkegaard and Existentialism" (2008). Accessed March 6, 2016. http://www.neo-philosophy.com/Phil101Week14.html.

D'Amato, Paul. *The Meaning of Marxism*. Chicago, IL: Haymaker Books, 2006.

Dart, John. *Decoding Mark*. London: Trinity Press International, 2003.

Derrida, Jacques. *Of Grammatology*. Translated by Gayatri Chakravorty Spivak. London: The Johns Hopkins University Press, 1997.

Donahue, John R., and Daniel J. Harrington. *The Gospel of Mark*. Collegeville, MN: The Liturgical Press, 2002.

Draper, Jonathan A., Cynthia Briggs Kittredge, and Ellen Bradshaw Aitken, eds. *The Bible in the Public Square: Reading the Signs of the Times*. Minneapolis, MN: Fortress Press, 2008.

Dube, Musa W. "Toward a Postcolonial Feminist Interpretation of the Bible." *Semeia* 18 (1997): 11–26.

———. "Reading for Decolonization (John 4:1–42)." In *The Postcolonial Bible*, edited by R. S. Sugirtharajah, 11–26. Sheffield, UK: Sheffield Academic Press, 1998.

Dube, Musa W., and Gerald O. West, eds. *The Bible in Africa: Transactions, Trajectories and Trends*. Leiden, Netherlands: Brill, 2000.

———. *Postcolonial Feminist Interpretation of the Bible*. St. Louis, MO: Chalice Press, 2000.

———, ed. *Other Ways of Reading: African Women and the Bible*. Atlanta, GA: Society of Biblical Literature, 2001.

———. "Looking Back and Forward: Postcolonialism, Globalization, God and Gender." *Scriptura* 92, no. 93 (2006): 178–93.

Edwards, James R. "The Authority of Jesus in the Gospel of Mark." *JETS* 37, no. 2 (1994): 217–33.

England, Frank. "Mapping Postcolonial Biblical Criticism in South Africa." *Neotestamentica* 31, no. 8 (2004): 62–87.
Eugene, Njeri, Alphonce Shiundu, and Caroline Wafula. "MPs Approve Bill to Control Opinion Polls." *Daily Nation*, 31 May 2012, 36.
Exum, J. Cherry, ed. *Feminist Criticism: Whose Interests Are Being Served?* Minneapolis, MN: Fortress Press, 1995.
Fairclough, Newton. *Discourse in Organization Studies: The Case of Critical Realism.* London: Sage, 2005.
Feston Kalua. "Homi Bhabha's Third Space and African Identity." *Journal of Cultural Studies* 21, no. 1 (2009): 23–32.
Fewell, Danna Nolan. "Reading the Bible Ideologically: Feminist Criticism." In *An Introduction to Biblical Criticisms and Their Applications: To Each Its Own Meaning*, edited by Stephen L. Mackenzie and Stephen R. Haynes, 269–82. Louisville, KY: Westminster John Knox Press, 1999.
Fiorenza, Elizabeth Schüssler. "Paul and the Politics of Interpretation." In *Paul and Politics*, edited by Richard A. Horsley, 45–68. Harrisburg, PA: Trinity Press International, 2000.
Fitzmyer, Joseph A. *Luke the Theologian: Aspects of His Teaching.* Mahwah, NJ: Paulist Press, 1989.
Forbes, Greg W. *The God of Old: The Role of Lukan Parables in the Purpose of Luke's Gospel.* Sheffield, UK: Sheffield Academic Press, 2000.
Foucault, Michel. *Power/Knowledge: Selected Writings and Other Interviews.* New York: Pantheon, 1980.
Fowler, Robert M. "The Rhetoric of Direction and Indirection in the Gospel of Mark." In *The Interpretation of Mark*, edited by William R. Telford, 45–78. Edinburgh: T&T Clark, 1995.
———. *Let the Reader Understand: Reader-Response Criticism and the Gospel of Mark.* Harrisburg, PA: Trinity Press International, 2001.
Freire, Paulo. *Pedagogy of the Oppressed.* Translated by Myra Bergman Ramos. London: Penguin Books, 1972.
Garland, David. *Punishment and Modern Society: A Study in Social Theory.* Oxford, UK: Oxford University Press, 1990.
Getui, Mary, Tinyiko Maluleke, and Justin Ukpong, eds. *Interpreting the New Testament in Africa.* Nairobi: Acton, 2001.
Gitari, David M. *In Season and Out of Season: Sermons to a Nation.* Oxford, UK: Regnum, 1996.
———. *Responsible Church Leadership.* Nairobi: Acton, 2005.
Gitau, Wilson. "Context, Timing and the Dynamics of Transitional Justice: A Historical Perspective." *Human Rights Quarterly* 31, no. 1 (2005): 13–22.

Githiga, Gideon. *The Church as the Bulwark against Authoritarianism: Development of Church-State Relations in Kenya, with Particular Reference to the Years after Political Independence 1963–1992*. Oxford, UK: Regnum, 2001.

Githu, Muigai. "Ethnicity and the Renewal of Competing Politics in Kenya." In *Ethnic Conflicts and Democratization in Africa*, edited by H. Glickman, 238–67. Atlanta, GA: The African Studies Association Press, 1995.

Gottwald, Norman K., ed. *The Bible and Liberation: Political and Social Hermeneutics*. Maryknoll, NY: Orbis Books, 1983.

———. *The Hebrew Bible: A Socio-Literary Introduction*. Philadelphia, PA: Fortress Press, 1985.

Gould, Ezra P., ed. *International Critical Commentary: Mark*. Edinburgh: T&T Clark, 1961.

Gramsci, Antonio. *Selections from the Political Writings 1910–1920*. London: The Electric Book Company, 1999.

———. *Selections from the Prison Notebooks*. London: Lawrence & Wishart, 1971.

Graves, Benjamin. "Can the Subaltern Speak?" (2012). Accessed September 12, 2012. http://www.postcolonialweb.org/poldiscourse/spivak/spivak2.html.

Griffins, Gareth, Bill Ashcroft, and Hellen Tiffin, eds. *The Post-Colonial Studies Reader*. London: Routledge, 1995.

Guardian UK. "Corruption Index 2011 from Transparency International: Find Out How Countries Compare" (2012). Accessed June 8, 2012. http://www.guardian.co.uk/news/datablog/2011/dec/01/corruption-index-2011-transparency-international.

Haddad, Beverly. "Women, Gender and Contexts: Engaging the Contextual Bible Study Model." In *Grant Me Justice: HIV/AIDS and Gender Readings of the Bible*, edited by Musa W. Dube, 23–45. Pietermaritzburg, South Africa: Cluster Publications, 2000.

Hargreaves, John. *A Guide to St Mark's Gospel*. London: SPCK, 1994.

Haugerud, Angelique. *The Culture of Politics in Modern Kenya*. Cambridge, UK: Cambridge University Press, 1995.

Holladay, Carl. *New Testament Introduction: Reference Edition*. Louisville, KY: Westminster John Knox Press, 2017.

Hooker, Morna D. *A Commentary on the Gospel According to St Mark*. London: A&C Black, 1991.

———. *The Gospel According to St Mark*. 3rd ed. London: A&C Black, 1995.

Horsley, Richard A. "Submerged Biblical Histories and Imperial Biblical Studies." In *The Bible and Postcolonialism*, edited by R. S. Sugirtharajah, 152–73. Sheffield, UK: Sheffield Academic Press, 1998.

———. *Paul and Politics: Ekklesia, Israel, Imperium, Interpretation*. London: T&T Clark, 2000.

Hutchinson, John C. "Servanthood: Jesus' Countercultural Call to Christian Leaders." *Bibliotheca Sacra* 166, no. 166 (2009): 53–69.
ICPC Africa. *ICPC 2012 Annual Report* (2012). Accessed June 4, 2018. http://www.icpcafrica.org/.
Incigneri, Brian J. "My God, My God, Why Have You Abandoned Me? The Setting and Rhetoric in Mark's Gospel." Australian Catholic University. PhD diss., 2001.
International Commission of Jurists. "International Commission of Jurists: Annual Report 2011" (2012). Accessed June 6, 2018. http://www.icj.org/news.php3?id_article=3663&lang=en.
International Criminal Court. https://www.icc-cpi.int/kenya/rutosang.
Jacques, Genevieve. *Beyond Impunity: An Ecumenical Approach to Truth, Justice and Reconciliation.* Geneva: WCC Publications, 2000.
Jobling, David. "Very Limited Ideological Options: Marxism and Biblical Studies in Postcolonial Scenes." In *Postcolonial Biblical Criticism: Interdisciplinary Intersections*, edited by Stephen D. Moore and Fernando F. Segovia, 124–65. London: T&T Clark, 2005.
Joinet, Louis. Impunity Watch (July). Accessed June 3, 2017. http://www.impunitywatch.org/en/publication2.
Juel, Donald H. *A Master of Surprise: Mark Interpreted.* Minneapolis, MN: Fortress Press, 1994.
Kalilombe, Patrick A. "The Bible and Non-Literate Communities." In *Voices from the Margin: Interpreting the Bible in the Third World*, edited by R. S. Sugirtharajah, 442–53. London: SPCK, 1991.
Kanyoro, Musimbi R. A. "Reading the Bible in the Face of HIV and AIDS." In *Grant Me Justice: HIV/AIDS and Gender Readings of the Bible*, edited by Musa W. Dube and Musimbi R. A. Kanyoro, 45–73. Maryknoll, NY: Orbis, 2004.
Kannabiran, K. G., *The Wages of Impunity: Power, Justice and Human Rights.* New Delhi: Orient Longman, 2004.
Kenyatta, Jomo. *Facing Mount Kenya: The Traditional Life of the Gikuyu.* Nairobi: General Printers, 1938.
K.H.R. Commission. "End Impunity Now" (2012). Accessed June 8, 2018. http://www.justice.go.ke/index2.php?option=com_content&do_pdf=1&id=25.
Kiambi, Julius Kithinji. "Bible and Impunity: Addressing Impunity in Kenya through a Postcolonial Reading of ἐξουσία in Mark 1:21–28." Kenyatta University. PhD diss., 2013.
———. *Postcolonial "Redaction" of Social-Economic Parables in Luke's Gospel: Bible and Making of the Poor in Kenya.* Berlin: LAP Lambert Academic Publishing, 2011.
Kgalemang, Malebogo. "Ngũgĩ's Postcolonial Bible: Devil on the Cross." *Scriptura* 92, no. 1 (2006): 218–24.

Kimathi, Leah. "Whose Truth, Justice and Reconciliation? Enhancing the Legitimacy of the Truth, Justice and Reconciliation Commission among Affected Communities in Kenya." *International Peace Support Training Centre* 6, no. 1 (2010): 1–40.

Kimonye, Klaper. "KNHCR Condemns Tana River Killings" (2012). Accessed October 28, 2012. http://www.citizennews.co.ke/news/2012/local/item/3774-knchr-tana-river-killings.

Kierkegaard, Søren. *Fear and Trembling*. Translated by Alastair Hannay. London: Penguin Books, 2003.

Kingsbury, Jack Dean. *Conflict in Mark: Jesus, Authorities, Disciples*. Minneapolis, MN: Fortress Press, 1989.

Kinyua, Johnson Kiriaku. "The Agikuyu, the Bible and Colonial Constructs: Towards an Ordinary African Readers' Hermeneutics." University of Birmingham, 2010.

Knight, Douglas A. *Methods of Biblical Interpretation*. Nashville, KY: Abingdon Press, 2004.

Kurtz, Leon. *The Language of War and Peace*. San Diego, CA: Academic Press, 1999.

Lacan, Jacques. *The Seminar of Jacques Lacan: The Ethics of Psychoanalysis*. Vol 1. New York: Norton, 1997.

LaVerdiere, Eugene. *The Beginning of the Gospel: Introducing the Gospel According to Mark*. Vol. 1. Collegeville, MN: The Liturgical Press, 1999.

Leander, Hans. *Discourses of Empire: The Gospel of Mark from a Postcolonial Perspective*. Atlanta, GA: Society of Biblical Literature, 2013.

Lewis, Mudge. *Impunity Is the Wife of Power*. Nairobi: Wazum Press, 2000.

Liew, Tat-Siong Benny, "The Gospel of Mark." In *A Postcolonial Commentary on the New Testament*, edited by Fernando F. Segovia and R. S. Sugirtharajah, 105–32. London: T&T Clark, 2009.

———. "Tyranny, Boundary and Might: Colonial Mimicry in Mark's Gospel." *Journal for the Study of New Testament* 73 (1999): 7–31.

Loomba, Ania. *Colonialism/Postcolonialism: The New Critical Idiom*. 2nd ed. London: Routledge, 2005.

Lumumba, P. L. O. *A Call for Hygiene in Kenya Politics*. Nairobi: Mvule Africa Publishers, 2008.

Lynch, Richard A. "Foucault's Theory of Power." In *Michael Foucault: Key Concepts*, edited by Dianna Taylor, 23–39. Durham, NC: Acumen, 2011.

Maathai, Wangari. *Unbowed: A Memoir*. New York: Anchor Books, 2006.

Machen, J. Gresham, and Dan G. McCartney. *New Testament Greek for Beginners*. 2nd ed. New York: Pearson, 2014.

Machira, Apollos. *Armed Conflict and the Law*. Nairobi: Centre for Conflict Resolution, 2010.

Machuka, Mark. "Ray of Hope for Ndung'u Land Report Proposals" (2009). Accessed June 8, 2017. http://www.standardmedia.co.ke/?id=1144019353&cid=4&articleID=1144019353.

Mack, L. Burton. *A Myth of Innocence: Mark and Christian Origins*. Philadelphia, PA: Fortress Press, 1991.

Maier, John, and Vincent Tollers, eds. *The Bible in Its Literary Milieu*. Grand Rapids, MI: William B. Eerdmans, 1979.

Maluleke, Tinyiko. "Black and African Theologies in New World Order: A Time to Drink from Our Own Wells." *Journal of Theology for Southern Africa* 96, no. 6 (1996): 3–19.

———. "African 'Ruths,' Ruthless Africans: Reflections of an African Mordecai." In *Other Ways of Reading: African Women and the Bible*, edited by Musa W. Dube, 237–51. Geneva: WCC Publications, 2001.

Masinde, Sheila. "Citizen Action: Key in Ending Longstanding Impunity in Kenya." *Transparency International—Kenya: Adili* (March 2011): 1–12.

Masoga, Alpheus. "Redefining Power: Reading the Bible in Africa from the Peripheral and Central Positions." In *Reading the Bible in the Global Village: Cape Town*, edited by Justin S. Ukpong, 45–60. Atlanta, GA: Society for Biblical Literature, 2002.

Manus, Ukachukwu Chris. *Intercultural Hermeneutics in Africa: Methods and Approaches*. Nairobi: Acton Publishers, 2003.

Marcus, Joel. *Christological Exegesis of the Old Testament in the Gospel of Mark*. Edinburgh: T&T Clark, 1993.

Mbai, Odhiambo. "The Rise and Fall of the Autocratic State in Kenya." In *The Politics of Transition in Kenya*, edited by Odhiambo Mbai, P. Wanyande, and W. Oyugi, 51–95. Nairobi: Heinrich Boll Foundation, 2003.

McGuigan, Jim. *Culture and the Public Sphere*. London: Routledge, 1996.

McLeod, John. *Beginning Postcolonialism*. Manchester, UK: Manchester University Press, 2000.

Miller, Norman. *Kenya: The Quest for Prosperity*. London: Gower House, 1984.

Moore, Stephen D., and Fernando F. Segovia. "Postcolonial Criticism: Beginnings, Trajectories, Intersections." In *Postcolonial Criticism: Interdisciplinary Intersections*, edited by Stephen D. Moore and Fernando F. Segovia, 1–38. London: T&T Clark, 2005.

———. *Empire and Apocalypse: Postcolonialism and the New Testament*. Sheffield, UK: Phoenix Press, 2006.

Morton, Andrew. *Moi: The Making of an African Statesman*. Nairobi: Michael Omara, 1999.

Mugenda, Olive, and Bank Mugenda. *Research Methodology: Quantitative and Qualitative Approaches*. Nairobi: Jomo Kenyatta Foundation, 1999.

Muigai, Githu. "Ethnicity and the Renewal of Competing Politics in Kenya." In *Ethnic Conflicts and Democratization in Africa*, edited by H. Glickman, 65–84. Atlanta, GA: The African Studies Association Press, 1995.

Munene, Macharia. *Historical Reflections on Kenya: Intellectual Adventurism, Politics and Intercultural Relations*. Nairobi: University of Nairobi Press, 2012.

Muñoz-Larrondo, Rubén. *A Postcolonial Reading of the Acts of the Apostles*. New York: Peter Lang, 2012.

Murfin, Ross, and Supryia M. Ray. *The Bedford Glossary of Critical and Literary Terms*. London: Bedford Books, 1998.

Muriuki, Geoffrey. *A History of the Kikuyu: 1500–1900*. Nairobi: Oxford University Press, 1974.

Murunga, Godwin R. "Governance and the Politics of Structural Adjustment in Kenya." In *Kenya: The Struggle for Democracy*, edited by Godwin R. Murunga and Shadrack W. Nasong'o, 13–34. London: Zed Books, 2007.

Murray, Martin J., and Garth A. Myers, eds. *Cities in Contemporary Africa*. London: Palgrave Macmillan, 2006.

Mutua, Martin. "Republic of Kenya Report of the Task Force on the Establishment of a Truth, Justice and Reconciliation Commission." *Human Rights Review* 10, no. 25 (2004): 1–22.

Mwaniki, Lydia M. "Paul's Construction of Imago Dei in 1 Corinthians 11:7–9 and Its Implications for Gender Power Relations in the Anglican Church of Kenya: A Postcolonial Feminist Examination." *UKZN*, 2010.

Mwaura, Philomena. "Religion and Leadership: The Creation of a Just Society." In *Governance and Development: Towards Quality Leadership in Kenya*, edited by Kimani Njogu, 14–38. Nairobi: Twaweza Communications, 2007.

Myers, Ched. *Binding the Strong Man: A Political Reading of Mark's Story of Jesus*. Maryknoll, NY: Orbis Books, 1988.

Nadar, Sarojini. "Barak God and Die!: Women, HIV and a Theology of Suffering." In *Voices from the Margin: Interpreting the Bible in the Third World*. Edited by R. S. Sugirtharajah. Maryknoll: Orbis, 2006.

———. "Sacred Stories as Theological Pedagogy." *Journal of Constructive Theology: Gender, Religion and Theology in Africa* 14, nos. 2 and 15 (2009): 9–23.

Nayar, Pramod K., ed. *Postcolonial Studies: An Anthology*. Hoboken, NJ: Wiley Blackwell, 2016.

Ndegwah, David J. *Biblical Hermeneutics as a Tool for Inculturation in Africa: A Case Study of the Pokot People of Kenya*. Nairobi: Creations Enterprises, 2007.

Ndüng'ü, Ruth Wangeci. "Socialization and Violence: Ideas and Practices in Kenya." In *(Re)Membering Kenya; Identity, Culture and Freedom*, edited by Mbugua wa-Mungai and George Gona, 230–75. Nairobi: Twaweza Communications, 2010.

Ngala, Denis. "Man Eat Man Society" (2011). Accessed December 8, 2019. http://nationofafrica.blogspot.com/2011/08/man-eat-man-society.html.

Nyaga, Daniel. *Customs and Traditions of the Ameru.* Nairobi: East African Educational Publishers, 1997.

Ogot, Bethwell. *Decolonization and Independence in Kenya, 1940–93.* London: Curry, 1995.

———. "Boundary Changes and Invention of Tribes." In *Kenya: The Making of a Nation 1895–1995*, edited by Bethuel Ogot and William Ochieng, 44–71. Kisumu, Kenya: Maseno University, 2000.

Okello, Duncan, and M. J. Gitau, eds. *Readings on Inequality in Kenya.* Nairobi: Regal Press, 2006.

Okure, Teresa. "Feminist Interpretation in Africa." In *Searching the Scriptures: A Feminist Interpretation*, edited by Elizabeth Schüssler Fiorenza, 38–51. New York: Crossroads, 1993.

Olbricht, Thomas H., and Jerry L. Sumney. *Paul and Pathos.* Atlanta, GA: Society of Biblical Literature, 2001.

Ombati, Cyrus. "MRC Leader Arrested, Two Killed in Raid" (2012). Accessed October 2, 2018. www.standardmedia.co.ke/?articleID=2000068457.

Orengo, Peter. "How NHIF Plan May Have Been Turned into Cash Cow" (2012). Accessed June 6, 2017.
http://www.standardmedia.co.ke/?articleID=2000059152&story_title=How-NHIF-plan-may-have-been-turned-into-cash-cow.

Penchansky, David. "Up for Grabs: A Tentative Proposal for Doing Ideological Criticism." *Semeia* 9, no. 34 (1999): 35–56.

Perkinson, Jim. "A Canaanitic Word in the Logos of Christ; or the Difference the Syro-Phoenician Woman Makes to Jesus." *Semeia* 75 (1998): 61–85.

Pero, Cheryl S. *Liberation from Empire: Demonic Possession and Exorcism in the Gospel of Mark.* New York: Peter Lang, 2013.

Perry, John Michael. *Exploring the Messianic Secret in Mark's Gospel.* New York: Sheed & Ward, 1997.

Powell, Mark Allan, ed. *Methods for Matthew.* Cambridge, UK: Cambridge University Press, 2009.

Prior, Michael. *The Bible and Colonialism: A Moral Critique.* Sheffield, UK: Sheffield Academic Press, 1997.

Pui-lan, Kwok. "Discovering the Bible in the Non-Biblical World." *Semeia* 47 (1989): 25–42.

Punt, Jeremy. "Postcolonial Biblical Criticism in South Africa: Some Mind and Road Mapping." *Neotestamentica* 37, no. 1 (2003): 59–85.

———. "Why Not Postcolonial Biblical Criticism in (South) Africa: Stating the Obvious or Looking for the Impossible?" *Scriptura* 91 (2006): 63–82.

Research Advisors. "Sample Size Table." 2010. Accessed August 11, 2016. http://research-advisors.com/tools/SampleSize.htm.

Rieger, Joerg. *Christ and Empire: From Paul to Postcolonial Times.* Philadelphia, PA: Fortress Press, 2007.

Rhoads, David, and Donald Michie, eds. *Mark as Story: An Introduction to the Narrative of a Gospel.* Philadelphia, PA: Fortress Press, 1982.

Robinson, Martha R. *Matriarchy, Patriarchy and Imperial Security in Africa: Explaining Riots in Europe and Violence in Africa.* New York: Lexicon Books, 2012.

Rukundwa, Lazare S. "The Formation of Postcolonial Theory." *HTS* 63, no. 3 (2007): 23–46.

Said, Edward W. *Culture and Imperialism.* London: Vintage, 1993.

———. *Orientalism.* New York: Vintage, 1979.

———. *Reflections on Exile and Other Essays.* Cambridge, MA: Harvard University Press, 2000.

Samuel, Simon. *A Postcolonial Reading of Mark's Story of Jesus.* New York: T&T Clark, 2007.

Santos, Narry F. "The Paradox of Authority and Servanthood in the Gospel of Mark." *Bibliotheca Sacra* 154, no. 2 (1997): 452–60.

Schermerhorn, Rick Ash. "Ethnicity in the Perspective of the Sociology of Knowledge." *Ethnicity April* 1, no. 1 (1974): 23–39.

Schildgen, Brenda Deen. *Power and Prejudice: The Reception of the Gospel of Mark,* Detroit, MI: Wayne State University Press, 1999.

Schreiner, Thomas R. *Interpreting the Pauline Epistles.* Louisville, KY: Baker Academic, 2011.

Schwarz, Henry, and Sangeeta Ray, eds. *A Companion to Postcolonial Studies.* Oxford, UK: Blackwell Publishing, 2005.

Scott, John, and Gordon Taylor. *A Dictionary of Sociology.* 2nd ed. Oxford, UK: Oxford University Press, 1998.

Segovia, Fernando F, and Mary Ann Tolbert, eds. *Reading from This Place: Social Location and Biblical Interpretation in the United States.* Vol. 1. Minneapolis, MN: Fortress, 1995.

Segovia, Fernando F. *Decolonizing Biblical Studies: A View from the Margins.* Maryknoll, NY: Orbis Books, 2000.

———. *Decolonizing Biblical Studies: A View from the Margins.* 2nd ed. Maryknoll, NY: Orbis Books, 2005.

Segovia, Fernando F., and R. S. Sugirtharajah, eds. *A Postcolonial Commentary on the New Testament.* London: T&T Clark, 2009.

Shannak, Rifat O., and Fairouz M. Aldhmour. "Grounded Theory as a Methodology for Theory Generation in Information Systems Research." *European Journal of Economics, Finance and Administrative Sciences,* issue no. 15 (2009): 1–19.

Sherwood, Yvonne, ed. *Derrida's Bible: Reading a Page of Scripture with a Little Help from Derrida*. New York: Palgrave Macmillan, 2004.
Shillington, V. G. *Reading the Sacred Text: An Introduction to Biblical Studies*. London: T&T Clark, 2002.
Shipp, Horace. *Lives That Moved the World: Brief Biographies of Famous Men and Women*. 3rd ed. London: Evans Brothers, 1946.
Shiner, Whitney. "Applause and Applause Lines in the Gospel of Mark." In *Rhetorics and Hermeneutics*, edited by James D. Hester, 62–76. London: T&T Clark, 2004.
Sinfield, Allan. *Faultlines: Cultural Materialism and the Politics of Dissident Reading*. Berkeley: University of California Press, 1992.
Sobania, N. W. *Culture and Customs in Kenya*. Westport, CN: Greenwood Press, 2003.
Spivak, Gayatri Chakravorty. "Can the Subaltern Speak?" In *Marxism and the Interpretation of Culture*, edited by Cary Nelson and Lawrence Grossberg, 34–49. London: Macmillan, 1988.

———. *Subaltern Studies: Deconstructing Historiography*. London: Oxford University Press, 1988.

Spurr, David. *The Rhetoric of Empire: Colonial Discourse in Journalism, Travel, Writing and Imperial Administration*. Durham, NC: Duke University Press, 1993.
Stein, Robert H. *Mark*. Grand Rapids, MI: Baker Academic, 2008.

———. "Mark." In *Baker Exegetical Commentary on the New Testament*. Grand Rapids, MI: Baker Academic, 2008.

Stewart, Susan. *On Longing: Narratives of the Miniature, the Gigantic, the Souvenir, the Collection*. Baltimore, MD: Johns Hopkins University Press, 1984.
Sugirtharajah, R. S., ed. *The Postcolonial Bible*. Sheffield, UK: Sheffield Academic Press, 1998.

———. *The Bible and the Third World: Precolonial, Colonial and Postcolonial Encounters*. Cambridge, UK: Cambridge University Press, 2001.

———. *Postcolonial Criticism and Biblical Interpretation*. Vol. 1. Oxford, UK: Oxford University Press, 2002.

———. *Postcolonial Reconfigurations: An Alternative Way of Reading the Bible and Doing Theology*. London: SCM Press, 2003.

———. *The Bible and Empire: Postcolonial Explorations*. London: Cambridge University Press, 2005.

———, ed. *Voices from the Margin: Interpreting the Bible in the Third World*. London: SPCK, 2006.

Swartley, Willard M. "The Role of Women in Mark's Gospel: A Narrative Analysis." *Biblical Theological Bulletin* 22, no. 1 (1997): 16–22.
Taylor, Vincent. *The Gospel According to St. Mark: The Greek Text with Introduction, Notes and Indexes*. 2nd ed. Grand Rapids, MI: Baker Book House, 1981.
Thiong'o, Ngũgĩ wa. *Decolonizing the Mind*. London: Heinemann, 1986.

Thitu, Gladys. "The Impact of Corruption on Governance: An Appraisal of the Practice of the Rule of Law in Kenya" (2012). Accessed June 8, 2018. http://repository.up.ac.za/handle/2263/1222.

Throup, David. "Elections and Political Legitimacy in Kenya." *Africa: Journal of the International African Institute* 63, no. 3 (1993): 371–96.

———. "Elections and Political Legitimacy in Kenya" (2012). Accessed June 8, 2018. http://www.jstor.org/stable/pdfplus/1161427.pdf.

Tolbert, Mary Ann. *Sowing the Gospel: Mark's World in Literary-Historical Perspective*. Minneapolis, MN: Fortress Press, 1989.

Transparency International. "The Role of Legal Aid in the Fight Against Corruption Underscored (2012)." Accessed June 8, 2017. http://www.tikenya.org/.

Trible, Phyllis. *Texts of Terror: Literary-Feminist Readings of Biblical Narratives*. Philadelphia, PA: Fortress Press, 1984.

Troch, Lieve. "A Method of Conscientization: Feminist Bible Study in Netherlands." In *Searching the Scriptures: A Feminist Introduction*, edited by Fiorenza Elizabeth Schüssler, 230–58. London: SCM Press, 1993.

Tutu, Desmond Mphilo. *No Future without Forgiveness*. New York: Hodder & Stoughton, 1999.

Ukpong, Justin S. "Development in Biblical Interpretation in Africa: Historical and Hermeneutical Directions." In *The Bible in Africa: Transactions, Trajectories and Trends*, edited by Musa W. Dube and Gerald O. West, 189–94. Leiden, Netherlands: Brill, 1996.

———. "Development in Biblical Interpretation in Africa: Historical and Hermeneutical Directions." In *The Bible in Africa: Transactions, Trajectories and Trends*, edited by Musa W. Dube and Gerald O. West, 11–28. Leiden, Netherlands: Brill, 2000.

———. "Reading the Bible with a Community of Ordinary Readers." In *Interpreting the New Testament in Africa*, edited by Mary Getui, Maluleke Tinyiko, and Justin Ukpong, 186–221. Nairobi: Acton, 2001.

———, ed. *Reading the Bible in the Global Village: Cape Town*. Atlanta, GA: Society for Biblical Literature, 2005.

UNDP. "UNDP Kenya Annual Report 2016" (2018). Accessed April 20, 2018. http://www.ke.undp.org.

Venn, Couze. *The Postcolonial Challenge: Towards Alternative Worlds*. London: Sage, 2006.

Virkama, Arthur, ed. *From Othering to Understanding*. Edited by Victor Korhonen. Tampere, Finland: Tampere University Press, 2010.

Waetjen, Herman C. *A Reordering of Power: A Social-Political Reading of Mark's Gospel*. Collegeville, MN: Fortress Press, 1989.

Wafula, R. S. *Biblical Representations of Moab: A Kenyan Postcolonial Reading*. New York: Peter Lang, 2014.

Wallis, Jim. "Liberation and Conformity" In *Mission Trends 4: Liberation Theologies*, edited by Gerald H. Anderson and Thomas F. Stansky, 67–85. Grand Rapids, MI: William B. Eerdmans, 1979.

wa-Mungai, Mbugua, and George Gona, eds. *(Re)Membering Kenya: Identity, Culture and Freedom*. Nairobi: Twaweza Communications, 2010.

Wanyonyi, Pius Kakai. "Historicizing Negative Ethnicity in Kenya." In *(Re)Membering Kenya; Identity, Culture and Freedom*, edited by Mbugua wa-Mungai and George Gona, 57–64. Nairobi: Twaweza Communications, 2010.

Watson, Mary Anne. *Modern Kenya: Social Issues and Perspectives*. Lanham, MD: University Press of America, 2000.

Waweru, Humphrey. "Postcolonial and Contrapuntal Reading of Revelation 22:1–5." *Churchman* 121, no. 1 (2007): 23–38.

———. "Postcolonial and Contrapuntal Reading of Revelation 22:1–5 Part 2." *Churchman* 121, no. 2 (2007): 139–62.

———. *The Bible and African Culture; Mapping Transactional Inroads*. Limuru, Kenya: Zapf Chancery Publishers Africa, 2011.

Weems, Renita J. "Ideological Criticism of Biblical Texts." *Semeia* 59: 3 (1992): 26–47.

Werbner, Richard, and Terence Ranger, eds. *Postcolonial Identities in Africa*. London: Zed Books, 1996.

Wekesa, John. "Historicizing Negative Ethnicity in Kenya." In *(Re)Membering Kenya; Identity, Culture and Freedom*, edited by Mbugua wa-Mungai and George Gona, 68–72. Nairobi: Twaweza Communications, 2010.

West, Gerald. *Doing Contextual Bible Study: A Resource Manual*. Accessed May 9, 2019. http://www.diohuron.org/what/HR/clergy_conference/2012/Ujamaa%20CBS%20Manual%20part%201.pdf.

———. *Biblical Hermeneutics of Liberation: Modes of Reading the Bible in the South African Context*. 2nd ed. Pietermaritzburg, South Africa: Cluster Publications, 1991.

———. "Finding a Place among the Posts for Postcolonial Criticism in Biblical Studies in South Africa." *Old Testament Essays* 2, no. 10 (1997a): 322–42.

———. "On the Eve of an African Biblical Studies: Trajectories and Trends." *Journal of Theology for Southern Africa* 99 (1997b): 99–115.

———. "Mapping African Biblical Interpretation: A Tentative Sketch." In *The Bible in Africa: Transactions, Trajectories and Trends*, edited by Musa W. Dube and Gerald O. West, 29–43. Leiden, Netherlands: Brill, 2000.

———. "Mapping African Biblical Interpretation." In *Interpreting the New Testament in Africa*, edited by Mary Getui, Tinyiko Maluleke, and Justin Ukpong, 83–98. Nairobi: Acton, 2001.

———. "Unpacking the Package That Is the Bible in African Biblical Scholarship." In *Reading the Bible in the Global Village: Cape Town*, edited by Justin S. Ukpong, 23–47. Atlanta, GA: Society of Biblical Literature, 2002.

———. *The Academy of the Poor: Towards a Dialogical Reading of the Bible*. Pietermaritzburg, South Africa: Cluster Publications, 2003.

———. "Reading Shembe 'Re-Membering' the Bible: Isaiah Shembe's Instructions on Adultery." *Neotestamentica* 40, no. 1 (2006): 157–84.

———. "Interpreting 'the Exile' in African Biblical Scholarship: An Ideo-Theological Dilemma in Postcolonial South Africa." *OTSSA* 2, no. 34 (2007): 1–18.

Wimbush, Vincent L. "Historical/Cultural Criticism as Liberation: A Proposal for an African American Biblical Hermeneutic." *Semeia* 47 (1989): 43–55.

———. "Other Ways of Reading: African Women and the Bible Review." *Shofar: An Interdisciplinary Journal of Jewish Studies* 21, no. 3 (2003): 167–69.

———. 2003. "Other Ways of Reading." *Shofar: An Interdisciplinary Journal of Jewish Studies* 21, no. 167 (2003): 1–32.

Wrong, Michela. *It is Our Turn to Eat: The Story of a Kenyan Whistle-Blower*. London: Fourth Estate, 2009.

Yamasky, Gary. *Watching a Biblical Narrative: Point of View in Biblical Exegesis*. London: T&T Clark, 2008.

Yoder, John Howard. *The Politics of Jesus*. Grand Rapids, MI: William B. Eerdmans, 1972.

Young, Robert C. *Colonial Desire: Hybridity in Theory, Culture and Race*. New York: Routledge, 1995.

———. *Postcolonialism: A Very Short Introduction*. Oxford, UK: Oxford University Press, 1999.

———. *Postcolonialism: An Historical Introduction*. Oxford, UK: Blackwell Publishing, 2001.

Zemke, R., and T. Kramlinger. *Figuring Things Out: A Trainer's Guide to Needs and Task Analysis*. Boston, MA: Wesley Publishing, 1986.

INDEX

ἅγιος 5, 9
ἀκαθάρτον 9
ἀκοὴ 10
ἀνέκραξεν 9
αὐτοὺς 130
γραμματεῖς 7
διδαχὴ 10
ἐθαμβήθησαν 10, 138
ἐξεπλήσσοντο 9
εὐαγγελίον 7, 27
εὐθὺς 6, 9, 10
θεοῦ 5, 9
πνεύμα 9
Φιμώθητι 10, 138

A

Agikuyu 36, 52, 151
alshabab 128
ambivalence 21, 40
Ameru 34, 65, 154
applause 121, 122, 123
Ashcroft, Bill 20, 21, 22, 49, 50, 51, 145, 149
askaris 39
authority 1, 2, 3, 4, 5, 6, 7, 8, 9, 10, 11, 12, 13, 14, 17, 18, 19, 21, 22, 23, 24, 25, 26, 30, 37, 38, 40, 48, 52, 59, 67, 68, 70, 85, 86, 87, 88, 89, 90, 91, 92, 99, 100, 101, 102, 103, 104, 106, 107, 114, 118, 119, 121, 122, 123, 127, 130, 134, 136, 137, 138, 142, 147

B

Bhabha, Homi 31, 40, 104, 146, 148
binary 3, 13, 18, 20, 21, 63, 103, 120
Botswana 115, 116
bourgeois 69, 72, 134, 136
British 25, 48, 50, 54, 64, 125, 128, 146

C

canons 116
colonial, colonialism, coloniality 4, 5, 11, 13, 14, 17, 18, 19, 21, 22, 27, 29, 31, 34, 36, 37, 39, 40, 41, 50, 51, 52, 53, 59, 60, 61, 64, 66, 67, 68, 69, 71, 72, 81, 96, 103, 104, 109, 117, 125, 128, 133, 138, 139, 140, 141, 142, 143, 144
community 2, 3, 11, 17, 18, 26, 27, 35, 36, 52, 53, 58, 84, 107, 113, 120, 130, 131
conformist 129, 130
connectedness, connections 38, 46
conscientization 55, 118
consulting
 Reader 115, 116, 117
Contextual Bible Study vii, 60, 78, 79, 85, 90, 158
contrapuntal, contrapuntalism 111, 112, 113, 114, 136
corruption, corrupt 30, 34, 41, 42, 43, 44, 45, 46, 47, 71, 72, 93, 98, 104, 139, 149
counter 27, 56, 70, 113, 134, 135, 136

counterpoint 112, 113, 114, 121
criticism 11, 13, 80, 83, 91, 102, 105, 117, 124, 133, 137, 141
cultural 15, 16, 20, 21, 27, 29, 34, 35, 37, 39, 48, 50, 51, 64, 69, 71, 73, 77, 104, 105, 109, 127, 133, 134, 139, 141
culture, cultures 26, 29, 30, 33, 35, 37, 41, 49, 50, 64, 67, 72, 73, 74, 75, 91, 92, 96, 97, 99, 107, 108, 109, 112, 113, 115, 128, 132, 134, 136, 137, 139, 141, 143

D

democracy 15, 90, 102, 128
disciples 12, 16, 23, 24, 25, 26, 86, 99, 101
Divination 115, 117
divine 4, 24, 25, 75, 89, 114, 115, 136
Divining 115, 118, 121
dominant 17, 20, 26, 27, 32, 33, 38, 41, 50, 52, 68, 69, 70, 78, 80, 81, 85, 86, 106, 112, 121, 126, 128, 133
Dube, Musa 15, 16, 107, 108, 109, 111, 115, 116, 131, 142, 146, 147, 149, 150, 152, 153, 157, 158

E

ecclesiastical 114, 140
empire vii, 4, 8, 12, 14, 15, 16, 21, 22, 26, 27, 30, 31, 32, 38, 41, 44, 46, 53, 62, 68, 72, 73, 75, 102, 106, 112, 121, 124, 125, 126, 128, 133, 135, 137, 139, 140, 141, 143
epistemology 80
ethics 131
ethnic 31, 32, 33, 34, 48, 49, 50, 51, 52, 53, 54, 55, 56, 57, 58, 59, 60, 61, 73, 74, 126
ethnicity 15, 30, 47, 48, 49, 50, 51, 52, 53, 54, 55, 56, 57, 58, 59, 61, 75, 97, 139

evangelism 119
exousia 1, 3, 4, 5, 6, 7, 9, 10, 11, 12, 13, 14, 17, 18, 19, 21, 22, 23, 24, 26, 27, 30, 75, 78, 103, 108, 112, 113, 114, 118, 119, 120, 121, 122, 123, 124, 126, 129, 135, 136, 137, 138, 140, 141, 143

F

feminist 38, 107, 116, 133

G

Galilee 87, 122, 129
GEMA ix, 56, 57
gender, gendered 16, 37, 107, 139
global, globalization 34, 65, 66, 71

H

hegemonic 19, 26, 30, 42, 47, 68, 69, 70, 71, 72, 73, 74, 78, 80, 84, 115, 123, 132, 135
hegemony 14, 33, 48, 62, 63, 123, 125, 126, 128, 132, 133
hermeneutics 18, 80, 83, 111, 132, 133, 134, 136, 141
historicizing 113
hybridity, hybrid 39, 63, 64, 65, 67, 104, 128

I

identity, identities 12, 21, 22, 38, 48, 49, 50, 51, 53, 59, 60, 61, 64, 68, 77, 86, 87, 104, 119, 124, 128

ideology, ideological 1, 13, 14, 15, 16, 18, 19, 21, 34, 41, 46, 53, 59, 64, 69, 75, 103, 107, 119, 121, 122, 123, 124, 128, 133, 139, 142, 143, 144
imagination 24, 27, 38, 114, 120, 133, 140

imperial 4, 6, 8, 12, 13, 14, 15, 16, 17, 21, 22, 26, 27, 30, 81, 106, 109, 119, 120, 123, 127, 129, 133, 134, 137, 138, 139, 140, 142, 143, 144
impunitism 132, 133, 134, 135, 136
impunity 3, 5, 12, 13, 14, 16, 18, 20, 22, 25, 26, 27, 29, 30, 31, 32, 33, 34, 35, 36, 37, 38, 39, 40, 41, 43, 47, 48, 53, 59, 60, 61, 67, 68, 69, 70, 71, 72, 75, 78, 79, 84, 85, 86, 89, 90, 91, 92, 93, 94, 95, 96, 97, 98, 99, 100, 101, 102, 103, 104, 105, 106, 107, 108, 111, 114, 115, 117, 118, 120, 124, 125, 126, 127, 128, 129, 130, 131, 132, 133, 134, 135, 136, 137, 138, 139, 140, 141, 142, 143, 144
independence 30, 33, 62, 63, 64, 67, 72, 106, 126
indigenous 33, 48, 64, 115, 117
infantilization 26

J

judiciary 70, 100

K

KAMATUSA ix, 56
Kenyatta vii, 45, 51, 54, 55, 56, 58, 59, 62, 63, 127, 150, 152
Kibaki 51, 57, 58
Kierkegaard 130
kipande 53, 60

L

liberation 83, 131
local 52, 53, 71, 151

M

Maasai ix, 52, 56

madoadoas 60
margins vii, 8, 12, 16, 31, 62, 78, 79, 80, 102, 117
marital impunity 35
marriage 35, 58
matatu 39
Mbiti, John 35
Methodist vii, x, 89
Michuki, Hon 98, 101
mimicry 13, 17, 18, 21, 29, 33, 39, 41, 64, 104, 128, 138, 142
miracle 6, 10, 19
Moi, Arap 51, 55, 56, 57, 58, 60, 73, 74, 128, 152
mungiki 34

N

narratives 23, 27, 61, 80, 82, 107, 109, 124, 135
Ngugi, wa Thiong'o 133, 150
njuri
 nceke 34, 35

O

Oginga, Odinga 33, 54
ordinary 51, 77, 79, 80, 81, 82, 83, 84, 85, 108, 111
Orientalism 112, 155
other 126
othering 12, 16, 20, 22, 29, 32, 46, 54, 58, 59, 61, 103, 109, 126

P

parable 23, 82
patriarchy 37, 38, 107, 108, 139
patron 63
patronage 30
patronizes 103
pericope 7, 86
Pilate Pontius 100, 101
police 39, 47, 97, 98

possessed 2, 105, 123, 125, 126, 127
postcolonial, postcolonialism vii, 4, 5, 11, 12, 13, 14, 15, 16, 18, 22, 27, 29, 30, 31, 32, 38, 39, 41, 51, 52, 60, 61, 63, 65, 67, 68, 71, 72, 75, 77, 78, 80, 83, 91, 102, 103, 104, 105, 106, 107, 108, 109, 111, 112, 115, 116, 117, 118, 124, 129, 130, 133, 134, 136, 137, 138, 139, 140, 141, 142, 143
poverty ix, 61, 65, 66, 67, 126
power 1, 3, 4, 8, 9, 10, 13, 14, 16, 17, 18, 19, 20, 21, 22, 23, 24, 25, 26, 27, 30, 32, 34, 37, 38, 39, 40, 41, 42, 45, 46, 47, 52, 56, 58, 59, 62, 63, 64, 66, 67, 70, 72, 78, 79, 85, 86, 87, 88, 89, 90, 97, 99, 100, 102, 103, 104, 105, 106, 107, 109, 114, 118, 119, 120, 121, 123, 124, 127, 128, 132, 133, 134, 135, 136, 137, 139
prophetic imagination 85, 120
public 19, 34, 36, 39, 42, 43, 44, 46, 49, 55, 72, 98, 105, 114, 122, 141, 142

R

Raila, Odinga 58
reformers 128
religion 15, 64, 75, 87, 119, 120, 131

S

Said, Edward 15, 112, 113, 145, 147, 155
Spivak, Gayatri 22, 77, 78, 80, 147, 156
subaltern 13, 14, 15, 27, 31, 32, 33, 39, 45, 61, 63, 64, 68, 69, 70, 71, 73, 77, 78, 80, 85, 104, 113, 114, 116, 117, 121, 123, 124, 126, 133, 136
Subalternity 61
submerged viii, 12, 65, 67, 106, 112, 116

Sugirtharajah 4, 15, 41, 52, 61, 78, 146, 147, 149, 150, 155, 156
sultanate 118
systemic 3, 62, 63, 66, 120, 126, 127

T

temple 3, 18, 23, 24, 87, 101, 129
terrorist 129
tyranny, tyrant, tyrannical 4, 11, 13, 14, 27, 142

V

violence 13, 30, 31, 33, 39, 48, 57, 65, 73, 74, 75, 77, 97, 100, 116

W

Wamwere, Koigi 51, 55
wanjiku 73, 81
worlding 18, 52, 68, 69, 70, 85, 113, 139, 141